Law, Governance and Technology Series

Volume 74

The *Law, Governance and Technology Series* is intended to attract manuscripts arising from an interdisciplinary approach in law, artificial intelligence and information technologies. The idea is to bridge the gap between research in IT law and IT-applications for lawyers developing a unifying techno-legal perspective. The series will welcome proposals that have a fairly specific focus on problems or projects that will lead to innovative research charting the course for new interdisciplinary developments in law, legal theory, and law and society research as well as in computer technologies, artificial intelligence and cognitive sciences. In broad strokes, manuscripts for this series may be mainly located in the fields of the Internet law (data protection, intellectual property, Internet rights, etc.), Computational models of the legal contents and legal reasoning, Legal Information Retrieval, Electronic Data Discovery, Collaborative Tools (e.g. Online Dispute Resolution platforms), Metadata and XML Technologies (for Semantic Web Services), Technologies in Courtrooms and Judicial Offices (E-Court), Technologies for Governments and Administrations (E-Government), Legal Multimedia, and Legal Electronic Institutions (Multi-Agent Systems and Artificial Societies).

Natalia Menéndez González • Giuseppe Mobilio
Editors

Next Democratic Frontiers for Facial Recognition Technology (FRT)

The Legal, Ethical and Democratic Implications of FRT

Springer

Editors
Natalia Menéndez González
European University Institute
Florence, Italy

Giuseppe Mobilio
Department of Legal Science
University of Florence
Florence, Italy

ISSN 2352-1902 ISSN 2352-1910 (electronic)
Law, Governance and Technology Series
ISBN 978-3-031-89796-2 ISBN 978-3-031-89794-8 (eBook)
https://doi.org/10.1007/978-3-031-89794-8

This Springer imprint is published by the registered company Springer Nature Switzerland AG
The registered company address is: Gewerbestrasse 11, 6330 Cham, Switzerland

Contents

Contents

Facial Recognition Technology and the Challenges to Democratic Systems: An Introduction

Natalia Menéndez González and Giuseppe Mobilio

Abstract This chapter discusses the state of the art of Facial Recognition Technology (FRT) and the legal implications that its biometric nature and use pose, particularly for fundamental rights and democracy. It also highlights the need of a contribution such as the one this book proposes, with a specific focus on the threat the use of FRT poses for democratic societies, particularly in the current evolving digital landscape.

1 Introduction

Facial Recognition is a disruptive technology with global implications. Its high level of accuracy, bolstered by Artificial Intelligence (AI) and the exponential growth of available data and computing power, has significantly expanded its reach. A 2019 Stanford Report revealed that Facial Recognition Technology (FRT) secured $4.7B, accounting for 6.0% of the total global investment between January 2018 and October 2019, and witnessed substantial growth in global private investment from 2015 to 2019.[1]

Facial Recognition Technology offers innovative solutions to current needs for identification and verification, as '[t]hese technologies brought together the promise of other biometric systems that tie identity to individual, distinctive features of the

[1] Perrault et al. (2019).

N. Menéndez González (✉)
Centre for a Digital Society, Robert Schumann Centre for Advanced Studies, European University Institute, Florence, Italy
e-mail: Natalia.Menendez@eui.eu

G. Mobilio
Department of Legal Science, University of Florence, Florence, Italy
e-mail: giuseppe.mobilio@unifi.it

N. Menéndez González, G. Mobilio (eds.), *Next Democratic Frontiers for Facial Recognition Technology (FRT)*, Law, Governance and Technology Series 74,
https://doi.org/10.1007/978-3-031-89794-8_1

body, and the more familiar functionality of video surveillance systems.'[2] A good example of FRT's increasing relevance is the technical advantage it provided during the COVID-19 health emergency.[3] Further, in various policy fields public authorities and private actors are experimenting with different practical applications for less costly and more effective activities or services, such as in border management and law enforcement.[4] As opposed to other biometrics, 'it imposes fewer demands on subjects and may be conducted at a distance without their knowledge or consent.'[5] This characteristic of the technology has led to the proliferation of what are known as remote facial recognition systems.[6] These systems normally operate with so-called 'non-cooperative subjects'. The adjective non-cooperative refers to subjects who do not voluntarily submit to facial recognition. Such a lack of cooperation can be active, meaning that the subject opposes, for instance, for ideological reasons, or passive, when the subject is not aware of being subjected to facial recognition.

However, despite the potential benefits, the scholarly literature has identified a multitude of potential risks that Facial Recognition Technology specifically poses for fundamental rights,[7] especially but not only privacy and data protection,[8] and specific subjects, such as minors in educational contexts.[9] Moreover, the addition of AI to FRT allows applications based on categorisation (e.g., sentiment analysis or predictive policing), escalating the level of risk that it poses. Compared to other biometric technologies such as fingerprint, iris or palm scanners, FRTs operate contactless, being remote and non-intrusive.[10] The face image can be processed without the individual noticing and consenting. This makes the technology particularly worthy of attention amongst other AI-empowered surveillance tools. In this sense, its ground-breaking character and potentially harmful uses pose a significant threat to the right to privacy and threaten a potential revolution to it, in a similar manner to the advent of instant photography.[11] Moreover, in a similar way to surveillance cameras, facial recognition systems do not require large deployments at the infrastructure level. This may seem like an advantage at first glance since they do not introduce visual noise, for instance, in the public spaces in which they are installed. However, it also has a counterpart, being that it is very difficult for 'non-cooperative' citizens potentially subject to such systems to refuse their surveillance control.

[2] Anderson et al. (2019).

[3] Menéndez González (2022).

[4] Mobilio (2023).

[5] Introna and Nissenbaum (2010).

[6] Wheeler et al. (2010).

[7] European Union Agency for Fundamental Rights (2019).

[8] Kindt (2016); European Union Agency for Fundamental Rights (2019); European Data Protection Board (2023).

[9] Mobilio (2024).

[10] Berle (2020), pp. 2 ff.

[11] Warren and Brandeis (1890).

Along these lines, numerous organisations and academics have warned of the danger that the non-invasiveness of facial recognition systems entails from the point of view of data protection.[12] The remote and non-invasive nature of facial recognition systems makes them a technology that is particularly suitable to be installed in general in a multitude of both public and private settings. Furthermore, the technological advantage it provides in contexts where there is a need for large-scale identification/verification has made facial recognition a very attractive option for many actors, as it is a very effective tool for managing large groups of people in settings such as large events. Democratic states are not the only ones to have recognised the advantages of exploiting these biometric technologies. In particular, private actors are currently leading the way in the research and development of FRT, driven by profit motives, while authoritarian regimes are not unaware of the potential for the repression of dissent, as the recent *Glukhin* case of the European Court of Human Rights demonstrates.[13] The proliferation of these technologies carries with it an unimaginable power of surveillance, control and manipulation that can seriously threaten democracy, the rule of law and fundamental rights.

This volume explores such an impact. Building on the existing legal and technical scholarship on FRT, which has recently been further developed,[14] it goes one step further. It proposes novel contributions that focus on specific issues and uses of FRT, never discussed before following a systematic and coherent perspective. The *fil rouge* that keeps all the contributions connected is the impact of FRT on democracy. While other research has focused on the impact of FRT on fundamental rights, particularly privacy and data protection, this volume will focus on concrete FRT applications that endanger democracy and how such danger can be prevented.

This book becomes especially relevant within the current moment when the European Union (EU) is involved in a long-term project that plans to ensure biometric recordings of all citizens by using fingerprints and facial images. EU citizens are bound by these provisions since EU Regulation No. 2252/2004 includes obligatory biometric attributes (such as facial images) in passports and travel documents issued by the Member States (MS). Moreover, most governments all over the world and in Europe are currently implementing biometric IDs.[15] The initiative will initially concentrate on non-citizens by storing biometrics on databases such as Visa Information System (photos and fingerprints of short-term visa applicants) and Eurodac. Additionally, MS are also invited to ensure that biometric data from people accused of criminal offences is obtained for storage in European Criminal History Database Systems (ECRIS-TCN). But, above all, this analysis

[12] Selinger and Woodrow (2019).

[13] ECtHR, *Glukhin v. Russia*, App no 11519/20, 4 July 2023.

[14] Matulionyte and Zalnieriute (2024).

[15] World Privacy Forum (2021).

seems timely considering the European Union's efforts to develop a critical position and a general policy on biometric surveillance means in relation to the general regulation of AI. In this sense, the High-Level Expert Group on AI set up by the European Commission, in its Ethics Guidelines for Trustworthy AI of April 2019, underlined that '[i]dentification of individuals is sometimes the desirable outcome', but 'automatic identification raises strong concerns of both a legal and ethical nature, as it may have an unexpected impact on many psychological and sociocultural levels'.[16] Thereafter, the White Paper on AI officially published by the European Commission in 2020 stressed the need for 'a broad European debate' on remote biometric identification systems, considering the 'specific risks for fundamental rights',[17] even though a leaked version of the White Paper was suggesting the possibility of placing a moratorium on these technologies.[18] This path resulted in the Regulation of the European Parliament and of the Council laying down harmonised rules on Artificial Intelligence and amending certain union legislative acts (Artificial Intelligence Act) (hereafter AI Act),[19] proposed by the European Commission in April 2021, and which entered into force in August 2024 . The AI Act states that FRT is either a prohibited or high-risk AI application, or in some cases even out of scope (such as biometric authentication). However, the debate is very heated, considering that many actors, such as the European Data Protection Board (EDPB) and the European Data Protection Supervisor (EDPS), have called for a general ban on any use of AI for automated recognition of human features in publicly accessible spaces and for categorising individuals into clusters.[20] Thanks also to the progress made at European Union level, there is a growing awareness of the opportunities and dangers of FRT, which makes a study such as the one proposed here all the more useful and opportune.

This chapter will introduce the whole volume, and it is structured in the following way: section one introduced the context and justification of the volume, section two explains what FRT is and how it works, section three discusses the research approach and the contributions of the volume.

[16] High-Level Expert Group on Artificial Intelligence (2019), p. 33.

[17] European Commission (2020), pp. 21–22.

[18] Delcker and Smith-Meyer (2020).

[19] Regulation (EU) 2024/1689 of the European Parliament and of the Council of 13 June 2024 laying down harmonised rules on artificial intelligence and amending Regulations (EC) No 300/2008, (EU) No 167/2013, (EU) No 168/2013, (EU) 2018/858, (EU) 2018/1139 and (EU) 2019/2144 and Directives 2014/90/EU, (EU) 2016/797 and (EU) 2020/1828 (Artificial Intelligence Act).

[20] EDPB and EDPS (2021).

2 What Is Facial Recognition Technology and How It Works

According to the Guidelines 05/2022 on the use of facial recognition technology in the area of law enforcement by the European Data Protection Board, '[f]acial recognition is a probabilistic technology that can automatically recognise individuals based on their face in order to authenticate or identify them.'[21] It belongs to the wider area of biometric technologies which refer to automated methods that quantify an individual's morphological, physiological, or behavioural traits, such as fingerprints, iris structure, voice, gait, and blood vessel patterns. These traits are classified as 'biometric data' since they enable or confirm the unique identity of that person.[22]

To be able to recognise individuals, the technology performs a series of subprocesses. Such processes are, according to Article 29 Data Protection Working Party,[23] image acquisition,[24] face detection,[25] normalisation,[26] feature extraction,[27] enrolment[28] and comparison.[29] However, since the incorporation of Machine Learning techniques into FRT systems, the sequence of subprocesses has been affected. For instance, some state-of-the-art FRT systems do not process biometric templates,[30] which might affect the data processing from a legal perspective.

Facial Recognition Technology has two modalities: 'real-time' and 'post'. Real-time FRT, also known as Live FRT, LFRT, Automated FRT or AFR, entails that 'the capturing of biometric data, the comparison and the identification all occur without a significant delay and comprises not only instant identification but also limited short

---

[21] Paragraph 6.

[22] European Data Protection Board (2023).

[23] Data Protection Article 29 Working Party was an independent European advisory body on data protection and privacy set up under Article 29 of Directive 95/46/EC (also known as the Data Protection Directive). It was replaced by the European Data Protection Board (EDPB) on 25 May 2018 (entry into application of the EU General Data Protection Regulation, also known as the GDPR). See Article 29 Data Protection Working Party (2012a).

[24] 'The process of capturing the face of an individual and converting to a digital form (the digital image).'

[25] 'The process of detecting for the presence of a face within a digital image and marking the area.'

[26] 'The process to smooth variations across detected facial regions, e.g. converting to a standard size, rotating or aligning colour distributions.'

[27] 'The processing of isolating and outputting repeatable and distinctive readings from the digital image of an individual. Feature extraction can be holistic, feature-based or a combination of the two methods. The set of key features may be stored for later comparison in a reference template.'

[28] 'If this is the first time an individual has encountered the facial recognition system the image and/or reference template may be stored as a record for later comparison.'

[29] 'The process of measuring the similarity between a set of features (the sample) with one previously enrolled in the system.'

[30] According to the European Data Protection Board, a biometric template is the 'digital representation of distinct characteristics of [a] face.' (European Data Protection Board 2023).

delays in order to avoid circumvention'.[31] Post FRT means an FRT system other than a real-time one.[32] Traditionally, Live FRT is considered more 'dangerous' since it allows the performing of real-time mass surveillance as opposed to post FRT, which is usually aimed at targeted surveillance. In this line, the High-Level Expert Group on AI stated apropos FRT that '[c]learly defining if, when and how AI can be used for automated identification of individuals and differentiating between the identification of an individual vs the tracing and tracking of an individual, and between targeted surveillance and mass surveillance, will be crucial for the achievement of Trustworthy AI.'[33]

Essentially, FRT can perform three functions: identification, verification and categorisation. Identification means 'the automated recognition of physical, physiological, behavioural, or psychological human features for the purpose of establishing the identity of a natural person by comparing biometric data of that individual to biometric data of individuals stored in a database'.[34] Verification entails 'the automated, one-to-one verification, including authentication, of the identity of natural persons by comparing their biometric data to previously provided biometric data'.[35] Last but not least, categorisation consists of 'assigning natural persons to specific categories on the basis of their biometric data, unless it is ancillary to another commercial service and strictly necessary for objective technical reasons'.[36]

The categorisation function of biometric technologies in general and FRT in particular is its most controverted one due to two reasons. First, technically speaking, categorisation is not facial recognition since this only covers identification and verification.[37] However, supervisory authorities, such as Article 29 Data Protection Working Party, consider face recognition a means of categorisation.[38] Therefore, there is no agreement between technical and socio-legal stakeholders on whether face analysis, as it is also known, constitutes facial recognition. Second, the categorisation function of FRT has been subject to high criticism due to the lack of scientific evidence supporting such a research stream.[39] Further, this research has also been coined as 'physiognomic AI' and accused of perpetuating systemic societal bias, racism, and colonialism.[40]

Precisely, the categorisation function of FRT is one of the two main technological advantages provided by the introduction of AI to modern FRT systems. FRT

---

[31] Article 3(42) AI Act.

[32] Article 3(43) AI Act.

[33] High-Level Expert Group on Artificial Intelligence (2019).

[34] Article 3(35) AI Act.

[35] Article 3(36) AI Act.

[36] Article 3(40) AI Act.

[37] See ISO/IEC 2382-37:2022 definition of 'biometric recognition' in the harmonised biometric vocabulary.

[38] Article 29 Data Protection Working Party (2012a).

[39] Stark and Hutson (2022).

[40] Coalition for Critical Technology (2021).

categorisation systems ranging from sentiment analysis,[41] depression diagnosis,[42] sexual orientation,[43] lie,[44] and political ideology detectors[45] are all empowered by AI. However, as previously mentioned, the scientific value of this research has been highly questioned by academics all over the world, including campaigns against the publication of certain papers.[46]

Finally, the second technological advantage provided by AI was an exponential improvement in the accuracy of modern FRT. Before AI, facial images of people in movement, not directly looking into the camera, with glasses, hats, facial hair, and/or facial masks, were impossible to recognise. Further, low-quality images or images lacking perfect 'studio' conditions were also poorly recognised.[47] The combined power of AI and Big Data has entailed a revolution in the entire field of computer vision, of which FRT has taken advantage.

The reconstruction of the technical process may seem relatively simple, and there are relatively few modalities that can be adopted and functions that FRT can perform. However, this biometric technology can be used in many different areas and for many different purposes in a way that allows both targeted and large-scale tracking, prediction and manipulation that goes to the very heart of fundamental rights and democratic systems.[48]

3 The Research Approach and the Contents of This Book

The essays featured in this volume have considered the democratic challenges posed by FRT, from its design to its deployment by various actors in different contexts. Each chapter frames how the characteristics of FRT, as described in the previous section, are intertwined and eventually collide with democracy, fundamental rights and the rule of law.

The book approaches this challenging issue from a legal point of view, although the analysis cannot fail to consider studies dealing with the technical characteristics of these revolutionary technologies or their socio-economic impact. This broader perspective is necessary in order to delve more deeply into the issues covered, which have not yet been dealt with in a comprehensive manner.

This volume is mainly addressed to people who wish to gain a better knowledge and understanding of the impact of FRTs on the daily life and activities of

[41] Patel et al. (2020).
[42] Kong et al. (2022).
[43] Wang and Kosinski (2018).
[44] Sánchez-Monedero and Dencik (2022).
[45] Rasmussen et al. (2023).
[46] Coalition for Critical Technology (2021).
[47] Gates (2011).
[48] Christakis et al. (2022).

contemporary society, as it offers reflections on the legal consequences of the widespread diffusion of these biometric technologies on democratic systems. The book is also aimed at legal academics or practitioners who are interested in critically reflecting on these issues and keeping abreast of the latest developments. However, the analysis offered may also be of interest to academics in other disciplines, such as engineering, ethics, sociology, and politics, or to policymakers, given that studies in this field must necessarily be carried out in a multidisciplinary and interdisciplinary fashion.

The study will focus primarily on the legal systems of the European Union and its Member States, but scenarios and considerations concerning other regions will not be disregarded, given that these technologies circulate very easily around the globe.

The authors involved in the project to produce this book are legal scholars who, from different perspectives, are already engaged in academic research on law and biometric technologies. They have agreed to share their expertise in order to address the challenging topic of this volume according to a common rationale.

Chapter two 'Facial Recognition Technologies: Threats or Opportunities for Democracy?', by **Giuseppe Mobilio**, introduces the general issue of the interrelationship between democracy and FRTs. The analysis shows how this kind of biometric technology can be an opportunity or a threat for democracy. Indeed, FRTs directly affect several pillars of legal systems based on liberal constitutions, such as free and fair elections, citizen participation, protection of fundamental rights and the rule of law. The chapter looks at relevant cases of current applications of FRTs that have the effect of discouraging political participation by repressing political dissent and manipulating political participation by using techniques of profiling and political microtargeting, while facilitating political participation by providing access to public activities, namely voting. For each application, the practical benefits and growing concerns are explored. The aim is also to assess the regulatory response offered by data protection legislation, the AI Act and other relevant legislation. The common feature of the overall regulation is the emerging need to 'democratise' FRTs.

In chapter three 'Technical Solutions for a Proportional Use of Facial Recognition Technology', **Natalia Menéndez González** begins the analysis of the legal principles that shape the regulation of FRT and condition the concrete uses of this surveillance technology. Here the focus is on the principle of proportionality. The analysis starts off from a description of how the principle of proportionality applies to FRTs, drawing on the main known decisions of courts, data protection authorities and the EDPB that have provided for the application of this principle. Then the chapter offers a critical overview of some technical solutions that have been applied to FRTs in order to operationalise the principle of proportionality. Each of these solutions has its strengths and weaknesses, but the author underlines how the 'proportionality by design' approach could be a preferred solution for making the legal regulation of FRT more effective and democratic.

Chapter four 'Facial Recognition in Public Spaces and the Principle of Necessity' by **Catherine Jasserand-Breeman** focuses on the controversial use of FRTs in public spaces by law enforcement authorities. Given the particular intrusiveness of this use when it comes to fundamental rights and democratic values, the chapter examines how another general principle, namely the principle of necessity, sets the conditions for the deployment of FRTs. Drawing on the example of the recent *Glukhin* case, the analysis reconstructs the main framework and tests for implementing the necessity principle, taking into account the case law of the ECtHR and the ECJ, the guidance provided by the EDPB and the doctrinal elaborations essential for defining the limits that FRTs must respect. With a view to the future, the author also considers the guidelines offered by the AI Act and questions whether the new regulation also meets the requirements imposed by the necessity principle.

In chapter five 'Enhancing Oversight and Addressing Gaps: Assessing the Impact of the AI Act on Biometric Identification Systems', **Federica Paolucci** explores some of the most prominent effects of the entry into force of the AI Act, which could be broadly considered as a nuanced manifestation of the 'Brussels effect'. In particular, the analysis examines how the new regulation on biometric identification systems and its inspiring principles will establish itself as a global standard for the rule of law. In this regard, the chapter examines both the internal impact within the EU legal framework, i.e. on other pieces of legislation, and the external impact, i.e. on the role of Member States in implementing the AI Act. In addressing these issues, the author highlights many critical aspects that are expected to influence the future of biometric identification technologies, not only within the EU, but also beyond its borders.

Chapter 'Biometric Data and Facial Recognition Technology in the EU' by **Theodoros Karathanasis** is dedicated to the crucial issue of cybersecurity. More specifically, the chapter analyses how various pieces of legislation may affect biometrics and FRTs, taking into account the GDPR, the NIS 2 Directive and the Cybersecurity Act, as well as the Cyber Resilience Act and the Cyber Solidarity Act, also mentioning the AI Act. The analysis looks at the main pillars of these complex and intertwined pieces of legislation. In outlining the general criticisms that have arisen in response to the various provisions, the author focuses on several specific cases, such as security breaches, data security, large-scale processing of biometric data for security purposes, the range of risk assessment and management techniques, and the systems of administrative penalties provided for under these legal regimes. The study shows that the security of FRTs and the data processed is bound to become as crucial as the disentanglement of the relevant legislation will be challenging.

Chapter "FRT and Access to Public Services: What Acceptable Uses in Smart Cities?" by **Isadora Neroni Rezende** reflects on the ability of FRTs to invade the most intimate and inner circle of people, to the extent that it is able to read and condition emotions. On this basis, the chapter analyses the use of FRT by law enforcement authorities to achieve what is called 'emotional dominance'. The massive proliferation and increasing use of biometric surveillance tools after 9/11 has contributed to a shift from their use for military purposes to the normalisation of their use for security purposes. The analysis challenges whether and how this kind of surveillance is compatible with democratic regimes by critically reconstructing the legal response, taking into account both key case law and the AI Act.

Finally, the volume closes with chapter "From Identity to Emotional Dominance? "Early Warnings" on Emotion Recognition Uses by Police Forces", where **Francesco Paolo Levantino** looks at one of the most widespread applications of FRT, which is the deployment of this biometric tool in smart city environments. Special attention is given to the challenge of using FRTs in public spaces to provide access to public services. The analysis starts from the difference between technology-driven and human-driven conceptions of smart cities, highlighting how these different approaches can influence the legal framework. The chapter focuses on FRT deployment to improve the efficiency of a service or to detect irregularities in the uses of services. For each of these situations, an assessment based on the principle of proportionality is carried out in order to provide some guidance on the legal acceptability of FRTs.

All the chapters in this book are the result of papers presented and discussed during the Conference 'Next Democratic Frontiers for Facial Recognition Technology. The Legal, Ethical and Democratic Implications of FRT', which took place in Florence on 29 September 2023. This event was organised by the Department of Legal Sciences of the University of Florence, the Chair of AI and Democracy at the School of Transnational Governance of the European University Institute and the Haifa Center for Cyber, Law and Policy.

References

Anderson K et al (2019) A.I. among us: Agency in a World of Cameras and Recognition Systems 2019 Ethnographic Praxis. Industry Conference Proceedings, 38, 40 https://onlinelibrary.wiley.com/doi/abs/10.1111/1559-8918.2019.01264. Accessed 2 July 2023

Article 29 Data Protection Working Party (2012a) Opinion 02/2012 on facial recognition in online and mobile services. 00727/12/EN. WP 192

Berle I (2020) Face recognition technology: compulsory visibility and its impact on privacy and the confidentiality of personal identifiable images. Springer International Publishing. https://doi.org/10.1007/978-3-030-36887-6

Christakis T et al (2022) Mapping the use of facial recognition in public spaces in Europe - Part. 3: Facial recognition for authorisation purposes. https://ai-regulation.com/wp-content/uploads/2022/05/Report3-MAPFRE-Christakis-et-al.pdf

Coalition for Critical Technology (2021, September 21) Abolish the #TechToPrisonPipeline. Medium. https://medium.com/@CoalitionForCriticalTechnology/abolish-the-techtoprisonpipeline-9b5b14366b16. Accessed 10 Aug 2023

Delcker J, Smith-Meyer B (16 January 2020) EU considers temporary ban on facial recognition in public spaces. Politico

European Commission (2020 February 19) White Paper "On Artificial Intelligence - A European approach to excellence and trust". COM(2020) 65 final

European Data Protection Board (2023 April 26) Guidelines 05/2022 on the use of facial recognition technology in the area of law enforcement. Version 2.0

European Data Protection Board, European Data Protection Supervisor (2021) EDPB-EDPS Joint Opinion 5/2021 on the proposal for a Regulation of the European Parliament and of the Council laying down harmonised rules on artificial intelligence (Artificial Intelligence Act). https://edpb.europa.eu/system/files/2021-06/edpb-edps_joint_opinion_ai_regulation_en.pdf. Accessed 19 Apr 2024

European Union Agency for Fundamental Rights (2019) Facial recognition technology: fundamental rights considerations in the context of law enforcement. Publications Office. https://data.europa.eu/doi/10.2811/52597

Gates KA (2011) Our biometric future: facial recognition technology and the culture of surveillance. NYU Press. https://www.jstor.org/stable/j.ctt9qg8xd. Accessed 25 Oct 2023

High-Level Expert Group on Artificial Intelligence (2019) Ethics Guidelines for Trustworthy Artificial Intelligence (AI)

Introna LD, Nissenbaum H (2010) Facial recognition technology a survey of policy and implementation issues. The Center for Catastrophe Preparedness & Response. New York University. 24

ISO/IEC 2382-37:2022(En). Information Technology — Vocabulary — Part 37: Biometrics. https://www.iso.org/obp/ui/#iso:std:iso-iec:2382:-37:ed-3:v1:en. Accessed 26 Mar 2024

Kindt EJ (2016) Privacy and data protection issues of biometric applications. Springer

Kong X et al (2022) Automatic identification of depression using facial images with deep convolutional neural network. Med Sci Monit 28:e936409

Matulionyte M, Zalnieriute M (eds) (2024) The Cambridge handbook of facial recognition in the modern state. Cambridge University Press

Menéndez González N (2022) 'Brave New (Normal) World': can the COVID-19 emergency serve as an excuse to increase the surveillance state with facial recognition technology? In: de Abreu Duarte F, Palmiotto Ettorre F (eds) Sovereignty, technology and governance after COVID-19: legal challenges in a postpandemic Europe. Oxford - Hart Publishing Bloomsbury Collections, pp 119–136. Web. 2 Jul. 2023. https://doi.org/10.5040/9781509956012.ch-007

Mobilio G (2023) Your face is not new to me – regulating the surveillance power of facial recognition technologies. Internet Policy Rev 12(1):1–31. https://doi.org/10.14763/2023.1.1699

Mobilio G (2024) When the kids aren't alright: the use of facial recognition technologies at school. In: Prifti K, Demir E, Krämer J, Heine K, Stamhuis E (eds) Digital governance. Confronting the challenges posed by artificial intelligence. Springer

Patel K et al (2020) Facial sentiment analysis using AI techniques: state-of-the-art, taxonomies, and challenges. IEEE Access 8:90495

Perrault R, Shoham Y, Brynjolfsson E, Clark J, Etchemendy J, Grosz B, Lyons T, Manyika J, Mishra S, Niebles JC (2019 December) The AI Index 2019 Annual Report, AI Index Steering Committee. Human-Centered AI Institute, Stanford University, Stanford, CA, 90

Rasmussen SHR, Ludeke SG, Klemmensen R (2023) Using deep learning to predict ideology from facial photographs: expressions, beauty, and extra-facial information. Sci Rep 13:5257

Sánchez-Monedero J, Dencik L (2022) The politics of deceptive borders: "biomarkers of deceit" and the case of iBorderCtrl. Inf Commun Soc 25:413. https://www.tandfonline.com/doi/full/10.1080/1369118X.2020.1792530. Accessed 27 Mar 2024

Selinger E, Woodrow H (2019) The inconsentability of facial surveillance. Loy Law Rev 66:101. https://scholarship.law.bu.edu/faculty_scholarship/3066

Stark L, Hutson J (2022) Physiognomic artificial intelligence. Fordham Intell Prop Media Ent Law J 32:922. https://ir.lawnet.fordham.edu/iplj/vol32/iss4/2

Wang Y, Kosinski M (2018) Deep neural networks are more accurate than humans at detecting sexual orientation from facial images. J Pers Soc Psychol 114:246

Warren SD, Brandeis LD (1890) The right to privacy. Harv Law Rev 4:–193. https://www.jstor.org/stable/1321160. Accessed 2 July 2023

Wheeler FW, Weiss RL, Tu PH (2010) Face recognition at a distance system for surveillance applications, 2010 Fourth IEEE International Conference on Biometrics: Theory, Applications and Systems (BTAS). https://ieeexplore.ieee.org/document/5634523. Accessed 30 Oct 2023

World Privacy Forum (2021) National IDs Around the World — Interactive Map. https://www.worldprivacyforum.org/2021/10/national-ids-and-biometrics/. Accessed 2 July 2023

Facial Recognition Technologies: Threats or Opportunities for Democracy?

Giuseppe Mobilio

Abstract The rule of law, democracy and fundamental rights are strictly entrenched in liberal constitutions. The widespread adoption of AI-based technologies can be seen as an opportunity or a serious threat to these pillars. In particular, facial recognition technologies (FRTs) open up a wide range of practical benefits, but they can also enable new forms of mass surveillance and interference with free and fair elections or citizens' participation in political life. This chapter examines the implications for democracy of the proliferation of FRTs. To this end, the analysis will focus on three paradigmatic deployments of FRTs, which are: identification, that allows people to be tracked in public spaces and thus discourages political participation; categorisation, that allows people to be profiled and thus manipulates political participation; and verification, that allows people to be granted access to voting and thus facilitates political participation. For each of these paradigmatic cases, the chapter underlines pros and cons of the use of FRTs, also in order to assess how the legal regulation addresses the concerns raised in the EU context. A fil rouge of the legal response is identified in the need to address threats to democracy by 'democratising' the same FRTs.

Keywords Facial recognition · Democracy · Political participation, transparency · Security

1 Introduction

Facial recognition technologies (FRTs) are biometric technologies that confer great surveillance power on public authorities and private actors. Their use has implications for some of the key pillars of liberal constitutions, such as the rule of law,

G. Mobilio (✉)
University of Florence, Department of Legal Science, Florence, Italy
e-mail: giuseppe.mobilio@unifi.it

N. Menéndez González, G. Mobilio (eds.), *Next Democratic Frontiers for Facial Recognition Technology (FRT)*, Law, Governance and Technology Series 74,
https://doi.org/10.1007/978-3-031-89794-8_2

human rights and democracy.[1] In particular, the issue of FRTs is closely linked to the idea of 'digital democracy', which investigates how the use of digital technologies may influence the conditions, institutions and practices of political engagement and democratic governance.[2] In this sense, the use of FRTs can directly or indirectly affect all the main elements of democratic systems as recently defined within the Council of Europe framework, namely: the choice and replacement of political bodies by means of free and fair elections; the participation of citizens in all aspects of social, political and economic life; human rights protection and the rule of law; and safeguards and guarantees to assure the equitable and fair application of laws and procedures to all citizens.[3]

FRTs, and AI-based technologies in general, have an ambiguous relationship with democracy. Technologies are not democratic per se: 'whether a technology is democratic or not depends on how it is used'.[4] Accordingly, FRTs can 'boost' democracy,[5] but they can also be a 'disruptive force'.[6] The model of liberal democracies has been challenged by several new conceptual categories, depending on whether these types of surveillance technologies are misused by governments, as in the case of 'digital authoritarianism',[7] thereby undermining the legitimacy of the democratic process, as for the risks of 'algocracy',[8] or even they are misused by private actors, as in the case of 'surveillance capitalism'.[9] In addition, there is still no clear perception of citizen support for AI in government and politics.[10] If unaccountable uses of AI, such as those for surveillance purposes, find acceptance among citizens, for example because they are viewed as bringing more convenience and efficiency, this could gradually lead to what has been called a kind of 'democratic paternalism'.[11] As a result, in the recent 'Draft Framework Convention on artificial intelligence, human rights, democracy and the rule of law', adopted on 14 March 2024, the Council of Europe's Committee on Artificial Intelligence stressed the importance of ensuring that 'artificial intelligence systems are not used to undermine the integrity, independence and effectiveness of democratic institutions and processes' (Article. 5).[12]

This chapter will address some of the most debated uses of FRTs that directly impact on democracy. In particular, the paper will focus on three cases of application

[1]Nemitz (2018).

[2]Berg and Hofmann (2021).

[3]EGE (2023), p. 7.

[4]Boehme-Neßler (2020), p. 80.

[5]Cavaliere and Graziella (2022).

[6]König and Wenzelburger (2020).

[7]Wright (2018).

[8]Danaher (2016).

[9]Zuboff (2019).

[10]König (2022).

[11]König (2022), p. 2.

[12]CAI (2024).

of FRTs to discourage (§2), manipulate (§3) and facilitate (§4) political participation, each associated with one of the main purposes that can be pursued through the use of these biometric technologies. For each of these cases, the analysis will also consider the EU legislation in force that seeks to protect the aforementioned elements underpinning democratic systems, such as data protection legislation (both Regulation (EU) 2016/679 (General Data Protection Regulation—GDPR) and Directive (EU) 2016/680 (Law Enforcement Directive—LED), the Regulation (EU) 2024/1689 (Artificial Intelligence Act—AI Act), and other relevant legislation. The aim of this Chapter is also to verify whether there are common features that shape the regulatory response to these challenges to democracy (§5). Finally, some brief conclusions will be drawn (§6).

2 Identification of People and the Risk of Discouraging Political Participation

The first relevant purpose of FRTs is *identification*. We have identification, also called 1-to-many comparison, when the biometric template extracted from a facial image is compared with a watchlist of many images. The main application of FRTs for identification purposes that has a relevant impact on democracy and the rule of law is the *tracking* of people in publicly accessible spaces. Biometric systems have been coupled with big data analytics and, as a result, it is now possible to capture live data, turn them into digital data and combine them with information available in public and private databases or online, including through social media.[13] In this way, FRTs can be used to monitor people, *discourage* political participation and restrict freedom of assembly and expression, as well as the right to data protection.

FRTs give to the public authorities, and in particular law enforcement agencies, a great capacity to pursue public interest tasks, such as the fight against crime. However, in 2012 the Article 29 Working Party already observed that in case of FRTs 'where biometric data can be easily captured without the knowledge of the data subject a widespread use would terminate anonymity in public spaces and allow consistent tracking of individuals'.[14] More recently, the EDPB declared that 'remote biometric identification of individuals in publicly accessible spaces poses a high risk of intrusion into individuals' private lives and does not have a place in a democratic society, as by its nature, it entails mass surveillance'.[15]

---

[13] Acquisti et al. (2014).

[14] ART29WP (2012), p. 9.

[15] EDPB (2022), §104.

Such concerns have recently been addressed by the European Court of Human Rights in the case of *Glukhin v. Russia*.[16] This case involved a Russian peaceful protester who had been arrested after the Russian authorities deployed FRTs, firstly, to identify him from the photographs and the video of the protest published on Telegram ('ex post' use of FRTs) and, secondly, to locate and arrest him while he was travelling on the Moscow underground ('live' and 'real-time' use of FRTs). The ECtHR stated that the Russian authorities unlawfully violated the freedom of expression (Article 10 ECHR) and the right to privacy (Article 8 ECHR) of the applicant because, inter alia, such interferences are not 'necessary in a democratic society'. Regarding *freedom of expression*, the demonstration was carried out in an indisputably peaceful and non-disruptive manner, while the only offence was the applicant's failure to notify the authorities of his demonstration. No reprehensible act was committed, but the authorities showed no tolerance towards the applicant's peaceful solo demonstration.[17] Regarding the *right to privacy and data protection*, the contested use of FRTs was qualified by the ECtHR as 'particularly intrusive' and, accordingly, 'a high level of justification is therefore required' ('the highest' in case of the use of 'live' FRTs), also considering the processing of data that reveal political opinions.[18] However, though the protester—as said—was never accused of committing any reprehensible acts, the domestic law permits the processing of biometric personal data in connection with the investigation and prosecution of any offence, irrespective of its nature and gravity.[19] In the end, the ECtHR concluded that such use of 'highly intrusive' FRTs 'is incompatible with the ideals and values of a democratic society governed by the rule of law, which the Convention was designed to maintain and promote.'[20]

From a regulatory perspective, the ECtHR stressed that restrictions on these rights need to be grounded in a law that meets several *qualitative conditions*. Thus, the ECtHR stated that it is 'essential' for the use of FRTs 'to have detailed rules governing the scope and application of measures as well as strong safeguards against the risk of abuse and arbitrariness'; such a need is even 'greater' where the use of live FRTs is concerned.[21] The Russian legal framework, by contrast, was 'widely formulated', so that the domestic law allows the processing of biometric data 'in connection with any judicial proceedings'. Moreover, Russian law does not contain any limitations 'on the nature of situations' which may lead to the use of FRTs, 'the intended purposes, the categories of people who may be targeted, or on processing of sensitive personal data'. Nor does it provide for 'any procedural safeguards', such as 'the authorisation procedures, the procedures to be followed for examining, using

[16] ECtHR, Glukhin v. Russia, no. 11519/20, 4 July 2023. See Palmiotto and Menéndez González (2023), Neroni Rezende (2023).

[17] ECtHR, Glukhin v. Russia, cit., § 55–56.

[18] ECtHR, Glukhin v. Russia, cit., § 86.

[19] ECtHR, Glukhin v. Russia, cit., § 86–88.

[20] ECtHR, Glukhin v. Russia, cit., § 90.

[21] ECtHR, Glukhin v. Russia, cit., § 82.

and storing the data obtained, supervisory control mechanisms and available remedies.'[22]

In the same vein, Article 52(1) CFREU states that any limitation on the exercise of fundamental rights 'must be provided for by law', and the CJEU has clarified that the law must lay down 'clear and precise rules' governing 'the scope and application of the measure' in question, imposing 'minimum safeguards' against the risk of abuse.[23]

The AI Act adds something extra to the existing rules governing FRTs, taking into account both the 'real-time' and 'ex post' use of FRTs considered in the *Glukhin* case. Firstly, the Regulation establishes a 'red line'[24] by prohibiting "real-time' remote biometric identification systems in publicly accessible spaces for law enforcement purposes', although there are broad exceptions provided in the Article 5.[25] However, Member States will have to specify the rules that apply to FRTs and may also provide for the option of restricting their use in relation to the offences to be prosecuted.[26] Thus, as also specified in Recital 38, national rules will be indispensable, as the AI Act cannot be relied upon as a sufficient legal basis under the provisions of data protection legislation, which requires that biometric data should only be processed where authorised by EU or national law.[27] Secondly, according to Article 26(10), the 'ex post' use of FRTs will be considered a 'high risk' system, resulting in the imposition of numerous burdens on all the operators in the value chain (such as providers, deployers, manufacturer, importers or distributors of AI systems).[28]

3 Categorisation of Voters and the Risk of Manipulating Political Participation

The second relevant purpose of FRTs is *categorisation*. In this case the aim is not strictly to identify a person, but rather to infer several characteristics from the facial image and to classify that person into one or more categories. One of the most important applications of categorisation affecting democracy is the *profiling* of people. As far as this aspect is concerned, FRTs enable the extraction of information

[22] ECtHR, Glukhin v. Russia, cit., § 83.

[23] CJEU, Digital Rights Ireland, Joined Cases C-293/12 and C-594/12, ECLI:EU:C:2014:238, 8 April 2014, § 54; V.S., C-205/21, ECLI:EU:C:2023:49, 26 January 2023, §65 ff. See also Article 10(a) Directive (EU) 2016/680.

[24] Smuha et al. (2021).

[25] Article 5 AI Act.

[26] Article 5(5) AI Act.

[27] Article 10 LED.

[28] Christakis et al. (2021).

from face images as never before.[29] They make it possible not only to infer whether an individual belongs to a particular group based on characteristics such as sex, age, or race, but also to deduce further information, such as political preferences. A recent and much discussed study shows that ML algorithms are able to establish a correlation between facial images and political orientation (liberal or conservative) with a success rate of around 70% when analysing image pairs of people with different political orientations, and just under 3% less when using faces of people of the same age, gender and ethnicity.[30] As a result, FRTs become a powerful tool for *manipulating* political participation, thanks to the practices of political marketing that they can enable.

In fact, if FRTs allow political orientation to be inferred simply through an analysis of facial images, these technologies can be deployed for broader political microtargeting. This is a technique of personalised communication that involves gathering information about people and using it to deliver targeted political advertisements that speak to their concerns and resonate with their opinions.[31] After the Cambridge Analytica scandal,[32] this 'weaponised'[33] form of propaganda has become well known for its power to massively alter free elections and voting.[34] However, political microtargeting also has several potential benefits:[35] it can increase the political participation of citizens, help them to make more informed voting choices and thus strengthen democracy; it can help political parties to run cheaper, more efficient and effective political campaigns; it can increase the diversity of political campaigns, emphasising the different positions of political actors to the benefit of public opinion. By contrast, political microtargeting combined with FRTs raises many concerns that are actually also related to the identification purposes described in §2.

The first set of concerns relates to the *accuracy* of FRTs. The above-mentioned study refers to a failure rate of nearly 30%, which is high. Furthermore, political orientation was not predicted by analysing the facial image of one person alone, but always by comparing two images. Accuracy is undermined by the inability to detect emotions, personal traits or inner beliefs, given the general technical and scientific failure to achieve such a result with certainty.[36] Moreover, as is well known, facial recognition can be inaccurate due to bias in training datasets.[37] The accuracy of ML algorithms that are used to automatically infer information, as well as for

[29] See chapter 8 in this volume by Levantino.

[30] Kosinski (2021).

[31] Council of Europe (2021), p. 23.

[32] https://www.theguardian.com/technology/2017/may/07/the-great-british-brexit-robbery-hijacked-democracy

[33] Manheim and Kaplan (2019), p. 134.

[34] Bradshaw and Howard (2018).

[35] Borgesius et al. (2018), p. 84 ff.

[36] Barrett (2020).

[37] Borgesius (2018), p. 17.

identification purposes, will be compromised if the training data reflect implicit biases.[38] In this regard, different studies have shown that dark-skinned people and women are significantly underrepresented in training datasets compared to light-skinned men of Caucasian origin.[39] As a result, FRTs are not reliable tools for political microtargeting and there is a risk that the potential benefits of this practice will be lost or, worse, that the inaccuracy may lead to discrimination.

Another set of concerns is related to the impact of FRT-supported political microtargeting on the same *fundamental rights* mentioned in §2. In the case of the right to data protection, this kind of political communication is based on the collection and combination of massive amounts of personal data about citizens in order to infer sensitivities and political preferences. Voters' data protection can thus be undermined. Citizens can also be manipulated by tailoring and distorting information, or they can even be ignored if not expected to vote.[40] In the case of freedom of expression, citizens have the right to inform themselves and receive political information from a diversity of sources and perspectives.[41] However, FRTs and AI in general contribute to shaping the information environment of citizens, intervening in their opinion formation and the social construction of reality for the wider public.[42] The creation of filter bubbles is one of the most serious consequences of this practice.[43]

Finally, FRTs and political microtargeting put significant power in the hands of *private actors*. Political parties are turning to data brokerage firms or social media platforms to purchase microtargeting services that exploit ML algorithms to predict and alter emotions and thoughts.[44] Mostly, as also noted at European level, these actors no longer serve as simple channels of communication between individuals and institutions but play an increasingly prominent role on their own, setting the agenda and shaping and transforming social and political models.[45] As a result, we are witnessing 'an unprecedented and un-checked concentration of data, information and power in the hands of a small group of major digital companies'.[46] Therefore, the authority of democratic States may be threatened by private actors who may use such algorithmic tools without adequate democratic oversight or control.[47]

---

[38] Leslie (2020).

[39] Buolamwini and Gebru (2018); Grother et al. (2019).

[40] Borgesius et al. (2018), p. 87 ff.

[41] See Bodó et al. (2017). Political advertising is protected speech pursuant to Article 10 ECHR, but, according to Article 3 of Protocol 1 to the Convention, the freedom of expression of a political party can be restricted in order to secure the 'free expression of the opinion of the people in the choice of the legislature' and to 'protect the electoral process'; see ECtHR, Bowman v UK, No. 24839/94, 19 February 1988, §43; Animal Defenders International v UK, No. 48876/08, 22 April 2013, § 111.

[42] König, Wenzelburger (2020), p. 5.

[43] Shaffer (2019).

[44] Barrett et al. (2019).

[45] Parliamentary Assembly of the Council of Europe (PACE) (2020).

[46] Parliamentary Assembly of the Council of Europe (PACE) (2020).

[47] Council of Europe (2019).

If FRTs are used for categorisation purposes, there is a regulatory framework to address the concerns raised, which strikes a balance between *prohibition* and *transparency* in the use of such techniques of political communication and manipulation.

On the one hand, there are now specific rules that relate directly to the technology itself. In particular, the AI Act includes a prohibition on biometric categorisation systems that categorise individuals 'based on their biometric data to deduce or infer [...] political opinions' (Article 5(1)(g)). This prohibition was added during the adoption process of the Regulation and could be intended to exclude the experimental uses of TRFs mentioned above, but also to avoid the problems related to accuracy and impact on fundamental rights. However, some doubts remain as long as it is not clear which uses will actually be covered by this ban. These rules will certainly apply to exclude attempts to identify a person's political affiliation, for example on the basis of physiognomy. But it is not certain whether it will still be possible to set up a political information campaign that differentiates people on the basis of their facial features and, once this classification has been made, associates different information with them: for example, providing different information on the basis of somatic features, age or state of health.

On the other hand, even if there was space for this kind of biometric categorisation, the AI Act foresees some transparency obligations. Deployers of biometric categorisation systems must inform the persons exposed thereto of the operation of the system.[48] In addition, the AI Act includes provisions aimed at enhancing the accuracy of FRTs, such as those establishing data quality requirements, harmonised standards, or common specifications.[49] In addition, as a general rule, high-risk AI systems should be tested before being put on the market or otherwise put into service in order to ensure that such systems perform consistently with their intended purpose and are in compliance with the requirements set out by the new Regulation.[50] Deployers of a high-risk AI system must be duly informed of the system's characteristics, capabilities and limitations of performance (Article 13 AI Act).

Data protection legislation is also in line with the need to promote transparency. As is well known, biometric data and people's political opinions are included among the 'special categories of data', which cannot be processed unless the processing falls under certain exceptions.[51] In the cases of FRT-based political microtargeting, the legal ground must be 'explicit consent'.[52] Moreover, personal data must be

---

[48] Article 50(3) AI Act.

[49] Articles 10, 40, 41 AI Act.

[50] Article 9 AI Act.

[51] Article 9 GDPR.

[52] Article 9.2(a) GDPR. Unless data are 'manifestly made public by the data subject' (Article 9.2 (e) GDPR); but in this case it is not sufficient for a facial photo to have been made public on a social network, as the data subject must be aware that the data will be publicly available to everyone, including the authorities (ART29WP 2017a, p. 10).

processed in a fair and transparent way[53] and, accordingly, data subjects have the right to receive information 'in a concise, transparent, intelligible and easily accessible form'.[54] The same explicit consent is one of the legal bases required for profiling activities that significantly affect a person through the use of FRTs, accompanied by appropriate safeguards, at least the right to obtain human intervention, to express one's point of view or to contest the decision taken.[55] At the same time, however, the limits and mystification of the traditional principle of 'notice and consent' are well known, so that giving consent or receiving information does not necessarily imply a greater awareness of the nature of the processing.[56]

However, the issue of FRT-based political microtargeting is also addressed by other pieces of legislation that are not directly related to FRTs. With regard to political advertising, a particularly relevant set of rules are those on party financing, which must ensure transparency and fairness in the way parties receive and spend public and private money to fund their campaigns.[57] On the other hand, if we look at the private intermediaries that manage political communication, the most promising developments may be found in the provisions of Regulation (EU) 2022/2065 on a Single Market For Digital Services (DSA). Article 26 of the DSA imposes obligations on the platforms concerned to disclose political advertising and to provide some information, such as the person on whose behalf the advertisement is presented; who paid for the advertisement; and the parameters used to determine the recipient. In addition, advertising based on profiling using special categories of personal data, such as biometric data, is explicitly prohibited for online platform providers.[58] Finally, a more systematic legislation has been adopted with Regulation (EU) 2024/900, on 'the transparency and targeting of political advertising'.[59] This Regulation has recently introduced many additional transparency and due diligence obligations for providers of advertising services, publishers and sponsors.[60] Political advertisements must be made available with a transparency label and a transparency notice providing key information such as sponsors, the amounts paid or any use of targeting techniques.[61] Specific rules apply to targeting and ad delivery,[62] which are only allowed under strict conditions, such as an explicit and separate consent for the use of data for political advertising. Targeting is subject to additional transparency requirements, while profiling based on special categories of personal data is

[53] Article 5.1(a) GDPR.

[54] Article 12 GDPR.

[55] Article 22 GDPR.

[56] Custers et al. (2022), p. 466 ff.

[57] Bodó et al. (2017).

[58] Article 26(3) DSA.

[59] van Drunen et al. (2022).

[60] Chapter II of Regulation (EU) 2024/900.

[61] Articles 11-12, Regulation (EU) 2024/900.

[62] Chapter III of Regulation (EU) 2024/900.

explicitly prohibited.[63] This prohibition is a general rule that must be read in conjunction with the specific prohibition of biometric categorisation in the AI Act, thus confirming a restrictive approach to this type of categorisation.

4 Verification of Identities and the Promise of Facilitating Political Participation

The third relevant purpose of FRTs is *verification*. We have verification, also called 1-to-1 comparison, when the biometric template extracted from a facial image is compared with a single existing image of the same individual. In this case, the most relevant application of FRTs with a direct impact on democracy is tied to *providing access* to public activities, namely voting. The combination of biometric technologies and the electoral process is a relevant application of e-voting, which is the use of electronic means to cast and/or count the vote.[64] In this realm, FRTs can be used to verify whether an individual is eligible to vote by matching a person's facial features with the stored images in the database of eligible voters. There are also some variables to consider, such as whether this system can be used alone or as a means of verification supplemental to, for example, fingerprints. Moreover, FRTs can be used inside the polling booth under the supervision of an election officer or to allow access from personal devices and remote voting. This type of system is already available in some States in slightly different forms,[65] and a number of studies are proposing that it be combined with blockchain technology.[66] In this way, unlike the cases described in the previous sections, FRTs can be used to *promote* political participation.

FRT-based voting can potentially have many practical benefits in terms of *facilitating* participation in elections and voting:[67] enabling voters to cast their votes from a place other than the polling station in their electoral district; making it easier for voters with reduced mobility or those who have other physical difficulties to take part in the electoral process; and increasing voter turnout by providing additional voting channels. Moreover, it can make voting cheaper by reducing the overall cost of the electoral process over time, and more efficient by delivering voting results reliably and more quickly.

But we must not make the mistake of fetishising technology,[68] because *it doesn't bring progress per se*. Remote voting results in the loss of the symbolic and ritual

[63] Article 18(1)(c), Regulation (EU) 2024/900.

[64] Council of Europe (2017).

[65] Heiberg et al. (2021).

[66] Revathy et al. (2022); Sreekanth et al. (2022); Prathyusha et al. (2023).

[67] Council of Europe (2017).

[68] Cheeseman et al. (2018).

function of the vote, which contributes to the integration of citizens in democracy.[69] Also, many measures must be taken to prevent coercion and safeguard free and secret suffrage.[70] Moreover, voters who do not have cameras of sufficient quality are automatically excluded, with an impact on equal suffrage.[71]

In addition, the same concerns as mentioned in §3 arise here. In terms of accuracy, even the best current algorithms have a certain error rate, especially when the facial images are captured in an uncontrolled (wild) environment.[72] And if an error occurs, an eligible voter may be prevented from voting (false negative), or an ineligible voter may be substituted for an eligible one (false positive). In terms of data protection, we need to consider the risks associated with storing images, accessing data, etc. In terms of the increasing power of private actors, the use of smartphones and facial recognition services provided by third parties may be critical in elections. Again, issues of freedom, equality and secrecy in voting come to the fore.

Furthermore, in the case of FRT-based voting, specific problems are posed in relation to the *security* of the systems. The Council of Europe has recently clarified that the issue of security in e-voting is very complex, as it entails ensuring the different dimensions of integrity and authenticity, availability and reliability, secrecy and confidentiality, usability and accessibility.[73] However, with reference to FRTs in particular, specific threats to the electoral process may come from people's attempts to replace themselves with another person through spoofing attacks.[74] In this regard it would be crucial to detect subject liveness, i.e. to make sure that a still image is not shown into a camera instead of a real person. To this end, FRTs have been combined with active liveness detection, which prompt the users to follow given guidelines in order to prove that they are alive, or passive liveness detection, which checks the consistency of the captured data.[75]

From a regulatory perspective, the security of FRT-based voting is addressed based on the principle of *accountability*. If these systems are attacked, we need to refer to national criminal law that punishes identity theft or fraud. However, in the case of identity substitution resulting in a false positive, we must also refer to data protection legislation that protects the processing of one's personal data. Here the legislation reflects what has been called an accountability-oriented approach.[76] Indeed, according to the principle of accountability, the controller must implement 'appropriate technical and organisational measures' in order to comply and be able to

---

[69] Boehme-Neßler (2020), p. 83.

[70] Krips and Willemson (2019).

[71] Heiberg et al. (2021).

[72] https://pages.nist.gov/frvt/html/frvt11.html.

[73] Council of Europe (2022).

[74] Hao and Howell O'Neill (2020).

[75] Heiberg et al. (2021).

[76] Quelle (2018).

demonstrate compliance with data protection rules.[77] These measures are mainly aimed at ensuring the 'security of processing',[78] which is assessed on the basis of several parameters and the risks for the rights of people.[79] Moreover, according to the further principles of 'integrity and confidentiality', these measures must ensure appropriate security, including protection against unauthorised or unlawful processing and against accidental loss, destruction or damage.[80] Depending on the nature and level of the election, the authority to be held accountable for processing biometric data must therefore be identified and be subject to control and corrective powers by the national supervisory authorities.

The AI Act does not consider FRTs used for verification purposes to be high-risk AI systems per se,[81] and therefore the rules on 'accuracy, robustness and cybersecurity' do not apply.[82] However, there are other relevant pieces of legislation that address security issues of FRTs employed for e-voting, such as Directive (EU) 2022/2555 (NIS 2 Directive). These specific rules apply to public or private entities operating in the digital infrastructure sector or being public administrations, and can therefore be considered as 'essential entities'.[83] Those responsible for the management of FRT systems aimed at facilitating political participation are also responsible for taking appropriate and proportionate technical, operational and organisational measures to manage the risks posed to the security of network and information systems.[84]

5 The Common Need to 'Democratise' FRTs

The three cases of application of FRTs have a direct impact on all the elements that underpin democratic systems, as mentioned in the Introduction (§1). Political participation can be discouraged, manipulated or facilitated depending on the purpose and types of use of these technologies. However, the results that can be achieved are not clear.

Tracking and profiling activities are very likely to indirectly distort voting outcomes. These controversial uses of FRTs for identification and categorisation can also lead to problems of accuracy and expose the right to data protection and freedom of assembly to serious violations and abuses by public authorities and/or

[77] Article 24 GDPR; Article 19 LED.

[78] Article 32 GDPR; Article 29 LED.

[79] These parameters are the state of the art, the costs of implementation, and the nature, scope, context and purpose of the processing. See EDPB (2020), §87 ff.

[80] Article 5.1(f) GDPR; Article 4.1(f) LED.

[81] Annex III(1)(a) AI Act.

[82] Article 15 AI Act.

[83] Annex I NIS 2.

[84] Article 21 NIS 2.

private actors. This has implications for the rule of law and the equal and fair application of the law to all citizens. However, it is also possible that tracking activity, if properly regulated, can safeguard public order and thus allow citizens legitimately to exercise their democratic freedoms. Even profiling, if not weaponised, can be aimed at enhancing freedom of information and thus promoting a more informed vote. On the contrary, FRT-assisted voting may give rise to social, technical and legal problems that create barriers instead of promoting political freedoms. As a result, the discourse on FRTs is more about risks and promises than certainties.

As we have seen, there is an overlap between different regulatory frameworks, and different solutions are in place to address this ambiguity. However, each regulatory response seems to stem from a common root, which can be synthesised as the need for 'democratisation' of FRTs.[85]

The case of identification highlights the need for *clear legislation* to set out the conditions, procedures and limits for the use of FRTs. In particular, the parliamentary law intended for this purpose can be seen as 'a proxy for a democratic ex ante decision-making',[86] which provides a democratic justification for measures that affect fundamental rights. In addition, although the legal norms do not necessarily have to be provided by a parliamentary law, as in the case of the limitation of fundamental rights according to the ECHR,[87] the rules must meet certain quality requirements that reflect values typical of the rule of law and democratic regimes. For example, as specified by the ECtHR, rules governing FRTs must provide for their scope and the application of these technologies, as well as safeguards against the risk of abuse and arbitrariness.[88] Thus, the ECtHR confirms the requirements of 'foreseeability' and 'accessibility', stating that the legal rules must be 'sufficiently clear' in order to provide citizens with an adequate understanding of the conditions and circumstances under which the authorities are empowered to resort to surveillance and data collection measures.[89]

The case of categorisation, in addition to the need for clear and precise rules on FRTs, which can go as far as banning them, reveals another aspect of the demand of democratisation of these technologies, related to greater *transparency*. Transparency helps to make clear the level of accuracy of FRTs and to strengthen—or not – citizens' trust in these technologies; to raise awareness of the impact on the fundamental rights of people under surveillance; to make explicit the role of private actors (political parties, but also platforms) and algorithms in conditioning citizens' political participation. In this way, transparency supports some of the typical elements of a democratic regime identified by political theory, such as trust and awareness.[90]

---

[85] Djeffal (2019), p. 264 ff.

[86] Djeffal (2019), p. 265.

[87] Lupo and Piccirilli (2012).

[88] ECtHR, Glukhin v. Russia, cit., § 82.

[89] ECtHR, Shimovolos v. Russia, no. 30194/09, 21 June 2011, § 68.

[90] Cavaliere and Graziella (2022), p. 429.

To achieve these objectives, the principle of transparency is operationalised through mechanisms and procedures which, in turn, strengthen the control and participation of those subject to these forms of surveillance. This is the case with audits, which can also be used as a tool to ensure compliance with AI Act's requirements on accuracy. Audits can be carried out by technical experts, but also by civil society through descriptive and non-specialist language.[91] These techniques can be conducted internally or, more importantly, externally by independent auditors. They can be ethical-legal,[92] to establish compliance with laws and ethical principles such as transparency, or technical, to evaluate the technical elements (e.g. the outputs) of an algorithmic system in order to reveal harmful behaviour.[93] This makes it possible, for example, to determine whether FRTs are biased and to try to identify possible corrective measures.

Other tools that follow a similar rationale are impact assessment techniques, which are used to assess the risks to fundamental rights arising from the concrete use of technologies and to envisage measures to address them. These techniques can involve stakeholders and interested individuals in order to strengthen the democratic legitimacy of decisions on the use of FRTs. Among these assessment tools, the one that has been legally formalised for the longest time and that is actually in force is the 'data protection impact assessment' (DPIA) provided for in the data protection legislation.[94] However, the DPIA has a limited requirement to seek the views of stakeholders and there is no legal requirement to publish the results of the assessment.[95] Conversely, with regard to algorithmic technologies, many scholars have emphasised how greater citizen engagement could instead enforce the right to know how AI affects people's lives, to resist such decisions, and to strengthen trust in institutions.[96] In the case of FRTs, these tools have also been tailored by academic scholars to assess the deployment of surveillance technology in specific contexts, where it is crucial for all stakeholders to have a sound understanding of the legal and ethical implications.[97] Other proposals aim to address even more 'systemic' risks associated with the use of FRTs in our societies, including the impact on democratic systems.[98] Now that the AI Act has been passed, many hopes are pinned on the 'fundamental rights impact assessment' (FRIA). This new tool consists of 'an assessment of the impact on fundamental rights' that the use of several high-risk AI systems 'may produce'.[99] AI deployers must carry out this ex-ante assessment for

---

[91] Epstein DD et al. (2021).

[92] Radiya-Dixit and Neff (2023).

[93] Bandy (2021).

[94] Article 35 GDPR; Article 27 LED.

[95] Article 35(9) GDPR. See ART29WP (2017b), p. 15.

[96] Reisman et al. (2018), p. 5.

[97] Ho et al. (2021).

[98] Castelluccia and Le Métayer Inria (2020).

[99] Article 27 AI Act. FRIA must be performed for a high-risk AI system referred to in Article 6(2) and listed in Annex III (except those used for management and operation of critical

risk identification, analysis, and prevention/mitigation. However, the AI Act contains too generic provisions on many aspects, such as the stakeholder participation, which is crucial for improving risk awareness, reducing exclusion and biases, and better framing risks.[100]

These kinds of participatory processes can also be considered as part of a broader universe of deliberative democracy and civic engagement practices for the sensitive purpose of regulating technologies. The aim is to enhance interaction and generate awareness, debate and spaces for people to express their views, also as a possible solution to the crisis of representative democracy.[101] Attempts to invigorate democracy are then accompanied by the use of digital tools to develop new forms of 'digital democratic participation', which many scholars and policy-makers now question whether they actually undermine or enhance democracy,[102] especially when dealing with unanimously controversial technologies such as FRTs.[103]

The principle of transparency and the mechanisms for enforcing it are closely related to the third emerging need for democratisation of FRTs that arises from the verification case, which concerns *accountability*.[104] The principle of accountability, as commonly understood in the international ethical guidelines on AI, can be seen as acting with integrity and clearly defining the attribution of responsibility and legal liability against potentially harmful factors.[105] As mentioned above, accountability is a cornerstone of the data protection legislation in order to comply and be able to demonstrate compliance with legal rules. But this principle is also a fundamental pillar of democratic systems, where citizens should be able to understand the justification for decisions taken collectively, so as to hold their representatives accountable for their decisions and to give legitimacy to the decision-making process.[106] Both concepts share the idea of being called 'to account' by some authority for one's actions. Accountability implies a process of transparent interaction, in which a subject seeks answers and possible rectification, and also imposes sanctions if the organisation's 'account' is not accurate.[107] Therefore, accountability in the use of FRTs, both from a legal and political perspective, can be considered crucial within democratic systems.[108] Conversely, the lack of accountability and

infrastructure), when deployers are 'bodies governed by public law', 'private entities providing public services', and deployers of high-risk AI systems used to evaluate the creditworthiness of a person or for credit scoring (with the exception of AI systems used for detecting financial fraud), and for risk assessment and pricing in life and health insurance.

[100] Mantelero (2024).

[101] Ercan et al. (2022); Landemore (2020).

[102] Sgueo (2023).

[103] Center for AI and Digital Policy (2023), p. 3.

[104] Consultative Committee of the Convention 108, (2021).

[105] Jobin et al. (2019).

[106] Cavaliere and Graziella (2022), p. 431 ff.

[107] Bennett (2012), p. 33 ff.

[108] Menéndez González (2021), pp. 87–88.

transparency in the use of these biometric technologies creates an 'invisible layer'[109] between citizens and their public authorities, which may result in legal and political unaccountability.

6 Conclusions

FRTs are very versatile biometric technologies that can be used in many contexts. They can be both a threat and an opportunity to democratic systems. The chapter examined three cases that correspond to the main purposes of identification, categorisation and verification using FRTs. Each of these purposes can lead to different activities, i.e. tracking for aims such as law enforcement and the suppression of dissent; profiling to set up mass micro-targeting campaigns; and providing access to public activities such as voting. In this way, FRTs can discourage, manipulate or facilitate political participation. However, these effects depend on the specific modalities and situations in which these technologies are used.

Legal rules seek to address the many technical, ethical and legal issues that arise in the cases examined and, more generally, in the spread of these technologies. The analysis has revealed a common trend towards the 'democratisation' of FRTs, which is expressed in different demands: that legislation should preserve certain values typical of rule of law and democratic systems, such as certainty and foreseeability; that legislation should promote control over these technologies (e.g. through audits) and participation of people who are affected by surveillance (e.g. through impact assessment techniques); and that accountability (legal and political) of those using these technologies should be strengthened. These different solutions, especially if they work together, can help to make the use of FRTs more compatible with democratic systems and avoid situations such as those addressed in the *Glukhin* case by the ECtHR.

References

Acquisti A, Gross R, Stutzman F (2014) Face recognition and privacy in the age of augmented reality. Journal of Privacy and Confidentiality 6(2)

Article 29 Data Protection Working Party (27 April 2012) Opinion 3/2012 on developments in biometric technologies, WP193

Article 29 Data Protection Working Party (4 October 2017a) Guidelines on Data Protection Impact Assessment (DPIA) and determining whether processing is "likely to result in a high risk" for the purposes of Regulation 2016/679, WP 248 rev.01

Article 29 Data Protection Working Party (29 November 2017b) Opinion on some key issues of the Law Enforcement Directive (EU 2016/680), WP 258

[109] Duberry (2022), p. 94.

Bandy J (2021) Problematic machine behavior: a systematic literature review of algorithm audits. Proceedings of the ACM on Human Computer Interaction 5, CSCW1, Article 74. https://doi.org/10.1145/3449148

Barrett L (2020) Ban Facial Recognition Technologies For Children—And For Everyone Else. Boston University Journal of Science & Technology Law 26(2):223–285

Barrett LF, Adolphs R, Marsella S, Martinez AM, Pollak SD (2019) Emotional expressions reconsidered: challenges to inferring emotion from human facial movements. Psychol Sci Public Interest 20(1):1–68. https://doi.org/10.1177/1529100619832930

Bennett CJ (2012) The accountability approach to privacy and data protection: assumptions and caveats. In: Guagnin D et al (eds) Managing privacy through accountability. Palgrave Macmillan

Berg S, Hofmann J (2021) Digital democracy. Internet Policy Rev 10(4). https://doi.org/10.14763/2021.4.1612

Bodó B, Helberger N, de Vreese CH (2017) Political micro-targeting: a Manchurian candidate or just a dark horse? Internet Policy Rev 6(4). https://doi.org/10.14763/2017.4.776

Boehme-Neßler V (2020) Digitising democracy: on reinventing democracy in the digital era - a legal, political and psychological perspective. Springer International Publishing AG

Borgesius FJZ et al. (2018) Online political microtargeting: promises and threats for democracy. Utrecht Law Rev

Bradshaw S, Howard PN (2018). Challenging truth and trust: a global inventory of organized social media manipulation. Working Paper 2018.1. https://demtech.oii.ox.ac.uk/wp-content/uploads/sites/12/2018/07/ct2018.pdf

Buolamwini J, Gebru T (2018) Gender shades: Intersectional accuracy disparities in commercial gender classification. Proceedings of the 1st Conference on Fairness, Accountability and Transparency 81:77–91. http://proceedings.mlr.press/v81/buolamwini18a.html

Castelluccia C, Le Métayer Inria D (2020) Impact analysis of facial recognition: towards a rigorous methodology (hal-02480647). HAL Inria. https://hal.inria.fr/hal-02480647/document

Cavaliere P, Graziella R (2022) From poisons to antidotes: algorithms as democracy boosters. Eur J Risk Regul 13(3):421–443

Center for AI and Digital Policy (2023) Artificial Intelligence and Democratic Values Index. https://www.caidp.org/reports/aidv-2022/

Cheeseman N, Lynch G, Willis J (2018) Digital dilemmas: the unintended consequences of election technology. Democratization 25(8):1397–1418. https://doi.org/10.1080/13510347.2018.1470165

Christakis T, Becuywe M, AI-Regulation Team (2021) Facial recognition in the draft European AI Regulation: Final report on the high-level workshop held on April 26, 2021 [Report]. AI-Regulation.com. https://ai-regulation.com/facial-recognition-in-the-draft-european-ai-regulation-final-report-on-the-high-level-workshop-held-on-april-26-2021/

Committee on Artificial Intelligence (CAI) (2024 March 15) Draft Framework Convention on artificial intelligence, human rights, democracy and the rule of law. CM(2024)52-prov1. https://rm.coe.int/-1493-10-1b-committee-on-artificial-intelligence-cai-b-draft-framework/1680aee411

Consultative Committee of the Convention 108 (2021) Guidelines on Facial Recognition (T-PD (2020)03rev4). Council of Europe, Directorate General of Human Rights and Rule of Law. https://rm.coe.int/guidelines-on-facial-recognition/1680a134f3

Council of Europe (2017 June 14) Recommendation CM/Rec(2017)5 of the Committee of Ministers to member States on standards for e-voting. https://rm.coe.int/0900001680726f6f

Council of Europe (2019 February 13) Declaration of the Committee of Ministers on the manipulative capabilities of algorithmic processes, Decl(13/02/2019). https://search.coe.int/cm/pages/result_details.aspx?ObjectId=090000168092dd4b

Council of Europe, Committee of Ministers' (2022 February 9) Guidelines on the use of information and communication technology (ICT) in electoral processes in Council of Europe member

States, CM(2022)10-final. https://search.coe.int/cm/pages/result_details.aspx?objectid=0900001680a575d9
Council of Europe, European Committee on Democracy and Governance (26 July 2021) Study on the impact of digital transformation on democracy and good governance. CDDG(2021)4 Final. 26 July 2021
Custers B, Fosch-Villaronga E, van der Hof S, Schermer B, Sears A M, Tamò-Larrieux A (2022) The role of consent in an algorithmic society—Its evolution, scope, failings and re-conceptualization. In: Kosta E, Leenes E (eds) Research Handbook on EU Data Protection Law. Edward Elgar 455–473
Danaher J (2016) The threat of algocracy: reality, resistance and accommodation. Philosophy Technol 29(3):245–268
Djeffal C (2019) AI, democracy and the law. In: Sudmann A (ed) The democratization of artificial intelligence net politics in the era of learning algorithms. Transcript. https://doi.org/10.14361/9783839447192
Duberry J (2022) Artificial intelligence and democracy. Risks and Promises of AI-Mediated Citizen–Government Relations. Routledge
Epstein DD et al. (2021) An action-oriented AI policy toolkit for technology audits by community advocates and activists. Proceedings of the 2021 ACM conference on fairness, accountability, and transparency, 772–781
Ercan A et al (eds) (2022) Research methods in deliberative democracy. Oxford University Press
European Data Protection Board (2020) Guidelines 3/2019 on processing of personal data through video devices (Guidelines 3/2019 Version 2.0). European Data Protection Board. https://edpb.europa.eu/sites/default/files/files/file1/edpb_guidelines_201903_video_devices_en_0.pdf
European Data Protection Board (2022) Guidelines 05/2022 on the use of facial recognition technology in the area of law enforcement (Guidelines 05/2022 Version 1.0). European Data Protection Board. https://edpb.europa.eu/system/files/2022-05/edpb-guidelines_202205_frtlawenforcement_en_1.pdf
European Group on Ethics in Science and New Technologies (20 June 2023) Opinion on Democracy in the digital age, no. 33. https://op.europa.eu/en/web/eu-law-and-publications/publication-detail/-/publication/8b11a1bc-0f21-11ee-b12e-01aa75ed71a1
Grother P, Ngan M, Hanaoka K (2019) Face recognition vendor test part 3: Demographic effects (NIST IR 8280; p. NIST IR 8280). National Institute of Standards and Technology. https://doi.org/10.6028/NIST.IR.8280
Hao K, Howell O'Neill P (2020 August) The hack that could make face recognition think someone else is you. MIT Technol Rev https://www.technologyreview.com/2020/08/05/1006008/ai-face-recognition-hack-misidentifies-person/
Heiberg S et al (2021) Facial recognition for remote electronic voting – missing piece of the puzzle or yet another liability? In: Saracino A, Mori P (eds) Emerging technologies for authorization and authentication. ETAA 2021, Lecture Notes in Computer Science. Springer. https://doi.org/10.1007/978-3-030-93747-8_6
Ho DE et al (2021) Evaluating facial recognition technology: a protocol for performance assessment in new domains. Denv Law Rev 98(4):753–773
Jobin A, Ienca M, Vayena E (2019) Artificial intelligence: the global landscape of ethics guidelines. Nat Mach Intell 1(9):389–399. https://doi.org/10.1038/s42256-019-0088-2
König PD (2022) Citizen conceptions of democracy and support for artificial intelligence in government and politics. Eur J Polit Res. https://doi.org/10.1111/1475-6765.12570
König PD, Wenzelburger G (2020) Opportunity for renewal or disruptive force? How artificial intelligence alters democratic politics. Gov Inform Quart 37(3):101489
Kosinski M (2021) Facial recognition technology can expose political orientation from naturalistic facial images. Sci Rep 100
Landemore H (2020) Open democracy: reinventing popular rule for the twenty-first century. Princeton University Press. https://doi.org/10.1515/9780691208725

Lupo N, Piccirilli G (2012) European Court of Human Rights and the quality of legislation: shifting to a substantial concept of 'Law'? Legisprudence 6(2):229–242

Manheim K, Kaplan L (2019) Artificial intelligence: Risks to privacy and democracy. Yale J Law Technol 21(1):106–189

Mantelero A (2024) The Fundamental Rights Impact Assessment (FRIA) in the AI Act: roots, legal obligations and key elements for a model template (March 30, 2024). Available at SSRN: https://ssrn.com/abstract=4782126

Menéndez González, N (2021) Development or dystopia? An introduction to the accountability challenges of data processing by Facial Recognition Technology. Communications Law 26(2):81–96. https://www.bloomsburyprofessional.com/journal/communications-law-17467616/

Nemitz P (2018) Constitutional democracy and technology in the age of artificial intelligence. Phil Trans R Soc A 376(2133). https://doi.org/10.1098/rsta.2018.0089

Neroni Rezende I (2023 September) Glukhin and the EU regulation of facial recognition: Lessons to be learned?. European Law Blog. https://europeanlawblog.eu/2023/09/19/glukhin-and-the-eu-regulation-of-facial-recognition-lessons-to-be-learned/

Palmiotto F, Menéndez González N (2023) Facial recognition technology, democracy and human rights. Comput Law Secur Rev 50. https://doi.org/10.1016/j.clsr.2023.105857

Parliamentary Assembly of the Council of Europe (PACE) (2020) Need for democratic governance of artificial intelligence. Resolution 2341. https://pace.coe.int/en/files/28803/html

Prathyusha N et al. (2023) Blockchain based E-Voting system with Facial Recognition, 2023. International Conference on Inventive Computation Technologies (ICICT), Lalitpur, Nepal, 2023, 1203–1210. https://doi.org/10.1109/ICICT57646.2023.10134227

Quelle C (2018) Enhancing compliance under the general data protection regulation: the risky upshot of the accountability- and risk-based approach. Eur J Risk Regul 9(3):502–527

Radiya-Dixit E, Neff G (2023) A Sociotechnical Audit: Assessing Police Use of Facial Recognition. In: 2023 ACM Conference on Fairness, Accountability, and Transparency (FAccT '23). https://doi.org/10.1145/3593013.3594084

Reisman D, Schultz J, Crawford K, Whittaker M (2018) Algorithmic impact assessments: a practical framework for public agency accountability. AI Now Institute. https://ainowinstitute.org/publication/algorithmic-impact-assessments-report-2

Revathy G et al (2022) Investigation of E-voting system using face recognition using convolutional neural network (CNN). Theor Comput Sci 925(2022):61–67

Sgueo G (2023) The design of digital democracy. Springer. https://doi.org/10.1007/978-3-031-36946-9

Shaffer K (2019) Data versus democracy: how big data algorithms shape opinions and alter the course of history. Apress

Sreekanth D et al (2022) E-Voting system using facial recognition. Int J Anal Exp Modal Anal 14(6):1191–1201

van Drunen MZ, Helberger N, Fathaigh RÓ (2022) The beginning of EU political advertising law: unifying democratic visions through the internal market. Int J Law Inform Technol 30(2): 181–199. https://doi.org/10.1093/ijlit/eaac017

Wright N (2018 July 10) How artificial intelligence will reshape the global order. Foreign Affairs. https://www.foreignaffairs.com/articles/world/2018-07-10/how-artificial-intelligence-will-reshape-global-order

Zuboff S (2019) The Age of Surveillance Capitalism. The Fight for the Future at the New Frontier of Power. Profile BooksAcquisti

Technical Solutions for a Proportional Use of Facial Recognition Technology

Natalia Menéndez González

Abstract That the use of facial recognition technology (FRT) is subjected to the principle of proportionality to a greater or lesser extent comes with no surprise for everybody. However, in which terms can the principle of proportionality be operationalised as far as the use of FRT is concerned? What does this imply in practice? This chapter will discuss several technological solutions provided by the FRT industry in light of the proportionality principle to discern whether they comply with the proportionality test, namely the elements of suitability, necessity and proportionality *stricto sensu*. The paper will analyse the use of portable FRT systems, data augmentation techniques by generative adversarial networks and synthetic data for training databases, and dynamic data masking techniques to assess to what extent their use allows a suitable, necessary and proportional use of FRT without endangering fundamental rights.

Keywords Proportionality principle · European Union law · Data protection · Artificial intelligence act · Proportionality by design

1 Introduction

That the use of Facial Recognition Technology (FRT) is subjected to the principle of proportionality probably comes as no surprise for the different stakeholders involved with the technology in one way or another. The principle of proportionality, apart from a well-established principle within several legal traditions all over the world, is also a value in life. Everybody, related to the legal field or not, makes balancing operations between contradictory interests numerous times in a day. Therefore, the use of FRT will be no different in this respect. From citizens when asked whether

N. Menéndez González (✉)
Centre for a Digital Society, Robert Schumann Centre for Advanced Studies, European University Institute, Florence, Italy
e-mail: Natalia.Menendez@eui.eu

N. Menéndez González, G. Mobilio (eds.), *Next Democratic Frontiers for Facial Recognition Technology (FRT)*, Law, Governance and Technology Series 74,
https://doi.org/10.1007/978-3-031-89794-8_3

they feel comfortable being subjected to FRT for security purposes[1] to FRT developers when they decide to sacrifice accuracy in favour of algorithmic fairness,[2] the balancing operation is an intrinsic part of FRT's deployment.

This chapter will operationalize what proportionality entails in practice regarding the use of FRT. While there is a great deal of legal scholarship on the principle of proportionality,[3] most of it adopts an eminently theoretical point of view. Further, the small stream of scholarship that focuses on a concrete dimension of the proportionality test or applies it to a particular field of law[4] still lacks the granularity necessary for FRT developers. Therefore, this chapter will look at several technological solutions provided by the FRT industry considering the proportionality of such proposals.

The piece will proceed in five parts. Part one has introduced the context and justification of the research. Part two will discuss the application of the proportionality principle to the use of FRT from a legal perspective. Part three will discuss three technical solutions provided by the FRT industry, namely the use of portable FRT systems, data augmentation techniques by generative adversarial networks for training data, and dynamic data masking techniques to assess to what extent their use allows a proportional FRT. Such solutions were selected for the chapter after extensive research and conversations with the industry. They are not the only ones, neither the best nor the most cutting-edge. However, as the chapter will unveil, they seem to be the ones with a more proportional approach, even from a technical perspective.

Further, the chapter does not intend to be an exhaustive repository of all technical solutions for FRT that contemplate, in one way or another, proportionality. It intends to foster a discussion on more tecno-legally oriented approaches to FRT, with the proportionality principle as a case study. The timing for such a discussion might be more relevant than ever with the European Union (EU) having recently passed its Artificial Intelligence Act (AI Act).[5] Such regulation has been criticised for its market-oriented approach and lack of understanding of the fundamental rights challenges that the technologies it tries to regulate pose.[6] In this line, this chapter will study to what extent current technical approaches comply with fundamental rights, democracy and the rule of law. Part four will debate how "proportionality by

[1]Pew Research Center (2019), Ada Lovelace Institute (2019) and Kostka and others (2023).

[2]Krishnapriya and others (2020) and Buolamwini and others (2018).

[3]It is impossible (and out of the scope of this chapter) to summarize all the literature on the proportionality principle. For a comprehensive overview, see Barak (2012) and Tridimas (2007). For a critique, see Urbina (2017).

[4]Dalla Corte (2022) and Gayrel (2016).

[5]Regulation (EU) 2024/1689 of the European Parliament and of the Council of 13 June 2024 laying down harmonised rules on artificial intelligence and amending Regulations (EC) No 300/2008, (EU) No 167/2013, (EU) No 168/2013, (EU) 2018/858, (EU) 2018/1139 and (EU) 2019/2144 and Directives 2014/90/EU, (EU) 2016/797 and (EU) 2020/1828 (Artificial Intelligence Act).

[6]Edwards (2021).

design" approaches are in line with the AI Act. Part five will summarise the conclusions of the chapter.

2 The Application of the Proportionality Principle to the Use of Facial Recognition Technology

The seed for the proportionality principle, as it is understood and applied nowadays, especially in EU law, comes from German administrative law.[7] It arose as a way to control discretional activity from public powers and to shield the fundamental rights of citizens against the State's actions, especially within a post-war era.[8] From this, it evolved and spread throughout the whole world[9] until its current formulation nowadays. In EU law, both the Court of Justice of the European Union (CJEU) and the European Court of Human Rights (ECtHR) have greatly contributed to the development and spread of the principle up to the point where the CJEU named it 'one of the general principles of Community law'.[10]

There is no absolute consensus about the elements that form the proportionality principle. While the most traditional formulation (provided by Alexy)[11] subdivides proportionality into three sub-principles, other authors, for instance, talk about a five-tier process.[12] Even the two European courts do not fully agree on their formulations of the proportionality test. Whereas the CJEU's doctrine is more aligned with Alexy, adding the pre-condition of a legitimate aim, the ECtHR only considers such a pre-condition and proportionality as a whole.

According to the CJEU, to be proportional a measure must pursue a legitimate aim, be suitable to fulfil such an aim, necessary further than suitable (the less restrictive means) and proportional *stricto sensu*. The legitimate aim pre-condition implies that the measure in question fulfils an objective contemplated within a legal instrument. I consider the legitimate aim not a proper element of the proportionality test but a pre-condition to trigger such a test since the lack of a legitimate aim precludes the application of the proportionality principle. The suitability element is understood as the fitness of the measure to attain the legitimate aim. The necessity element goes one step further, and it discerns, from the different suitable measures, which is the less restrictive one.[13] The element of proportionality *stricto sensu*, also known as the balancing test, entails that the burden implied by the application of the measure is surpassed by the benefit such application provides. Finally, the ECtHR

---

[7] Cohen-Eliya and others (2008).

[8] Engle (2009).

[9] Barak (2012).

[10] Case C-265/87 *Schroeder v. Hauptzollamt Gronau* [1989] ECR 2237 para 21.

[11] Alexy (2003).

[12] Bernal Pulido (2003).

[13] For a deeper review on the principle of necessity see chapter 4 in this volume by Jasserand.

also applies its doctrine on the margin of appreciation when assessing the State's conformity with the principle of proportionality. The margin of appreciation 'stands for the notion that the authorities of each state party to the European Convention ought to be allowed a certain measure of discretion in implementing the standards enshrined in the Convention.'[14] Therefore, the Court grants States some leeway to, according to their national idiosyncrasy, decide on the suitability, necessity and proportionality of the measure in question.

For this chapter, the use of FRT will be considered proportionate when it fulfils a legitimate aim (meaning an aim that is established within a legal instrument) and its deployment is suitable and necessary to attain such an aim. Finally, the use of FRT will be considered proportionate when the burden it places on the ones subjected to the technology is less than the technological advantage it provides.

The application of the proportionality principle to FRT mainly comes from the interference its use poses against both human and fundamental rights. The use of FRT might infringe on several human and fundamental rights such as human dignity; liberty and security; freedom of thought, conscience and religion; freedom of expression;[15] freedom of assembly and association; equality before the law; non-discrimination and the rights of the child and the elderly and people with disabilities.[16] But probably the rights more and most intuitively affected by FRT are privacy and data protection. This is because FRT processes personal data (facial images) intending to uniquely identify, authenticate, or profile a person.

Even when the EU General Data Protection Regulation (hereinafter, GDPR), does not contemplate proportionality within its Article 5 (Principles relating to processing of personal data), its imprint can be seen throughout the regulation. It is mentioned within the regulation recitals,[17] and 'an assessment of the necessity and proportionality of the processing operations in relation to the purposes'[18] is one of the minimum contents of Data Protection Impact Assessments (DPIAs).[19] Further, according to the Norwegian Data Protection Authority (DPA), the data minimisation principle[20] 'stipulates proportionality' in intervening with the data subject's privacy.[21] Therefore, many stakeholders, from national[22] to European

---

[14] Gross and others (2001).

[15] ECtHR, *Glukhin v. Russia,* App no 11519/20, 4 July 2023.

[16] Menéndez González *(forthcoming).*

[17] Recitals 4, 156 and 170 GDPR.

[18] Article 35(7)(b) GDPR.

[19] See Article 35 GDPR.

[20] Article 5(1)(c) GDPR.

[21] Datatilsynet (2018)

[22] *The Queen (on application of Edward Bridges) v The Chief Constable of South Wales Police* [2020] EWCA Civ 1058; Tribunal Administratif de Marseille (9ème chambre) N° 1901249 *La Quadrature Du Net et autres* (27 février 2020) and Conseil d'Etat, Décision n° 442364, 26 April 2022.

courts,[23] to DPAs,[24] have continuously discussed the application of the proportionality principle to the use of FRT concerning its privacy and data protection dimensions.

Such a discussion mainly touches upon its legitimacy, necessity and proportionality as a whole. Regarding the legitimate aim, FRT processes biometric sensitive data and, according to the GDPR (Article 9), such processing is in principle forbidden with some exceptions. The most frequently used grounds for biometric data processing are consent (Article 9(2)(a) GDPR), personal data manifestly made public by the data subject (Article 9(2)(e) GDPR), reasons of substantial public interest (Article 9(2)(g) and reasons of public interest in the area of public health (Article 9(2)(i)). However, both DPAs and courts have questioned the use of such lawful grounds for biometric data processing. For instance, consent to the use of FRT has been deemed unlawful when provided by students and employees due to the imbalance of power between these and their academic institutions and employers.[25]

Regarding 'data manifestly made public', whether facial images uploaded to Social Network Services (SNS) open profiles can be considered to fit within such a category, has also been questioned as a legitimate aim and it is at the core of the discussion on the compliance with the GDPR of the activities carried out by Clearview AI. Clearview AI is a FRT US company whose main clients are law enforcement agencies. They allege to have built an impressive facial image database only by using public information from the open web. However, several DPAs have deemed the use of Clearview AI within the EU unlawful in breach of the GDPR and, consequently, fined the company and prohibited them to continue carrying out their activities.[26]

Regarding the necessity of the use of FRT, both domestic courts and DPAs have considered that, when less restrictive means were available, the use of FRT should be avoided. This was the case with the use of FRT in schools. When other remedies such as having a badge, are (almost) equally effective to monitor children's attendance, such an intrusive technology as FRT should be overruled. A different scenario would be, for instance, according to the Dutch DPA, that of a nuclear power plant.[27] Because identity theft or trespassing in such a securitised environment could have dangerous consequences, the use of FRT for monitoring entrance could be justified.

[23] ECtHR, *Glukhin v. Russia,* App no 11519/20, 4 July 2023.

[24] European Data Protection Board (2023).

[25] See, for instance, Catalan Data Protection Authority (2022) and Garante per la protezione dei dati personali (2021).

[26] Der Hamburgische Beauftragte für Datenschutz und Informationsfreiheit (2021), IMY (2021), Garante per la protezione dei dati personali (2022), Hellenic Data Protection Authority (2022), CNIL (2022) and NOYB (2023).

[27] European Data Protection Board (2021).

Finally, regarding proportionality as a whole, the EDPB has stated, apropos the use of FRT by law enforcement, that proportionality also encompasses calling ‘for rules which would serve, in particular, to govern the protection and security of the data in question in a clear and strict manner in order to ensure their full integrity and confidentiality’.[28] Data security obligations have been widely argued as red lines for lawful biometric data processing by regulators,[29] and a proportionality requirement. As we will see within the following section of this chapter, data security considerations will be crucial within “proportionality by design” FRT solutions.

3 Technically Operationalizing Proportional Facial Recognition Technology

In light of the previous section, the importance of the application of the proportionality principle to the use of FRT cannot be questioned. However, as previously stated, proportionality is a very wide principle. Therefore, from a technical perspective, it is very difficult to operationalize what proportionality requirements might mean in practice. This part will discuss a few solutions that the FRT industry has come up with which, from a proportionality point of view, might entail an alignment with the suitability and necessity sub-principles. These solutions were selected following a “proportionality by design” approach. This means that, to the best of the knowledge of this author, they were the ones which better embedded the proportionality requirements into the technical design of the technology.

3.1 Portable FRT

One of the main legal conundrums of FRT from the proportionality perspective is the sunk cost effect. According to Olivola, ‘individuals are more likely to pursue alternatives if they have invested substantial amounts of time or money to obtain them.’[30] As far as FRT is concerned, such a technology requires huge money investments to be acquired and deployed. Especially when it is installed as part of a surveillance effort to control a certain area (i.e. the city centre of a city).[31] When such an investment is spent, it is very unlikely that if the reason which caused the deployment disappears, the FRT systems will follow. A very pragmatic example in this respect is the use of FRT within the context of border control. According to a report from the Samuelson-Glushko Canadian Internet Policy & Public Interest

[28] European Data Protection Board (2023) Paragraph 53.

[29] See Article 32 GDPR.

[30] Olivola (2018).

[31] Dearden (2019).

Clinic, '[b]order control systems have been repurposed for general law enforcement investigatory objectives, as a general purpose identity service for private and public sector bodies, as a general surveillance tool and as a digital identity management mechanism.'[32] Another example was the repurposing of an FRT system initially installed during the COVID-19 pandemic by the Russian government to enforce compliance with quarantine and the use of face masks, repurposed once the pandemic was over for surveillance purposes.[33]

However, repurposing of FRT systems is contrary to the principle of proportionality. It is very unlikely that a solution for a problem (for instance, border management) is also going to be the most suitable, necessary, and least restrictive means to achieve a secondary aim (for instance, a law enforcement investigation). In this scenario, the use of portable FRT might seem a fit solution. If one thinks about facial recognition systems working on mobile phones for unlocking or payment verification,[34] it is not very difficult to picture the idea of portable FRT devices.

Portable FRT are standalone systems that can be deployed autonomously. Such portability allows them to be deployed and withdrawn almost effortlessly. In this way, these systems might be deployed, for instance, in certain sports events with high risk (such as matches between two rival teams[35] or final matches in particularly unsafe competitions[36]). They could also be useful in cases such as the COVID-19 pandemic. In this line, if necessary, FRT could be deployed for reasons of substantial public interest within the area of public health and, once the sanitary alert is over, be removed.[37] If that is the case, the use of portable FRT will be very much in line with the sub-principle of necessity and the less restrictive means test. In this way, FRT will be only deployed for as long as it is necessary and its intrusiveness will decrease since it will be only applied to the people attending that specific sports competition or during the reduced timeframe that lasts the health emergency.

In principle, portable FRT functions in a very similar way to *static* FRT, meaning FRT systems that cannot be relocated. In plain sight, the main difference is on the hardware side. Further, different portable FRT systems will have different configurations, depending on the model. Other variables that might be taken into account, from a more legal perspective, will be wireless connectivity which might facilitate security breaches.[38] However, wireless connection is not exclusive to portable FRT. Along the same lines, in case portable FRT favours centralised data storage solutions, this could restrict the access and distribution of FRT data, thus enhancing the

---

[32] Israel (2020).

[33] Borak (2023).

[34] Pascu (2020).

[35] Strang and others (2018).

[36] Conn (2022).

[37] Menéndez González (2022).

[38] Canadian Centre for Cyber Security (2022). For a more comprehensive review on the cybersecurity issues of FRT, see chapter 6 in this volume by Karathanasis.

privacy and data protection by design character of these solutions, making their use more proportional. Finally, the portable character of these systems might make them more vulnerable to vandalism or theft. In case of theft, apart from the economic loss, the data loss will be as important, if not even more.

3.2 *Data Augmentation by Generative Adversarial Networks*

Algorithmic bias has been one of the main obstacles to the use of FRT and one of the main criticisms it has faced.[39] Even though state-of-the-art FRT has significantly improved its accuracy,[40] algorithmic bias has still been one of the main reasons argued by regulators,[41] and NGOs[42] against its use. As scholarship has repeatedly stated,[43] one of the reasons for algorithmic bias in FRT systems is the training data used. As certain profiles are overrepresented within the FRT training datasets (mainly white males), accuracy with those profiles does not present many problems. However, people from ethnic minorities, women, and people with transgender experiences or health conditions or impairments are frequently underrepresented within those training datasets and, consequently, misidentified by FRT.

According to Shorten and others, '[d]ata [a]ugmentation encompasses a suite of techniques that enhance the size and quality of training datasets such that better Deep Learning models can be built using them.'[44] In the same line, Mumuni and others argue that '[t]he main goal of data augmentation is to increase the volume, quality and diversity of training data.'[45] One of the most efficient techniques to do data augmentation is by using Generative Adversarial Networks (GAN).[46] According to Goodfellow (considered the father of GAN) and others,

> In the proposed adversarial nets framework, the generative model is pitted against an adversary: a discriminative model that learns to determine whether a sample is from the model distribution or the data distribution. [...] This framework can yield specific training algorithms for many kinds of model and optimization algorithm.

Therefore, by enlarging FRT training datasets, also including representation from underrepresented groups, such datasets will gain in volume and diversity. Further, the use of data augmentation techniques by GAN is also a privacy-enhancing solution. This is because the origin of facial images for FRT training datasets has

---

[39] Buolamwini and others (2018), Castelvecchi (2020), David Leslie (2020) and Gentzel (2021).

[40] Grother and others (2019).

[41] European Parliament (2021).

[42] Jakubowska and others (2020) and 'Look inside the NYPD's Surveillance Machine' (*Ban the Scan*) <https://nypd-surveillance.amnesty.org> accessed 25 July 2023.

[43] See, for instance, Buolamwini and others (2018) and Leslie (2020).

[44] Shorten and Khoshgoftaar (2019).

[45] Mumuni and others (2022).

[46] Antoniou and others (2018).

been sometimes questioned from a privacy and data protection point of view.[47] Data augmentation techniques will allow to increase in the volume of training datasets, without further data collection. However, since data augmentation 'builds' on data, the privacy and data protection problems of the 'original' data will not be solved but at least will not be perpetuated either.

To counterbalance this risk, another solution along the same line as data augmentation is the use of synthetic data for FRT training datasets. According to Fontanillo and others, 'synthetic data is, at a fundamental level, data artificially generated from original data that preserves the statistical properties of said original data.'[48] The strengths of synthetic data are twofold: on the technical side, as data augmentation, the possibility to enlarge FRT training datasets without further data collection. On the legal side, synthetic data can be used to generate FRT training datasets including a wide and rich range of diverse facial images. This might help out in reducing algorithmic bias and accuracy issues. Further, data artificially generated should not, in principle, pose any questions from a privacy and/or data protection point of view. However, this is not entirely true. Since synthetic data are generated from original data, they could 'inherit' the privacy and/or data protection issues that the use of such data could pose. As Fontanillo and others argue, in some cases 'synthetic data can still show sufficient structural equivalence with the original dataset or share essential properties or patterns to trigger attribution.'[49] In this line, more research is needed to truly discern whether synthetic data could be considered anonymous data or whether, as some opponents of synthetic data argue, it 'is far from the holy grail of privacy-preserving data publishing.'[50]

Even with its shortcomings, the use of FRT systems trained on augmented data and/or synthetic data could entail a step forward within both algorithmic discrimination and privacy and/or data protection issues within the data collection for FRT training datasets. Advancements in such fronts might make those FRT systems more proportional, since the balancing operation between the technological advantage provided by the technology and the interference on fundamental rights will be mitigated on the fundamental rights side, at least as far as the two abovementioned points are concerned.

3.3 Dynamic Data Masking

According to Microsoft, '[d]ynamic data masking (DDM) limits sensitive data exposure by masking it to nonprivileged users.'[51] It 'helps prevent unauthorized

[47] Raji and Fried (2021).
[48] Fontanillo and Elbi (2022).
[49] Ibid.
[50] Stadler and others (2022).
[51] VanMSFT (2023).

Fig. 1 Examples of DDM techniques applied to real-time CCTV video feeds. Source: 'AXIS Live Privacy Shield | Axis Communications' <https://www.axis.com/products/axis-live-privacy-shield> Accessed 29 January 2025

access to sensitive data by enabling customers to specify how much sensitive data to reveal with minimal effect on the application layer.'[52] Finally, '[t]he purpose of dynamic data masking is to limit exposure of sensitive data, preventing users who shouldn't have access to the data from viewing it.'[53] DDM techniques might be applied to real-time CCTV video feeds, masking moving and still objects such as humans, license plates, or backgrounds. As far as FRT is concerned, DDM could be used to restrict the content of CCTV footage that, for instance, law enforcement agents have access to (See Fig. 1).

[52]Ibid.

[53]VanMSFT (n 51).

On the other side, DDM could serve other purposes rather than just privacy and/or data protection. Consider the case of FRT's use within the Chinese province of Xinjiang to surveil and oppress people from the Uyghur ethnic minority.[54] If it was possible to dynamic mask Uyghur people from the CCTV footage from the Xinjiang government, DDM will be also contributing to preventing a violation of the rights to equality before the law and non-discrimination.

The use of DDM techniques would be mainly directed to live FRT, one of the most controversial uses of an already controverted technology. Live FRT is considered one of the most intrusive modalities of FRT since it allows continuous monitoring of people.[55] For instance, the Guidelines on Facial Recognition (2021) by the Consultative Committee of the Convention for the Protection of Individuals with regard to Automatic Processing of Personal Data (ETS 108) argued that

> The use of live facial recognition technologies in uncontrolled environments [the notion of 'uncontrolled environment' covers places freely accessible to individuals, which they can also pass through, including public and quasi-public spaces such as shopping centres, hospitals, or schools], in light of its intrusiveness on the right to privacy and the dignity of individuals, coupled with the risk of an adverse impact on other human rights and fundamental freedoms, should be subject to a democratic debate and the possibility of a moratorium pending a full analysis.

Further, the European Court of Human Rights in its decision on *Glukhin v. Russia*,[56] stated that '[a] high level of justification is therefore required in order for them [FRT] to be considered "necessary in a democratic society", with the highest level of justification required for the use of live facial recognition technology.'[57] Therefore, the use of DDM could make FRT more proportional by controlling the live feeds of CCTV on which FRT could run. In this way, the balancing operation between the technological advantage provided by FRT and the interference with fundamental rights, in this case, privacy and data protection and non-discrimination, will be more offset.

Finally, the question of who decides which data should be masked should be tackled. In principle, this will be a design decision. However, the introduction of privacy and data protection by design and, along the same line, accountability instruments such as Data Protection Impact Assessments and Fundamental Rights Impact Assessments[58] might ensure that developers align their design choices with more fundamental-rights-oriented approaches. The next section will briefly cover how the AI Act rules developers to comply with these kinds of criteria.

---

[54] Healy (2021).

[55] Sinmaz (2023).

[56] ECtHR, *Glukhin v. Russia,* App no 11519/20, 4 July 2023. For a more detailed analysis of the Glukhin case, see chapter 2 in this volume by Mobilio.

[57] ECtHR, *Glukhin v. Russia,* App no 11519/20, 4 July 2023 paragraph 86.

[58] Article 27 AI Act.

4 What About the AI Act?

The Artificial Intelligence Act establishes in its Recital 176 that 'In accordance with the principle of proportionality as set out in that Article, this Regulation does not go beyond what is necessary in order to achieve that objective.' The (legitimate) objective in question is to 'improve the functioning of the internal market and promoting the uptake of human centric and trustworthy AI, while ensuring a high level of protection of health, safety, fundamental rights enshrined in the Charter, including democracy, the rule of law and environmental protection against harmful effects of AI systems in the Union and supporting innovation.'[59] Therefore, AI products, particularly FRT systems, whose design follows the abovementioned 'proportionality by design' approach, might be expected to comply with the AI Act requirements as long as its use also complies with the risk-based approach of the regulation. Further, the regulation points out, particularly regarding the use of real-time biometric systems, that the proportionality and necessity requirements should be considered in the light of the period of time and geographical and personal scope of the use of the technology (Articles 5(2) and (3) AI Act). However, products whose design goes further to the protection of democracy, fundamental rights and the rule of law and the objectives established by the regulation in favour of innovation, could be expected to be found not in compliance. In this way, the 'proportionality by design' approach could help members of the industry to discern the principles underlying the criteria required for compliance with the AI Act. The AI Act does not specifically mention technical solutions such as portable FRT or DDM. However, nothing seems to contradict that, as long as such technical solutions follow the rules from Articles 5 and following of the AI Act,[60] they will be allowed under the same regulation. The use of synthetic data is explicitly mentioned within Article 10(5)(a) AI Act which allows the processing of special categories of personal data (such as biometric data) when 'bias detection and correction cannot be effectively fulfilled by processing other data, including synthetic or anonymised data'. Thus, it seems that the AI Act favours the interpretation proposed within this chapter of using synthetic data, when possible, for bias mitigation.

5 Conclusion

This chapter has discussed the practical application of the proportionality principle to the use of FRT. First, it has reviewed the theoretical basis of the proportionality principle, with a special emphasis on EU law and the jurisprudence of both the CJEU and the ECtHR. Further, it has more concretely operationalized the application of the

[59] Recital 176.

[60] For a deeper analysis on the application of the AI Act to biometric systems in general and FRT in particular, see chapter 5 in this volume by Paolucci.

proportionality principle to the use of FRT as a balancing operation between the technological advantage provided by FRT and the intrusion with human rights, especially but not only, privacy and data protection its use entails. After that, the chapter has discussed three technological solutions namely portable FRT, data augmentation by generative adversarial networks (also briefly synthetic data) and dynamic data masking techniques in light of the proportionality principle.

Portable FRT systems might mitigate the application of the sunk cost effect to the use of FRT, especially by governments when they invest in huge surveillance infrastructures. On the other hand, they might be more vulnerable to security breaches than *static* FRT. Data augmentation techniques by GAN might allow bigger and more diverse datasets without more intensive (and potentially rights-violating) data collection practices. The same applies to synthetic data for FRT training databases. However, it should be considered that ‘traces’ of the ‘original data’ will not prevent de-anonymisation or re-identification. Further, relevant stakeholders should put more emphasis on the lawfulness of the origin of facial images that form FRT training databases. Finally, DDM techniques would allow CCTV video feeds to be ‘manipulated’, only allowing authorised people to have access to biometric sensitive data. This would allow a reduction in the level of intrusiveness that live FRT might pose.

Finally, the chapter has discussed whether this approach to the design of FRT, named “proportionality by design”, would help industry members to operationalize the criteria imposed by regulations that apply to the design and use of such technologies such as the AI Act. This piece does not intend to advocate for the blanket use of FRT if these (or similar) technical solutions are applied. It aims to argue that, before claiming such drastic solutions as banning, all involved stakeholders should sit at the table and discuss what requirements should apply and what solutions are available. Even though the abovementioned technical solutions do not solve all the legal problems posed by using FRT, they could move the pendulum towards a more proportional deployment of such a technology. As this chapter stated within its introduction, this kind of techno-legal approach could better help to balance, the classical operation within the proportionality test. Only by merging state-of-the-art techniques with democracy, fundamental rights and rule of law requirements, we could seize the technological advantages provided by FRT without risking human rights.

References

Ada Lovelace Institute, Beyond face value: public attitudes to facial recognition technology, September 2019

Alexy R (2003) Constitutional rights, balancing, and rationality. Ratio Juris 16:131 https://onlinelibrary.wiley.com/doi/abs/10.1111/1467-9337.00228 Accessed 18 July 2023

Antoniou A, Storkey A, Edwards H (2018) Data augmentation generative adversarial networks (arXiv, 21 March 2018) http://arxiv.org/abs/1711.04340 Accessed 25 July 2023

'AXIS Live Privacy Shield | Axis Communications'. https://www.axis.com/products/axis-live-privacy-shield accessed 26 July 2023
Barak A (2012) Proportionality: constitutional rights and their limitations. Cambridge University Press
Bernal Pulido C (2003) El principio de proporcionalidad y los derechos fundamentales: el principio de proporcionalidad como criterio para determinar el contenido de los derechos fundamentales vinculante para el legislador https://dialnet.unirioja.es/servlet/libro?codigo=165029 Accessed 18 July 2023
Borak M (2023) Inside Safe City, Moscow's AI Surveillance Dystopia, Wired https://www.wired.com/story/moscow-safe-city-ntechlab/ Accessed 29 March 2024
Buolamwini J, Gebru T (2018) Gender shades: intersectional accuracy disparities in commercial gender classification. Proceedings of the 1st Conference on Fairness, Accountability and Transparency (PMLR 2018) https://proceedings.mlr.press/v81/buolamwini18a.html Accessed 17 July 2023
Canadian Centre for Cyber Security, 8 April 2022, Security CC for C, Wi-Fi Security (ITSP.80.002) Accessed 25 July 2023
Castelvecchi D (2020) Is facial recognition too biased to be let loose? Nature 587:347. https://www.nature.com/articles/d41586-020-03186-4 Accessed 25 July 2023
Catalan Data Protection Authority, Opinion CNS 2/2022
CNIL, Restricted Committee Deliberation No. SAN-2022-019 of 17 October 2022 concerning CLEARVIEW AI
Cohen-Eliya M, Porat I (2008) American Balancing and German Proportionality: The Historical Origins (23 September 2008) https://papers.ssrn.com/abstract=1272763 Accessed 18 July 2023
Conn D (2022) Uefa Apologises to Liverpool and Madrid Fans over Champions League Chaos. The Guardian (3 June 2022) https://www.theguardian.com/football/2022/jun/03/uefa-apologises-to-fans-at-liverpool-v-real-madrid-champions-league-final Accessed 25 July 2023
Dalla Corte L (2022) On proportionality in the data protection jurisprudence of the CJEU. Int Data Priv Law 12(4):259–275. https://doi.org/10.1093/idpl/ipac014
Datatilsynet (2018) Artificial intelligence and privacy (January 2018), 11 https://www.datatilsynet.no/globalassets/global/english/ai-and-privacy.pdf Accessed 18 July 2023
Dearden L (2019) Police Spent £200,000 on Facial Recognition Trials That Resulted in No Arrests (The Independent, 19 January 2019) https://www.independent.co.uk/news/uk/home-news/facial-recognition-uk-police-met-arrests-london-cost-false-positives-accuracy-a8723756.html accessed 25 July 2023
Der Hamburgische Beauftragte für Datenschutz und Informationsfreiheit (2021) Letter to Clearview AI Inc. Consultation prior to an order pursuant to Article 58(2):(g) GDPR
Dutch DPA Issues Formal Warning to a Supermarket for Its Use of Facial Recognition Technology | European Data Protection Board. https://edpb.europa.eu/news/national-news/2021/dutch-dpa-issues-formal-warning-supermarket-its-use-facial-recognition_en Accessed 19 July 2023
Edwards L (2021) Three Proposals to Strengthen the EU Artificial Intelligence Act https://www.adalovelaceinstitute.org/blog/three-proposals-strengthen-eu-artificial-intelligence-act/ Accessed 17 July 2023
Engle E (2009) The History of the General Principle of Proportionality: An Overview (7 July 2009) https://papers.ssrn.com/abstract=1431179 Accessed 18 July 2023
European Parliament (2021) corresponds to this reference: Use of Artificial Intelligence by the Police: MEPs Oppose Mass Surveillance | News | European Parliament' (6 October 2021) Accessed 25 July 2023
European Data Protection Board (2021) Dutch DPA Issues Formal Warning to a Supermarket for Its Use of Facial Recognition Technology. Accessed 19 July 2023
Fontanillo CA, Elbi A (2022) On synthetic data: a brief introduction for data protection law dummies. European Law Blog, 22 September 2022. https://europeanlawblog.eu/2022/09/22/on-synthetic-data-a-brief-introduction-for-data-protection-law-dummies/ Accessed 26 July 2023
Garante per la protezione dei dati personali, Ordinanza ingiunzione nei confronti di Università Commerciale "Luigi Bocconi" di Milano - 16 settembre 2021 [9703988]

Gayrel C (2016) The principle of proportionality applied to biometrics in France: review of ten years of CNIL's deliberations. Comput Law Secur Rev 32:450 https://www.sciencedirect.com/science/article/pii/S0267364916300279 Accessed 17 July 2023

Gentzel M (2021) Biased face recognition technology used by government: a problem for liberal democracy. Philos Technol 34:1639 https://doi.org/10.1007/s13347-021-00478-z Accessed 25 July 2023

Gross O, Aoláin FN (2001) From discretion to scrutiny: revisiting the application of the margin of appreciation Doctrine in the context of Article 15 of the European Convention on Human Rights. Human Rights Quart 23:625. https://www.jstor.org/stable/4489350 Accessed 18 July 2023

Grother P, Ngan M, Hanaoka K (2019) Face Recognition Vendor Test (FRVT) Part 2: Identification. [2019] NIST https://www.nist.gov/publications/face-recognition-vendor-test-frvt-part-2-identification Accessed 25 July 2023

Guidelines on Facial Recognition (2021) by the Consultative Committee of the Convention for the Protection of Individuals with regard to Automatic Processing of Personal Data (ETS 108)

Healy C (2021) IPVM Uyghur Surveillance & Ethnicity Detection Analytics in China Expert Report Presented to the Uyghur Tribunal August 20, 2021 https://uyghurtribunal.com/wp-content/uploads/2021/09/Conor-Healy.pdf Accessed 26 July 2023

Hellenic Data Protection Authority (2022) corresponds to this reference: Επιβολή προστίμου στην εταιρεία Clearview AI, Inc (dpa.gr, 13 July 2022) Accessed 4 July 2023

IMY (2021) Beslut efter tillsyn enligt brottsdatalagen – Polismyndighetens användning av Clearview AI Diarienummer: DI-2020-2719 Ert diarienummer: A126.614/2020 Datum: 2021-02-10

Israel T (2020) Facial Recognition at a Crossroads: Transformation at our Borders and Beyond (September 30, 2020). Samuelson-Glushko Canadian Internet Policy & Public Interest Clinic (CIPPIC), Available at SSRN: https://ssrn.com/abstract=3714297

Jubowska and others, Ban Biometric Mass Surveillance: A set of fundamental rights demands for the European Commission and EU Member States on the use of technology for the untargeted mass processing of special categories of personal data in public spaces (13 May 2020) https://edri.org/wp-content/uploads/2020/05/Paper-Ban-Biometric-Mass-Surveillance.pdf accessed 25 July 2023

Kostka G, Steinacker L, Meckel M (2023) Under big brother's watchful eye: cross-country attitudes toward facial recognition technology. Gov Inform Q 40:101761 https://www.sciencedirect.com/science/article/pii/S0740624X22000971. Accessed 17 July 2023

Krishnapriya KS, Albiero V, Vangara K, King MC, Bowyer KW (2020) Issues related to face recognition accuracy varying based on race and skin tone. IEEE-TTS 1(1):8–20, https://doi.org/10.1109/TTS.2020.2974996

'Law Enforcement' (Clearview AI) https://www.clearview.ai/law-enforcement. Accessed 4 July 2023

Leslie D (2020) Understanding bias in facial recognition technologies: an explainer. The Alan Turing Institute. https://doi.org/10.5281/zenodo.4050457

'Look inside the NYPD's Surveillance Machine' (Ban the Scan) https://nypd-surveillance.amnesty.org accessed 25 July 2023

Menéndez González N (2022) 'Brave New (Normal) World': Can the COVID-19 Emergency Serve as an Excuse to Increase the Surveillance State with Facial Recognition Technology? In: Sovereignty, Technology and Governance after COVID-19: Legal Challenges in a PostPandemic Europe. Ed. Francisco de Abreu Duarte and Francesca Palmiotto Ettorre. Hart Publishing, Oxford, pp 119–136. Bloomsbury Collections. Web. 2 Jul. 2023. https://doi.org/10.5040/9781509956012.ch-007

Menéndez González N (forthcoming) Cultured Proportionality: Navigating the EU's Fragmented Facial Recognition Landscape

Mumuni A, Mumuni F (2022) Data augmentation: a comprehensive survey of modern approaches. Array 16:100258 https://www.sciencedirect.com/science/article/pii/S2590005622000911 Accessed 25 July 2023
NOYB (2023) 'Clearview AI Data Use Deemed Illegal in Austria, However No Fine Issued'. https://noyb.eu/en/clearview-ai-data-use-deemed-illegal-austria-however-no-fine-issued Accessed 4 July 2023
Olivola CY (2018) The interpersonal sunk-cost effect. Psychol Sci 29:1072 https://doi.org/10.1177/0956797617752641 Accessed 25 July 2023
Ordinanza ingiunzione nei confronti di Clearview AI - 10 febbraio 2022 [9751362] https://www.gpdp.it:443/web/guest/home/docweb/-/docweb-display/docweb/9751362 Accessed 4 July 2023
Pascu L (2020) Biometric Facial Recognition Hardware Present in 90% of Smartphones by 2024 | Biometric Update. (7 January 2020) https://www.biometricupdate.com/202001/biometric-facial-recognition-hardware-present-in-90-of-smartphones-by-2024 Accessed 25 July 2023
Pew Research Center (2019) More Than Half of U.S. Adults Trust Law Enforcement to Use Facial Recognition Responsibly
'Police Spent £200,000 on Facial Recognition Trials That Resulted in No Arrests' (The Independent, 19 January 2019) https://www.independent.co.uk/news/uk/home-news/facial-recognition-uk-police-met-arrests-london-cost-false-positives-accuracy-a8723756.html Accessed 25 July 2023
Raji ID, Fried G (2021) About face: a survey of facial recognition evaluation (arXiv, 1 February 2021) http://arxiv.org/abs/2102.00813 Accessed 25 July 2023
Shorten C, Khoshgoftaar TM (2019) A survey on image data augmentation for deep learning. J Big Data 6:60 https://doi.org/10.1186/s40537-019-0197-0 Accessed 25 July 2023
Sinmaz E (2023) Live facial recognition labelled "Orwellian" as met police push ahead with use. The Guardian (5 April 2023) https://www.theguardian.com/technology/2023/apr/05/live-facial-recognition-criticised-metropolitan-police Accessed 26 July 2023
Stadler T, Oprisanu B, Troncoso C (2022) Synthetic Data -- Anonymisation Groundhog Day (arXiv, 24 January 2022) http://arxiv.org/abs/2011.07018 Accessed 26 July 2023
Strang L and others (2018) Violent and antisocial behaviours at football events and factors associated with these behaviours: a rapid evidence assessment. RAND Corporation https://www.rand.org/pubs/research_reports/RR2580.html Accessed 25 July 2023
'Three Proposals to Strengthen the EU Artificial Intelligence Act'. https://www.adalovelaceinstitute.org/blog/three-proposals-strengthen-eu-artificial-intelligence-act/ Accessed 17 July 2023
Tridimas T (2007) The general principles of EU law, 2nd edn. Oxford University Press
Urbina FJ (2017) A critique of proportionality and balancing. Cambridge University Press
Use of Artificial Intelligence by the Police: MEPs Oppose Mass Surveillance | News | European Parliament' (6 October 2021) https://www.europarl.europa.eu/news/en/press-room/20210930IPR13925/use-of-artificial-intelligence-by-the-police-meps-oppose-mass-surveillance Accessed 25 July 2023
VanMSFT, Dynamic Data Masking - SQL Server (13 April 2023) https://learn.microsoft.com/en-us/sql/relational-databases/security/dynamic-data-masking?view=sql-server-ver16 Accessed 26 July 2023

Facial Recognition in Public Spaces and the Principle of Necessity

Catherine Jasserand

Abstract Facial recognition technologies (FRTs) are increasingly used around the world to monitor and police public spaces. In the EU, new rules will apply to the deployment of Remote Biometric Identification systems (RBIs), a generic category of biometric systems used for identification purposes, including FRTs. While the real-time use of RBIs for law enforcement in publicly accessible spaces is banned except in three situations, which must be allowed at national level, all other uses of the technologies fall into the category of high-risk systems. As acknowledged by various EU bodies and the European Court of Human Rights in the *Glukhin* case, the use of FRTs in public spaces interferes with fundamental rights, including the rights to privacy and data protection. Since these rights are not absolute, they can be limited by measures that pursue legitimate interests (including public security, national security, or prevention of disorder or crime), provided they comply with several requirements, among which the condition of necessity. Both the European Court of Human Rights and the European Court of Justice have established a test of necessity through their case law on fundamental rights. Building on the tests of necessity developed by the two Courts and the guidance of the European Data Protection Supervisor on the principle of necessity, this chapter will discuss whether the rules introduced by the AI Act on real-time and post-event use of RBIs for law enforcement purposes meet the necessity standard.

Keywords Facial recognition · Public spaces · Law enforcement · AI Act · Necessity

C. Jasserand (✉)
Faculty of Law, Transboundary Legal Studies Department, University of Groningen, Groningen, The Netherlands

Faculty of Law and Criminology, CiTiP, KU Leuven, Belgium
e-mail: c.a.jasserand@rug.nl

N. Menéndez González, G. Mobilio (eds.), *Next Democratic Frontiers for Facial Recognition Technology (FRT)*, Law, Governance and Technology Series 74,
https://doi.org/10.1007/978-3-031-89794-8_4

1 Introduction

On 4 July 2023, the European Court of Human Rights delivered its first judgment on the police use of facial recognition technologies (FRTs) in public spaces, in a case against Russia that involved a peaceful demonstrator in the Moscow underground.[1] Although the Court did not clarify the general issue of legitimate uses of FRTs by police in public spaces, the decision was published when the EU institutions were still negotiating the future Artificial Intelligence Act (AI Act). At that time, the European institutions had not found any consensus on the prohibited and allowed uses of FRTs and other similar biometric technologies, regrouped under the generic category of Remote Biometric Identification systems (RBIs). While the European Parliament was in favour of an almost complete ban applicable to both live and retrospective use of RBIs by the private and public sectors (with a limited exception for the retrospective use of the technologies for criminal investigations), the European Commission and Council supported a partial ban on the real-time use of RBIs for law enforcement purposes in public spaces only, with three possible exceptions. All the other uses of the technologies fell in the category of high-risk systems. The final text of the AI Act has introduced a partial ban on the real-time use of RBIs for law enforcement purposes with three exceptions subject to conditions and safeguards,[2] while the retrospective use of the technologies for law enforcement purposes is subject to the rules applicable to high-risk AI systems with additional safeguards. All other uses of RBIs, including by the private sector or for non-law enforcement purposes, fall into the category of high-risk systems.[3] While this chapter discusses the rules of the AI Act applicable to the use of RBIs, its focus will be on the justifications put forward to allow the deployment of technologies that are deemed highly intrusive.[4]

The deployment and use of facial recognition technologies in public spaces, and particularly, in real-time for surveillance and policing purposes, have been the topic of intense discussions in Europe and beyond.[5] In April 2021, the European

[1]ECtHR, *Glukhin v. Russia*, App no 11519/20, 4 July 2023. On the Glukhin case, see also chapter 'Facial Recognition Technologies: Threats or Opportunities for Democracy?' in this volume by Mobilio.

[2]Regulation (EU) 2024/1689 of the European Parliament and of the Council of 13 June 2024 laying down harmonised rules on artificial intelligence and amending Regulations (EC) No 300/2008, (EU) No 167/2013, (EU) No 168/2013, (EU) 2018/858, (EU) 2018/1139 and (EU) 2019/2144 and Directives 2014/90/EU, (EU) 2016/797 and (EU) 2020/1828 (Artificial Intelligence Act) Article 5(1)(h).

[3]*Ibid*, Article 6(2) and Article 26(10), and Annex III, 1(a) AI Act.

[4]E.g., Autoriteit Persoonsgegevens (Dutch DPA), 'Dutch DPA Imposes a Fine on Clearview Because of Illegal Data Collection for Facial Recognition' 3 September 2024 https://www.autoriteitpersoonsgegevens.nl/en/current/dutch-dpa-imposes-a-fine-on-clearview-because-of-illegal-data-collection-for-facial-recognition, European Commission (2020) *White Paper: on Artificial Intelligence – A European Approach to Excellence and Trust, COM (2020) 65 final.*

[5]E.g. Bacciarelli (2023).

Commission published the proposal for the Artificial Intelligence Act to regulate the development, placing on the EU market, and use of specific AI systems that present risks to fundamental rights, safety, or health.[6] After lengthy discussions and negotiations, the European institutions politically agreed on the AI Act on 8 December 2024.[7] The final text was adopted on 13 June 2024[8] and will apply in different stages.[9]

The question that arises is whether FRTs, understood as part of RBIs, deployed in real-time or post-event in publicly accessible spaces for law enforcement purposes, is necessary in a democratic society. The chapter will not address and assess the justifications for allowing FRTs to be deployed in public spaces for non-law enforcement purposes (such as the use of FRTs for security purposes around a construction area).[10] After describing the terms of the discussions and establishing that the deployment of FRTs in public spaces for law enforcement purposes interferes with the fundamental rights to privacy and data protection, Sect. 2 will describe the conditions under which fundamental rights can be restricted in application of Article 52(1) of the Charter. These conditions are the legality of a measure (i.e. legal basis), the respect for the essence of the fundamental rights and freedoms at stake (essence), the existence of an objective of general interest (legitimate aim), the necessity of the restriction to achieve that objective (necessity), and the proportionality *stricto sensu* of the measure (proportionality).[11] This chapter will focus on the necessity requirement, as this condition is often conflated with the proportionality requirement or not even addressed, including by the Courts. Section 3 will dissect the condition of necessity, explaining the test of *strict necessity* as shaped by the European Court of Justice (ECJ) in its case law on the fundamental rights to privacy and data protection and enriched by the test of necessity derived from the case law of the European Court of Human Rights (ECtHR) on the right to privacy. Concerning the use of FRTs in public spaces, the ECtHR ruled in *Glukhin v Russia*, that the police use of FRTs to identify, locate, and arrest a demonstrator was 'incompatible with ideals and values of a democratic society governed by the rule of law.'[12]

---

[6]Proposal for a Regulation of the European Parliament and of the Council laying down harmonised rules on artificial intelligence (Artificial Intelligence Act) and amending certain union legislative acts, COM/2021/206 final, 21 April 2021.

[7]Council of the European Union, 'Artificial Intelligence Act: Council and Parliament Strike a Deal on the First Rules for AI in the World', https://www.consilium.europa.eu/en/press/press-releases/2023/12/09/artificial-intelligence-act-council-and-parliament-strike-a-deal-on-the-first-worldwide-rules-for-ai/.

[8]AI Act (n2).

[9]Article 113 AI Act.

[10]This chapter is part of a research project that dealt with law enforcement use of FRTs in public spaces. See acknowledgment section.

[11]On proportionality, see also chapter 'Technical Solutions for a Proportional Use of Facial Recognition Technology' in this volume by Menéndez González.

[12]*Glukhin v Russia* (n1), para. 90. On the Glukhin case, see chapter 'Facial Recognition Technologies: Threats or Opportunities for Democracy?' in this volume by Mobilio.

Building on this case law, the chapter will discuss the wider issue of FRTs in public spaces through the lens of the principle of necessity. Section 4 will assess the provisions of the AI Act against the test of necessity and identify what might be missing.

2 Interference with the Rights to Privacy and Data Protection

2.1 Background

2.1.1 Functioning of the Technologies

Facial Recognition Technologies detect, capture, and transform measurable facial characteristics (such as eye distance and size, nose length, etc.) into machine-readable biometric data.[13] These data are available in different forms: facial images or templates, which are a mathematical representation of the salient features used for recognition purposes. Biometric recognition covers verification and identification operations. The first operation compares data presented at a sensor with another set of previously recorded data. The purpose of the verification modality, often wrongly named authentication, is to check if the person is who they claim to be or not to establish who they are. This functionality is used in access control, identity checks, or password replacement.[14] The second functionality, biometric identification, compares captured data with multiple sets of data to find who the person is, i.e. whether there is a match between the data presented at the sensor and any other data present in databases used for comparison purposes. From a technical perspective, identifying someone is not establishing a person's identity or knowing the name but determining if the person is known in any of the databases checked during the identification process. Identification is often used in criminal investigations. Biometric recognition covers both verification and identification processes.[15] However, FRTs can also be used for purposes other than biometric recognition. They can be used for biometric categorisation (linked to gender classification or age estimation, for example) or for emotion detection.[16]

Concerning the use of FRTs in public spaces, discussions have mainly focused on the use of the technologies to identify individuals, leaving aside their use for identity verification purposes. This is acknowledged in Annex III, 1(a) of the AI Act, which

[13] E.g., Hamsici and Martinez (2015).

[14] E.g., Ross and Jain (2015).

[15] 'Biometric recognition', Term 37.01.03, ISO/IEC Standard 2382-37:2022.

[16] For a detailed description of the functioning of FRTs, see chapter 'Facial Recognition Technology and the Challenges to Democratic Systems: An Introduction' in this volume by Menendez Gonzalez and Mobilio.

excludes from the scope of RBIs verification systems that are only used ‘to confirm that a specific natural person is the person he or she claims to be’. More details on the functioning of facial recognition technologies can be found in chapter ‘Facial Recognition Technology and the Challenges to Democratic Systems: An Introduction’ of this book.

2.1.2 Notion of Publicly Accessible Spaces

As observed by some authors, the deployment of biometric surveillance technologies affects public spaces. Public spaces, understood here as publicly accessible spaces, are spaces where individuals can exercise their fundamental rights, for instance, to participate in political life and have social interactions, and also where their fundamental rights,[17] such as their right to privacy, are protected.[18] Yet, due to different security concerns and threats (such as the threats to terrorist attacks for the past 20 years in Western democracies), the function of these public spaces is changing, and surveillance technologies to monitor these spaces are increasingly used. In *Exclusion from the Public Space*, Moeckli explains how public spaces have been transformed through the years into ‘controlled spaces’ with surveillance technologies, which include CCTVs and thus FRTs, and the change of nature of these spaces, which are ‘losing [their] character[s] as the space of liberty.’[19] Yet, if the AI Act regulates the use of biometric technologies in publicly accessible spaces,[20] it does not address the function of these spaces, how the use of surveillance biometric technologies restricts these spaces, and why these restrictions are necessary.[21] The particularity of ‘publicly accessible spaces’ is that their ownership, whether public or private, the potential capacity or security restrictions (including the payment of an entrance ticket) do not affect the nature of these spaces. However, restrictions of access to the public, such as a gate or areas reserved for employees or service providers, are delimiting spaces that are not publicly accessible.[22] Thus, in the category of publicly accessible spaces fall public spaces, in the sense of spaces being owned by public authorities, but also privately owned spaces, provided they are accessible to ‘an undetermined number’ of persons and ‘irrespective of the activity for which the space may be used.’ It could be a restaurant, a shop, parks, banks, public roads, cinemas, swimming pools, bus stations, airports, etc.[23]

[17] Bastida (2016).

[18] E.g., SURVEILLE (2014).

[19] Moeckli (2016).

[20] Rec. 19 and Article 3(44) AI Act; the term ‘public spaces’ is used as a synonym for ‘publicly accessible spaces’ in this chapter.

[21] No recital of the AI Act reflects these important issues.

[22] Rec. 19 AI Act.

[23] *ibid.*

2.2 Interference

As acknowledged by different European bodies[24] and the ECtHR in *Glukhin v Russia*,[25] using FRTs in public spaces affects several fundamental rights and freedoms beyond the rights to privacy and data protection. It also affects freedom of expression, freedom of religion, freedom of assembly and association, human dignity, the right to a fair trial, and the presumption of innocence. This contribution focuses, however, on their impact on the rights to privacy and data protection and the conditions under which these rights can be limited.

Concerning the right to data protection, the technologies collect and process personal data of individuals to transform them for comparison purposes. According to the EDPB, the interference with the fundamental right to data protection is constituted as soon as the facial characteristics are captured to be transformed, irrespective of any matching with other biometric data stored in an existing database. Thus, the processing of biometric data interferes with the fundamental rights of the Charter, even if a biometric template comparison does not lead to any identification.[26] For the ECtHR, the protection of personal data is a component of the right to privacy,[27] as protected by Article 8 of the European Convention on Human Rights. The storage of photographs by the police also constitutes an interference with the right to privacy.[28]

Beyond the collection and processing of personal data, the interference with the right to privacy is also constituted based on individuals' expectation of privacy, including in public spaces.[29] They have the right to control their image and develop their 'social identity'.[30] Knowing that they could be identified in public spaces could have a chilling effect on people's exercise of fundamental rights in public spaces, such as the right to assembly or freedom of expression.[31]

---

[24] E.g., EDPB (2023) Guidelines 05/2022 on the use of facial recognition technology in the area of law enforcement, version 2.0, 26 April 2023, Consultative Committee of the Convention for the Protection of Individuals with regard to Automatic Processing of Personal data (2021), CNIL (2019).

[25] *Gluhkin v Russia* (n1) paras 65 et seqs.

[26] EDPB (2023)(n24), pp. 14–15.

[27] *S and Marper v UK* Apps nos 30562/04 and 30566/04 (ECtHR, 4 December 2008), para 103.

[28] E.g. *Gaughran v UK* App no 45245/15 (ECtHR, 13 February 2020), paras 69–70; *Glukhin v Russia* (n1) para. 72.

[29] E.g. *P.G. and J.H. v UK* App no 44787/98 (ECtHR, 25 September 2001), para 57.

[30] As cited in *Bărbulescu v Romania* App no 61496/08 (ECtHR, 5 September 2017), para. 70.

[31] Galič (2019) and EDPB (2023)(n24), p. 14.

2.3 *Justifications*

Non-absolute fundamental rights, such as the rights to privacy and data protection, can be restricted provided they comply with specific conditions defined in Article 52(1) of the Charter. Following that article, restrictions to fundamental rights must be in accordance with the law, necessary, proportionate, and respect for the essence of the fundamental rights at stake. As the right to privacy in Article 7 of the Charter mirrors Article 8 of the European Convention on Human Rights (ECHR), it must be interpreted as having the same scope and meaning as Article 8 of the ECHR. This means that the European Court of Justice (ECJ) must interpret Article 7 and the restrictions on this right, as the European Court of Human Rights (ECtHR) interprets Article 8 of the ECHR and its restrictions thereof.[32] Concerning the right to data protection, a separate fundamental right prescribed in Article 8 of the Charter, while recognised as a component of the right to privacy in the European Convention, the same obligation does not apply. However, the ECJ usually takes into account the ECtHR's case law on Article 8 of the ECHR when it interprets Article 8 of the Charter. Consequently, as the case law of the ECtHR influences the way the ECJ interprets both Articles 7 and 8 of the Charter, references to the tests of necessity developed by both Courts will be used in assessing the necessity of the measure.

3 Necessity Tests

As analysed by the legal doctrine, the test of necessity is part of the proportionality test broadly understood. The proportionality test is composed of three elements: (1) the suitability test, (2) the necessity test, and (3) the proportionality test *stricto sensu*. This approach originates from the German legal theory, in particular, by Alexy,[33] but is also supported by the ECtHR and the ECJ.[34] While proportionality *stricto sensu* calls for balancing competing interests or rights, necessity means that the least restrictive but equally effective means have been chosen to achieve the legitimate aim of a measure.[35] Thus, not only should a measure pursue a legitimate objective that must be appropriate in reaching the aim (suitability test), but it should also not go beyond what is necessary (necessity test) and be proportionate (proportionality test *stricto sensu*). As observed by Afonso da Silva,[36] necessity 'stand[s] in the shadows of balancing' and is often conflated with proportionality *stricto sensu*. Yet, necessity implies examining less restrictive but equally effective means from a

[32] Art 52(3) Charter.

[33] Alexy (2002).

[34] As analysed in Meškić and Samardžić (2017).

[35] Although legal scholars have different understandings of what necessity means; see for instance Gerards (2013).

[36] Afonso da Silva (2023).

fundamental rights perspective. Necessity also requires a factual analysis. Both the ECtHR and the ECJ have developed a test of necessity in their respective case law. While the ECJ applies a test of 'strict necessity' for the restrictions on the exercise of fundamental rights, the ECtHR applies a different standard assessing whether a measure is 'necessary in a democratic society'. Can criteria be drawn from the Courts' judicial review on measures interfering with the rights to privacy and data protection to assess the necessity of the rules governing the use of FRTs in public spaces as introduced in the AI Act?

3.1 Necessary in a Democratic Society

Following Article 8(2) ECHR, an interference with the right to privacy should be:

> in accordance with the law and necessary in a democratic society in the interests of national security, public safety or the economic well-being of the country, for the prevention of disorder or crime, for the protection of health or morals, or for the protection of the rights and freedoms of others.

The ECtHR views an interference as being 'necessary in a democratic society' if it complies with several conditions.[37] First, as specified by the Court, 'necessary' is not synonymous with 'indispensable'. It also does not have 'the flexibility' of 'admissible', 'ordinary', 'useful', 'reasonable', or 'desirable.'[38] Instead, it needs to pursue a legitimate aim that answers a 'pressing social need.'

Although this expression is not defined by the Court, the European Data Protection Supervisor (EDPS) suggests understanding it as meaning 'critical for the functioning of society',[39] while the Article 29 Working Party calls for taking into account the impact a measure has on society and the 'broader views (societal, historical or political etc) of society on the issue in question.'[40] Second, that interference needs to be proportionate to the legitimate aim pursued. Third, it needs to be justified by relevant and sufficient reasons. If alternatives exist, i.e. less intrusive measures, the interference is unlikely to meet the necessity test. In some cases, the Court did not examine whether the interference answered a 'pressing social need' but 'whether the relationship between the aim sought to be achieved and the means employed [could] be considered proportionate.'[41] Thus, the Court seems to mix the test of necessity per se with that of proportionality *stricto*

[37] *S and Marper v UK* (n 27) para. 101.

[38] *Handyside v UK* App no 5493/72 (ECtHR, 7 December 1976) para. 48.

[39] EDPS (2017) Assessing the necessity of measures that limit the fundamental right to the protection of personal data: A Toolkit, p. 15.

[40] Article 29 Working Party (2014) Opinion 01/2014 on the Application of Necessity and Proportionality Concepts and Data Protection within the Law Enforcement Sector, WP211, p. 8.

[41] *Robathin v Austria* App no 30457/06 (ECtHR, 3 July 2012) para. 43.

sensu. For instance, the Court has examined whether the law under review provided 'adequate and effective safeguards against any abuse and arbitrariness.'[42]

As stated in *Handyside*, the initial assessment of the existence of a 'pressing social need' is left to the discretion of national authorities through their margin of appreciation.[43] The State is responsible for 'demonstrat[ing] the existence of the pressing social need behind the interference.'[44] The margin of appreciation depends on the level of consensus among Member States, as recalled in *S and Marper*, besides other factors (including the nature of the right at stake).[45] Without consensus, Member States have a wider margin of appreciation. But, ultimately, the Court makes the final assessment on whether an interference complies with the necessity requirement.[46]

Although the 'fight against crime, particularly against organised crime and terrorism'[47] depends on modern investigation and identification technologies, the Court is of the view that these technologies cannot be allowed 'at any cost and without carefully balancing the potential benefits of the extensive use of such techniques against private-life interests.'[48] In its case law relating to these technologies, which include DNA and fingerprint analysis, as well as facial recognition, the ECtHR did not identify what constitutes an interference *necessary in a democratic society*. Instead, the Court checked the existence of a legitimate aim, the margin of appreciation of Member States, the existence of safeguards, especially if the interference presents significant risks (such as a system of secret surveillance in the context of national security), and the proportionality of the interference. In *S and Marper*, the Court found the blanket retention of biometric information of suspected but not convicted individuals for an illimited period as being disproportionate and, therefore, not necessary in a democratic society.[49] In *Glukhin v Russia*, due to the nature of the technologies ('highly intrusive'), the offence at stake, and their use in real-time, the Court concluded that the deployment of FRTs did not answer a 'pressing social need.'[50] The Court conducted a proportionality test, weighing all factors at stake rather than defining which use of the technologies could answer a 'pressing social need.' In that sense, this decision does not help understand which uses of FRTs could answer such undefined 'pressing social need.' However, one has to agree with Article 29 WP that 'the very essence of a pressing social need will

---

[42] *ibid* para. 44.

[43] *Handyside v UK* App (n38) para. 48.

[44] *Piechowicz v Poland* App no 20071/07 (ECtHR, 17 April 2012), para. 212.

[45] *S and Marper v UK* (n27) para 102, and *Gaughran v UK* App no 45245/15 (n28), para. 77.

[46] *S and Marper v UK* (n27) para 101.

[47] *S and Marper v UK* (n27) para. 105.

[48] *ibid,* para. 112.

[49] *ibid,* paras 118 et seqs.

[50] *ibid*, paras 88–89.

mean that it is fluid and will have an element of subjectivity.'[51] In *Glukhin v Russia*, the Court gave a logical answer based on the minor offence committed and the use of intrusive and ubiquitous technologies, such as facial recognition technologies. The Court also seems to consider that certain uses of FRTs by police authorities would be allowed in democratic societies. In that sense, the ECtHR did not take a position on the general issue of police use of FRTs in public spaces and limited its decision to the circumstances of the case. But given the divided opinions among Member States to the Convention and EU Member States on the legitimate uses of these technologies by the police, was it the role of the Court to take a position in *Glukhin v Russia* on such a political and societal issue?[52]

On its side, the ECJ applies a different test of necessity, as described in the next section.

3.2 Strictly Necessary

The limitation clause to fundamental rights is provided in by Article 52(1) of the Charter, which reads as follows:

> Any limitation on the exercise of the rights and freedoms recognised by this Charter must be provided for by law and respect the essence of those rights and freedoms. Subject to the principle of proportionality, limitations may be made only if they are necessary and genuinely meet objectives of general interest recognised by the Union or the need to protect the rights and freedoms of others.

As already mentioned, Article 52(1) of the Charter requires several conditions to be met to justify an interference with fundamental rights. The condition of necessity is one of them and is interpreted as a condition of 'strict necessity' by the ECJ.[53] Before analysing the Court's test, it should be mentioned that the Court applies a test of strict necessity to assess an interference and conducts a 'strict' judicial review when it assesses interferences with the rights to privacy and data protection.[54]

In his Opinion delivered in *Tele2 Sverige*, AG Saugmandsgaards ØE explained that there were two ways to interpret the strict necessity of a measure. The first would view a measure as going beyond what is strictly necessary to achieve the legitimate aim independently of any safeguards; the second would consider that a measure does not go beyond what is strictly necessary precisely because it is accompanied by specific safeguards.[55] The Advocate General favoured the second interpretation and considered the existence of safeguards as a determining factor in finding a measure

---

[51] A29WP (n40) p. 8.

[52] On the limits of the *Glukhin v Russia's* judgment, see the analysis made by Neroni Rezende (2023).

[53] E.g., joined cases C-92/09 and 93/09 *Volker und Markus Schecke and Eifert*, [2010] ECLI:EU:C: 2010: 662, paras 77 and 86.

[54] Joined cases C-293/12 and C-594/12 *Digital Rights Ireland and Steilinger and others* [2014] ECLI:EU:C: 2014: 238, paras 47–48.

[55] AG Opinion in joined cases C-203/15 and C-698/15, *Tele2 Sverige v Post-och telestyrelsen et al.* [2016] ECLI:EU:C: 2016: 572, paras 192–193; AG Mengozzi called it 'a strict review of compliance' in his Opinion in Opinion 1/15 of the Grand Chamber, [2009] ECLI:EU:C:2016:656, para. 9.

to be strictly necessary. The Court followed the AG and looked at the existence or absence of safeguards to determine whether the measure was strictly necessary.[56] Therefore, the ECJ seems to rely on the existence of safeguards in its assessment of necessity. However, as Meškić and Samardžić observed in both *Digital Rights Ireland* and *Tele2 Sverige*, the Court did not examine the necessity of the measure in itself, as it only examined safeguards as part of the test of proportionality *stricto sensu.* Still, this is not per se part of the test of necessity, which should involve assessing alternative solutions that are less restrictive. In his Opinion in *Digital Rights Ireland*, AG General Cruz Villalón suggested looking at 'the quick freeze procedure' as an alternative to blanket data retention.[57] According to him, assessing the legitimacy of a measure amounts to assessing 'whether a measure less disruptive to the enjoyment of the fundamental rights at issue would allow the objective pursued to be attained.'[58] In its decision, the Court did not discuss this aspect and annulled the Data Retention Directive.[59] As analysed by Sajfert, the Court did not answer whether data retention measures were 'a valuable tool for criminal investigation' and thus did not assess their necessity.[60] When reviewing the necessity of new investigative tools, such as in the case of police use of FRTs in public spaces, the Court should review the existence of objective evidence justifying their necessity, i.e. whether that they are necessary to achieve the objective pursued and that no other less intrusive means could achieve it, instead of or beyond looking at existing safeguards.

The ECJ does not distinguish the test of necessity from that of proportionality. It might be because the task of assessing the strict necessity of a measure should be left at national level, rather than at EU level. In his Opinion in *Tele2 Sverige*, while AG Saugmandsgaards ØE viewed the strict necessity as being linked to the existence of safeguards, he also considered that national courts should assess the strict necessity of the general data retention obligation by 'not simply verify[ing] the mere utility of general data retention obligations, but [by] rigorously verify[ing] that no other measure or combination of measures, such as targeted data retention obligation accompanied by other investigatory tools, can be as effectiveness [sic] in the fight against serious crime.'[61] Adding to this, one should also observe that it is not the task

[56] Joined Cases C-203/15 and C-698/15 *Tele 2 Sverige v Post-och telestyrelsen et al.* [2016] ECLI: EU:C: 2016: 970, paras 96 et seqs; and in the earlier case on data retention, *Digital Rights Ireland* (n54) paras 61–64.

[57] *Ibid.*

[58] *Ibid*, para 143.

[59] *Digital Rights Ireland* (n54).

[60] In his PhD thesis entitled 'Resolving Legal Conflicts between Data Access Investigative Measures and Data Protection Law in the EU' *(forthcoming)*, Sajfert observed a common trend regarding the absence of objective evidence and empirical data behind the law enforcement authorities' requests to obtain new investigative tools through measures such as data retention, passenger name records, financial data.

[61] AG Opinion Joined Cases C-203/15 and C-698/15, *Tele2 Sverige v Post-och telestyrelsen et al.* (n55) para 209.

of the Courts 'to choose or to point to the supposed best way to achieve a given goal but to compare the means chosen by the legislature (…) which each possible alternative to it,' as rightly noted by Afonso da Silva.[62] Therefore, Courts should not substitute themselves for the legislator and provide for alternative measures that the legislator did not consider while reviewing the necessity of a measure.

To complete the tests of necessity developed by the ECtHR and the ECJ, it might be helpful to look at the practical guidance elaborated by the EDPS before assessing whether the provisions of the AI Act on RBIs comply with the condition of necessity.

3.3 EDPS Guidelines

The EDPS has elaborated two distinct guidelines on the principles of necessity and proportionality. In 2017,[63] he issued a toolkit on necessity, completed in 2019 with guidelines on the principle of proportionality.[64] This section will only deal with the first document. Although non-binding, the toolkit offers practical guidance on the application of the necessity requirement. The document is based on the case law of the ECJ, enriched by the interpretation of the ECtHR on the restrictions to the right to privacy. These guidelines provide a checklist to assess the necessity of new measures through a four-step approach based on the description of the measure (step 1), the fundamental rights and freedoms affected (step 2), the objectives of the measures (step 3) and the least intrusive but effective option (step 4).

As already observed, the EDPS links the principle of necessity and that of proportionality. The proportionality of a measure should be assessed only if the necessity has been established. However, the order between the two principles is not always clear.[65] Importantly, the EDPS identifies the need to provide 'sufficient and scientifically verifiable evidence supporting the existence of the problem.'[66] This objective evidence can include 'facts or statistical data' and should 'convincingly support the proposed measure' to prove that 'existing measures and less intrusive alternative measures cannot effectively address the problem.'[67] The assessment implies a factual-based analysis.

[62] Afonso da Silva (2023), p. 1748.

[63] EDPS (2017) (n39).

[64] EDPS (2019) Guidelines on Assessing the Proportionality of Measures that Limit the Fundamental Rights to Privacy and to the Protection of Personal Data, 19 December 2019.

[65] See for illustration, joined cases C-203/15 and C-698/15, *Tele 2 Sverige AB* (n56) paras 102–103.

[66] EDPS (2017) (n39), p. 15.

[67] *Ibid*, p. 19.

Applied to the deployment of FRTs in public spaces for surveillance and policing purposes, the questions to assess the necessity of the measure could be the following ones:

i. Which objective of general interest or protection of rights and freedoms does the use of FRTs in public spaces for surveillance and policing purposes answer?
ii. Why is this objective, if any, 'critical for the functioning of society'?
iii. Is there any scientific evidence that FRTs are necessary and effective to achieve the purposes of the measure?
iv. If so, is the measure effective and the least restrictive one? Concerning this last point, one should observe that the measure should be the least restrictive regarding the impact on fundamental rights, but it does not need to be more effective than the alternative measures. It should be, at least, equally effective.

It should be noted that the EDPS also examines the existence of safeguards, but only after having assessed the other elements of the test (including the objective justification and the effectiveness of the measure) and not instead of them.

This practical approach can guide the review of the rules adopted by the EU institutions on the use of RBIs in public spaces for law enforcement purposes as part of the future AI Act.

4 Application to AI Act Rules

The AI Act regulates the development, placing on the EU market, and use of certain AI systems that present risks to fundamental rights, safety, or health.[68] While AI systems that present unacceptable risks to fundamental rights are prohibited save for some exceptions, other AI systems that present serious interferences with fundamental rights, safety, or health are regulated as high-risk systems. Concerning RBIs, those used in publicly accessible spaces and real-time for a law enforcement purpose are prohibited except in three situations that need to be allowed by national law and comply with conditions and safeguards. All the other uses, as well as the development and placing of the EU market of RBIs, fall in the category of high-risk systems. Concerning the retrospective use of RBIs for a law enforcement purpose in publicly accessible spaces, their use is subject to additional safeguards, such as a fundamental rights impact assessment. The rules introduced in the AI Act will be analysed in this section, followed by a necessity assessment.

[68] AI Act (n2)

4.1 Rules on RBIs Deployed in Publicly Accessible Areas

The AI Act distinguishes two situations: live use of RBIs for a law enforcement purpose versus retrospective use.

4.1.1 Live ('Real-time') Use

According to the adopted rules, real-time use of RBIs in publicly accessible spaces for law enforcement purposes is, in principle, banned, except in three cases (Art 5(1)(h)(i)-(iii) AI Act).

Real-time use refers to the capture of biometric data, comparison with other biometric data and identification of individuals, occurring all at the same time or without any significant delay.[69] The definition of real-time is vague and does not rely on a scientific understanding of real-time. Law enforcement purposes are those described in Article 1(1) of the Law Enforcement Directive (LED)[70] and reproduced in Article 3(46) of the AI Act, i.e. 'the prevention, investigation, detection or prosecution of criminal offences or the execution of criminal penalties including safeguarding against and preventing threats to public security.'[71] These activities are performed by law enforcement authorities (which include entrusted bodies or entities) or on their behalf.[72] So not only police authorities or other law enforcement authorities are covered, but also private parties acting on behalf of those authorities (most likely through a contractual agreement). As for publicly accessible areas, they are defined as 'any publicly or privately owned physical place accessible to an undetermined number of natural persons, regardless of whether certain conditions for access may apply, and regardless of the potential capacity restrictions.'[73] These spaces can be both privately and publicly owned. They cover a broad range of spaces, including a shopping centre, a public park, or a train station, among others.[74]

Consequently, the live deployment of FRTs by the police in the context of crime prevention is not allowed in principle, whereas the same deployment in real-time to ensure the security of a shopping mall by private actors is not covered by the ban.[75]

[69] Recital 17 and Article 3(42) AI Act.

[70] Directive (EU) 2016/680 of the European Parliament and of the Council of 27 April 2016 on the protection of natural persons with regard to the prevention, investigation, detection or prosecution of criminal offences or the execution of criminal penalties, and on the free movement of such data, and repealing Council Framework Decision 2008/977/JHA.

[71] See Brewczyńska (2024) in the Commentary of Article 1 of the LED, pp. 58–63.

[72] Art 3(45) AI Act; see also Tosoni and Bygrave (2024) in the Commentary of Article 3 of the LED, pp. 99–104.

[73] Art 3(44) AI Act.

[74] See Sect. 2.1, notion of publicly accessible spaces.

[75] As this will not be considered a law enforcement activity. However, other rules will apply, such as data protection rules. But the study of these rules falls outside the chapter.

However, the ban on law enforcement use of RBIs is not absolute as the AI Act has introduced three exceptions applicable to:

(1) the targeted search for victims of kidnapping, trafficking in human beings, or sexual exploitation, as well as the search for missing persons (Article 5(1)(h)(i) AI Act).
(2) the prevention of a threat to the life or physical safety of persons, provided the threat is specific, imminent and substantial, or a genuine threat of a terrorist attack, that must be either present or foreseeable (Article 5(1)(h)(ii) AI Act).
(3) the localisation or identification of a criminal suspect or perpetrator to conduct a criminal investigation, prosecution or execution of a criminal penalty for serious crimes listed in Annex II and punishable by jail time (for a maximum period of at least four years) (Article 5(1))(h)(iii) AI Act).

Specific conditions and obligations must be implemented before law enforcement authorities or anyone acting on their behalf can deploy live RBIs in publicly accessible areas in one of these three situations.[76] First, the technologies can only be used to confirm the identity of a targeted individual, considering the nature of the situation and the impacts of the technologies' use on individuals' rights and freedoms. Second, their use must be authorised by law at national level. Authorisation can only be given if law enforcement authorities have conducted a fundamental rights impact assessment and registered the technologies in the EU database before use, except in 'duly justified cases of urgency.'[77]

From a procedural perspective, real-time RBIs are subject to a prior judicial or administrative authorisation based on 'objective evidence or clear indications' that their use is necessary and proportionate to one of the three objectives. Results obtained from real-time RBIs can only be used as lead information. In 'duly justified cases of urgency', their use can start without authorisation provided the authorisation is obtained within 24 h maximum. If the authorisation is rejected, their use should stop, and all the data and information should be deleted.[78]

Member States can fully or partially authorise the use of real-time RBIs. They are not obliged to allow the real-time use of RBIs and can also decide not to allow any of the exceptions in their national law. In case they allow the real-time use of RBIs, their national legislation should detail the rules to obtain the authorisation to use real-time RBIs. It should also include the objectives pursued by the deployment of RBIs and, in the case of localisation or identification of a criminal suspect, the criminal offences for which real-time RBIs are authorised to be used and the competent authorities allowed to use them. Member States must report the rules they adopt to the European Commission and can decide to adopt more restrictive rules.[79]

---

[76] Article 5(2)-(7) AI Act.

[77] Article 5(2) AI Act.

[78] Article 5(3) AI Act.

[79] Article 5(5) AI Act.

Market surveillance and national data protection authorities receive notifications of each RBIs use. Then, they submit an annual report to the European Commission on these uses based on a template report. Afterwards, the European Commission publishes annual reports on the use of real-time RBIs, based on those reports.[80]

4.1.2 Retrospective ('Post') Use

As proposed by the European Commission, the AI Act provides specific rules for the retrospective use of RBIs by law enforcement authorities in publicly accessible areas. First, post RBIs for law enforcement purposes cannot be used untargeted, i.e. without connection with a criminal offence, criminal proceeding, a genuine threat of a criminal offence, or the search for a specific missing person. It also has to be limited in terms of location, temporal scope, and linked to 'a closed data set of legally acquired video footage'.[81] The retrospective use of RBIs should be documented in a police file and made available for inspection. Before deploying RBIs for retrospective use, the deployer, i.e. the law enforcement authorities, should receive a judicial or administrative authorisation, except when the technologies are used to identify a potential suspect based 'on objective and verifiable facts' directly linked to the offence. Their use should be limited to what is strictly necessary for the investigation.[82] Post RBIs are considered high-risk and subject to the rules applicable to high-risk systems, which include the conduct of a fundamental rights impact assessment.[83]

4.2 Justifications

During the negotiations of the AI Act, the rules concerning the regulation of RBIs used by law enforcement authorities in publicly accessible spaces have been the subject of intense discussions from various stakeholders defending different interests, which were not easily conciliable. For instance, the European Parliament struggled to reach a consensus on the text due to disagreement among political groups. As a result, the adopted AI Act has expanded the list of prohibited AI practices based on the unacceptable risks they pose to fundamental rights.

Concerning the real-time use of RBIs in publicly accessible spaces for law enforcement purposes, the AI Act refers to their 'particularly intrusive' nature, to the number of individuals impacted by their use ('may affect the private life of a large number of the population'), the feeling of surveillance their use might create,

[80] Article 5(4), Article 5(6)-(7) AI Act.

[81] Recital 95 and Article 26(10) AI Act.

[82] Article 26(10) AI Act.

[83] Article 27 AI Act.

and the chilling effect they might have on the exercise of other rights.[84] Based on these elements, recital 33 explains that such use of the technologies should be prohibited, except in three situations, where according to that recital, 'the use is strictly necessary to achieve a substantial public interest, the importance of which outweighs the risks.' Those are the only justifications that can be found in the AI Act. To ensure that the technologies are used in 'a responsible and proportionate manner,' safeguards and conditions are required for each exception.[85]

Concerning the retrospective use of RBIs for law enforcement purposes in publicly accessible spaces, the AI Act does not justify why the use of RBIs post-event poses fewer risks for fundamental rights than their real-time use. Concerning the other uses of the technologies, such as their real-time use for non-law enforcement purposes in publicly accessible spaces,[86] the AI Act identifies 'technical inaccuracies' of RBIs and the resulting biases and discriminations, including based on 'age, ethnicity, race, sex or disabilities', as a reason to classify RBIs as high-risk systems.[87] But it does not explain why such use should not be banned, contrary to the position of the European Parliament on the AI Act.[88]

In the impact assessment accompanying the proposed AI Act, the European Commission had acknowledged the 'chilling effect [of these] technologies on democracy' while justifying their use 'when strictly necessary and proportionate safeguarding important public interests of public security.' The Commission based its position on the responses of several Member States (France, Finland, Denmark, and the Czech Republic) to its public consultation on the regulation of AI but did not go through a necessity test to provide evidence of the deployment of these biometric tools in publicly accessible spaces.[89]

The next sub-section will critically assess the adopted rules through the necessity test, taking into account the questions drawn from the EDPS Toolkit.

4.3 Strictly Necessary [in a Democratic Society]?

The AI Act distinguishes the real-time use of RBIs for law enforcement purposes from their retrospective use for the same purposes but does not mention the other uses of the technologies.

---

[84] Recital 32 AI Act.

[85] Recital 34 AI Act.

[86] Such as the use of live FRT in a supermarket to deter shoplifting.

[87] Recital 54 AI Act.

[88] See European Parliament, Amendments Adopted by the European Parliament on 14 June 2023 on the Proposal for a Regulation of the European Parliament and of the Council Laying Down Harmonised Rules on Artificial Intelligence (Artificial Intelligence Act) and Amending Certain Union Legislative Acts, P9-TA(2023) 0236, Amendment 41 (Recital 18).

[89] European Commission (2021) Impact Assessment Accompanying the Proposal for the Artificial Intelligence Act, SWD (2021) 84 final, Part 1, pp. 18–19.

Concerning the real-time use of the technologies for law enforcement purposes in publicly accessible spaces, the AI Act acknowledges that, due to their nature and their impacts on fundamental rights,[90] such use of RBIs should be prohibited. At the same time, it identifies a legitimate aim that would justify their use in three cases. Those are the search for the victims of specific crimes and missing persons (first exception), the threats to the life or physical safety of individuals or a terrorist attack (second exception), and the localisation or identification of suspects or perpetrators of serious crimes as listed in Annex II of the AI Act (third exception). The ECtHR has recognised the fight against serious crime, as well as the protection of others' rights and freedoms, as a legitimate aim justifying an interference with fundamental rights. These legitimate aims are of such importance that they 'outweigh the risks', rendering the use of the technologies strictly necessary.[91] This statement in Recital 33 seems to result from a test of proportionality (balancing the risks to individuals[92] against the substantial public interest) and a test of necessity (referring to 'strict necessity').[93]

However, there is no indication of whether, and how, the EU legislators conducted the proportionality and necessity tests. Looking back at the questions identified by the EDPS in its guidelines, once the objective of the measure has been identified, it should be checked whether such an objective answers a 'pressing social need.'[94] According to the EDPS, this means that the problem the measure addresses is 'not only real, present or imminent' but also 'critical for the functioning of the society.'[95] Although the EDPS has not defined what 'being critical for the functioning of the society is,' he criticized, together with the EDPB, the proposal for the AI Act and called for a complete ban on RBIs in publicly accessible spaces in 'any context', i.e. for law enforcement and non-law enforcement purposes.[96] Due to the risks of technical inaccuracies potentially leading to biases and discriminations on sensitive attributes and the risk of constant monitoring, the EU legislators should have evidenced that the exceptions to the ban were necessary in a democratic society. The EU institutions should have provided objective, verifiable, and scientific evidence that their use for those purposes was strictly necessary and that deploying RBIs for those purposes in publicly accessible spaces was the least restrictive measure. There is no indication that other less intrusive solutions were envisaged and discarded because they were not as efficient as real-time RBIs. It seems that the decision to allow exceptions was first a political issue. In policy documents and

[90] Recital 33 AI Act.

[91] Recital 33 AI Act.

[92] As identified in Recital 32.

[93] Recital 33 AI Act.

[94] As formulated by the ECtHR in its case law, see Sect. 3.1.

[95] EDPS (2017) (n39), p. 15.

[96] EDPB-EDPS, Joint Opinion 5/2021 on the Proposal for a Regulation of the European Parliament and of the Council Laying Down Harmonised Rules on Artificial Intelligence (Artificial Intelligence Act), 18 June 2021, pp. 11–12.

reports prior to the AI Act, there were already indications that certain uses of FRTs were considered justified. For instance, this was the case of FRT used to help find missing or abducted children,[97] to 'contribute to the protection of public spaces' for 'detecting terrorists on the move.'[98] In a 2021 Resolution, while the European Parliament called for a moratorium on the law enforcement use of FRTs,[99] it acknowledged that 'AI [was] in use by law enforcement in applications such facial recognition technologies, e.g. to search suspect databases and identify victims of human trafficking or child sexual exploitation and abuse.'[100]

Instead of explaining why the real-time use of RBIs is strictly necessary, the AI Act provides the conditions and safeguards under which the authorised technologies should be used.[101] One of the essential conditions is the existence of national legislation authorising the real-time use of the technologies in the different situations. According to Article 5(2) of the AI Act, it is the responsibility of the national authority (either a judicial authority or an independent administrative authority) delivering the authorisation of use to conduct a test of necessity (and proportionality). One could imagine that national legislation allowing the real-time use of RBIs for the exceptions to the ban would provide some justifications for the necessity of their deployment.

Concerning their retrospective use, similar remarks can be made, as no justification and evidence of the strict necessity of their use are put forward in the AI Act. Article 26(10) of the AI Act only states that their use should 'be limited to what is strictly necessary for the investigation of a specific criminal offence' and requires the adoption of safeguards due to their 'intrusive nature.' It seems that the EU legislators, like the ECJ, rely on the existence of safeguards instead of assessing the necessity of a measure. Before the negotiations of the AI Act, several Member States, including France,[102] had already adopted legal frameworks to allow the retrospective use of FRTs for criminal investigation purposes.[103] Therefore, they had an interest in keeping these rules in place and introducing a distinction between live and retrospective use of the technologies. In 2022, the French Council of State considered the retrospective use of FRTs for criminal investigations as being strictly necessary ('absolutely necessary') due to the number of images the French criminal database counted and the 'impossib[ility] for the competent authorities to carry out such a comparison [i.e. facial image comparison] manually.'[104] According

---

[97] As acknowledged in FRA (2020), p. 29.

[98] European Commission (2020), Communication, A Counter-Terrorism Agenda for the EU: Anticipate, Prevent, Protect, Respond, 9 December 2020, COM (2020) 795 final, p 4.

[99] European Parliament (2021) Resolution on Artificial Intelligence in Criminal Law and its Use by the Police and Judicial Authorities in Criminal Matters, 6 October 2021, para 27, P9_TA (2021) 0405.

[100] *ibid*, Point M.

[101] Article 5(2)-(7) AI Act; see Sect. 4.1.

[102] Through the French criminal facial database called TAJ, *Traitements des Antécédents Judiciaires*, established in 2012 by Decree no.2012-652.

[103] TELEFI (2021), pp. 11–12.

[104] Council of State, Decision no. 442364; as translated by the European Civic Forum.

to the French Council of State, it is, therefore, the volume of data to be processed that justifies using such intrusive technologies. Scholars have criticised this approach to strict necessity,[105] which also seems far from the EDPS' understanding of a strictly necessary measure.

Finally, the AI Act does not provide any justifications for the use of RBIs in contexts other than law enforcement, whether in real-time or post-event, while these systems function the same way and can have the same discriminatory consequences for individuals.

5 Conclusion

This chapter analysed the tests of necessity elaborated by the ECtHR and the ECJ, completed by the EDPS practical guidance on necessity to discuss the rules adopted in the AI Act on the real-time and retrospective use of RBIs, and thus FRTs, by law enforcement authorities in publicly accessible spaces. While the test of necessity should consist of comparing alternative solutions to protect the security of these spaces, the analysis did not find evidence of such a test. Indeed, no alternative solutions are discussed in the impact assessment, the proposal of the AI Act, and the AI Act itself. Instead, safeguards and conditions are imposed before the technologies can be deployed. The use of these technologies, either in real-time or post-event, is only authorised if it is targeted. Still, while the legislators acknowledge the risks and flaws of these technologies, they allow Member States to adopt national legislation to allow their use in three situations for their real-time use while asking national authorities that deliver the authorisation of use to conduct a proportionality and necessity assessment. One could wonder if the possibility to deploy FRTs and other RBI technologies in public spaces does not result from a political will, linked to security concerns, without evidence that this measure is adequate in a democratic society or that other measures posing fewer risks to individuals' fundamental rights exist. This observation echoes some scholars' views who consider that much of the discussion 'has taken for granted the existence of such technologies as a necessary means for securing public safety',[106] whereas discussions should also have been about the impact of these technologies on individuals in public spaces and the risks for these public spaces.

Acknowledgements This chapter results from the discussions held during the Next Democratic Frontiers for Facial Recognition Technology Conference organised by the European University Institute and the University of Florence in Florence on 29 September 2023. The chapter was written after the adoption of the AI Act but before the publication of the European Commission's guidelines on prohibited AI practices. This chapter builds on some ideas and analysis developed in 'The Future AI Act and Facial Recognition Technologies in Public Spaces: Nice to Have or Strictly

[105] Christakis and Lodie (2022).

[106] Leslie (2020), p 5.

Necessary?' (2023) 9(4) EDPL, written by the author during the negotiations of the AI Act. Part of the research carried out for the conference and the chapter was funded by the European Union's Horizon 2020 research and innovation programme under the Marie Skłodowska-Curie grant agreement no. 895978 (DATAFACE).

References

Afonso da Silva V (2023) Standing in the shadows of balancing: proportionality and the test of necessity. ICON 20(5):1738–1767
Alexy R (2002) A theory of constitutional rights, 2nd edn. OUP
Bacciarelli A (2023) Time to ban facial recognition from public spaces and borders. Human Rights Watch
Bastida F (2016) The concept of 'Public Space of Fundamental Rights' (Public Space and the Exercise of Fundamental Rights). Int J Hum Rights Const Stud 4(3):183–198
Brewczyńska M (2024) Article 1, Subject Matters and Objectives. In: Kosta E, Boehm F (eds) The EU Law Enforcement Directive (LED), a commentary. OUP
Christakis T, Lodie A (2022) The Conseil d'Etat finds the use of facial recognition by law enforcement agencies to support criminal investigations 'strictly necessary' and proportional. ERDAL 3:159–165
Commission Nationale de l'Informatique et des Libertés (CNIL) (2019) Facial Recognition: for a Debate Living up to the Challenges
Consultative Committee of the Convention for the Protection of Individuals with regard to Automatic Processing of Personal data (Convention 108) (2021) 'Guidelines on Facial Recognition'
European Union Agency for Fundamental Rights (FRA) (2020) Facial Recognition Technology: Fundamental Rights Considerations in the Context of Law Enforcement
Galič M (2019) Surveillance and privacy in smart cities and living labs: conceptualising privacy for public space
Gerards J (2013) How to improve the necessity test of the European Court of Human Rights. ICON 11(2):466–490
Hamsici OC, Martinez AM (2015) Face recognition, component-based. In: Li SZ, Jain AK (eds) Encyclopedia of biometrics, 1st edn. Springer Science, New York, pp 485–495
Leslie D (2020) Understanding bias in facial recognition technologies: an explainer. The Alan Turing Institute
Meškić Z, Samardžić D (2017) The strict necessity test on data protection by the CJEU: a proportionality test to face the challenges at the beginning of a new digital era in the midst of security concerns. CYELP 13:133–168
Moeckli D (2016) Exclusion from public space: a comparative constitutional analysis. Cambridge University Press, pp 65–67
Neroni Rezende I, Glukhin and the EU regulation of facial recognition: lessons to be learned? European Law Blog, 19 September 2019, Blogpost 39/2023
Ross A, Jain AK (2015) Biometrics, overview. In: Li SZ, Jain AK (eds) Encyclopedia of biometrics, 1st edn. Springer Science, New York, pp 289–294
SURVEILLE (2014) Deliverable D4.7. The Scope of the Right to Private Life in Public Places
TELEFI (2021) Towards the European Level Exchange of Facial Images, Summary of the Report. Version 1.0. https://www.telefi-project.eu/sites/default/files/TELEFI_SummaryReport.pdf
Tosoni L, Bygrave AL (2024) Article 3, Definitions. In: Kosta E, Boehm F (eds) The EU Law Enforcement Directive (LED), a commentary. OUP

Enhancing Oversight and Addressing Gaps: Assessing the Impact of the AI Act on Biometric Identification Systems

Federica Paolucci

Abstract Facial recognition technology (FRT) represents a pivotal force in modern society, with implications for both security and privacy. In response to concerns raised by incidents like the Clearview AI scandal, the European Union (EU) has crafted the Artificial Intelligence Act (AI Act) to regulate biometric recognition systems. This paper explores the EU's regulatory approach, focusing on the delicate balance between security imperatives and individual rights. It examines the internal influence of the AI Act within the EU, considering its potential as a regulatory model for biometric data use beyond law enforcement. Drawing parallels with the EU's influential General Data Protection Regulation (GDPR), the paper underscores the potential of the AI Act to set a protective standard for biometric tools, exemplified in initiatives like the Digital Identity Wallet. However, challenges persist in ensuring effective enforcement mechanisms, notably concerning the authorisation process and the balance between security imperatives and individual rights. The choice between judicial and administrative oversight remains contentious, with significant implications for privacy rights, the rule of law and democracy. As Member States navigate the implementation of biometric recognition systems, the paper emphasises the importance of procedural fairness and judicial independence in safeguarding fundamental rights. Ultimately, the paper advocates for a balanced approach that prioritises both security imperatives and individual rights, calling for continued vigilance in refining regulatory frameworks to address emerging challenges and uphold fundamental principles in the era of technological innovation.

Keywords AI Act · Brussels Effect · Privacy · Data protection · Biometric systems

F. Paolucci (✉)
Bocconi University, Baffi Research Centre, Milan, Italy
e-mail: federica.paolucci@unibocconi.it

N. Menéndez González, G. Mobilio (eds.), *Next Democratic Frontiers for Facial Recognition Technology (FRT)*, Law, Governance and Technology Series 74,
https://doi.org/10.1007/978-3-031-89794-8_5

1 Introduction

In an era where technological advancements redefine our daily interactions, facial recognition technology (FRT)[1] stands as a pivotal force shaping the contours of modern society. While the ability to identify individuals solely from a facial image is undeniably valuable in the realm of crime prevention, it also raises concerns regarding privacy protection,[2] which entails the right to safeguard against unwanted intrusions into one's personal sphere.[3] Within the territory of the European Union,[4] proposed uses of this technology covered a wide range of applications, from law enforcement purposes and installation in open public spaces[5] to the use in the workspace[6] or schools.[7]

As a reaction, at least in part, to the Clearview AI scandal,[8] since the first versions of the Artificial Intelligence Act (hereafter, AI Act),[9] dedicated provisions on biometric recognition systems have stood out for their representativeness. Particularly, the AI Act is the first hard law instrument on AI, and it sets out special rules for using biometric systems in the specific law enforcement sector. As stated by Rec. 3, 'this Regulation contains specific rules on the protection of individuals with regard to the processing of personal data concerning restrictions on the use of AI systems for remote biometric identification for the purpose of law enforcement'; for this reason, together with art. 114 TFEU, the legal basis of the Regulation is precisely Article 16 of the TFEU, which pertains to the protection of personal data and privacy in the European Union. In this balancing exercise between regulation and innovation,[10] the EU is positioning itself in the global race toward AI regulation.

---

[1] Regulation (EU) 2024/1689 of the European Parliament and of the Council of 13 June 2024 laying down harmonised rules on artificial intelligence and amending Regulations (EC) No 300/2008, (EU) No 167/2013, (EU) No 168/2013, (EU) 2018/858, (EU) 2018/1139 and (EU) 2019/2144 and Directives 2014/90/EU, (EU) 2016/797 and (EU) 2020/1828 (Artificial Intelligence Act). Facial recognition technology falls in the category of 'biometric identification systems', defined under Art. 3, no. 35 of the AI Act, as 'the automated recognition of physical, physiological, behavioural, or psychological human features for the purpose of establishing the identity of a natural person by comparing biometric data of that individual to biometric data of individuals stored in a database'.

[2] Menéndez González (2022); Mobilio (2023).

[3] In the 'negative' concept of privacy as per Art. 7 of the Charter of Fundamental Rights of the European Union (CFEU).

[4] Christakis et al. (2022).

[5] Italian Data Protection Authority (DPA), decision no. 65, 11 January 2024.

[6] Italian DPA, Italian Data Protection Authority (DPA), decisions nn. 105, 106, 107, 108 and 109, 22 February 2024. On the same matter, also the Information Commission Officer (ICO), Order against Serco Limited UK, 23 February 2024.

[7] Trib. Adm. de Marseille, n. 1901249, 3 February 2020.

[8] Rezende (2020).

[9] Proposal for a regulation of the European Parliament and of the Council on harmonised rules on Artificial Intelligence (Artificial Intelligence Act) and amending certain Union Legislative Acts, COM(2021)0206.

[10] Bradford (2024 - *forthcoming*).

As we delve deeper into this analysis, the AI Act introduces a regulatory framework aimed at permitting the deployment of biometric identification systems under specific circumstances. The regulation's risk assessment focuses less on how Artificial Intelligence (AI) is constructed or trained and more on its actual application in different contexts.[11] Thus, while real-time biometric identification systems are deemed unacceptable in terms of risk, post-remote biometric identification is categorised as high risk.[12] This division, along with the EU's chosen approach to classify and regulate the usage of this potentially intrusive technology, is poised to establish a precedent not only within the EU but also on the global stage. As a matter of fact, the EU exercised a prominent regulatory dominance, which is particularly pronounced in the realm of digital governance, where the EU is actively asserting its 'digital sovereignty' over critical domains such as digital platforms, data management, digital identities, and artificial intelligence.[13] Historically, it has been possible to observe how EU laws served as regulatory models for third countries, notably in the realm of data protection.[14] However, with the AI Act, predicting such an effect before its actual implementation proves challenging. Hence, to refrain from speculating and echoing the sentiment of avoiding 'bringing obviousness out of men's lips when anticipating the future,'[15] this commentary abstains from predicting the global ramifications of the AI Act.

This analysis takes a unique approach, focusing on the internal influence within the EU following the adoption and forthcoming enactment of regulations concerning facial recognition tools. Specifically, it examines the EU's legislative efforts regarding the broader use of biometric recognition tools, like the Digital Identity Wallet initiative, beyond law enforcement. Drawing from the principles outlined in the AI Act, particularly Articles 5 and 6, the analysis illustrates how these principles should guide other domains utilising biometric data. It also explores how EU regulations will impact Member States (MS) responsible for implementation. The goal is to show how the AI Act provisions could become a model for other European regulations, introducing checks and balances rather than outright condemnation of biometric data use. However, it also highlights potential conflicts in practical implementation, especially regarding procedural aspects of biometric system usage. Resolving this conflict, pivotal in nature, will heavily influence MS, who can lean on general legal principles and international law to mitigate any adverse effects on landmark legislation destined to shape history.

---

[11] This choice has been rebutted by Novelli et al. (2024).

[12] As it is well explained by the European Data Protection Board (EDPB), face recognition is one technology that serves one sole purpose, meaning the probability of the 'estimated match between templates: the one being compared and the baseline(s)'. EDPB (2022) Guidelines 05/2022 on the use of facial recognition technology in the area of law enforcement.

[13] Bradford (2023a, b).

[14] Svantesson (2022).

[15] Wharton (2021).

Hence, in Sect. 2, the paper explores the concept of the 'Brussels Effect' on AI, explaining how EU regulations influenced global standards in the data protection domain and explaining why it is not the moment to predict such an effect for the AI Act. Following this, Sect. 3 provides an in-depth analysis of the EU standard for regulating biometric identification systems, considering its implications and applications. Section 4 delves into the use of biometrics in other EU legislation, discussing the evolving discourse on biometric technologies and digital identity within the European context. Transitioning from internal considerations to external implications, Sect. 5 focuses on how Member States should ensure effective protection of fundamental rights in the enforcement process. Finally, Sect. 6 offers concluding remarks, synthesising key findings.

2 What Effect Should We Expect from the 'Brussels Effect'?

When it comes to speaking about digital technologies, a term above all has been globally used to describe the extensive application and rage of the European norms: the Brussels Effect. Such term, scholarly coined, has been used to describe how 'EU has become a global regulator not only because of the size of its internal market but also because it has built an institutional architecture that has converted its market size into a tangible regulatory influence'.[16] Saying differently, this term describes the extraordinary capacity of the European Union to exert a profound and far-reaching influence on global markets.

This influence spans a diverse array of sectors, ranging from competition policy and environmental protection to food safety, privacy regulations, and the governance of hate speech on social media platforms. At its core, the EU's ability to set and enforce standards has become a hallmark of its regulatory prowess. Moreover, this effect has been observed with respect to the Regulation (EU) 2016/679 (hereafter, GDPR),[17] where the legislation crafted a system that *de iure*—for the outreach of the compliance measure towards companies regardless of where the data processing takes place makes—and *de facto* has been established a European domain over the data protection regulation, as mentioned before. As observed by Bradford, 'incorporating GDPR compliance into the product design is a powerful way to globalise the EU norms',[18] and the 'instalment' of this 'default' requirements created a system

[16]Bradford (2020).

[17]Regulation (EU) 2016/679 of the European Parliament and of the Council of 27 April 2016 on the protection of natural persons concerning the processing of personal data and on the free movement of such data, and repealing Directive 95/46/EC (General Data Protection Regulation).

[18]Id:144.

of harmonisation that, even if perfectible, exported the EU data protection standard at the worldwide level.[19]

About AI, the EU, aware of both the potentials and pitfalls inherent in it, has taken proactive steps to regulate this domain. Its efforts aim to foster the advancement and implementation of AI technologies while simultaneously addressing and mitigating the various risks they pose, particularly those concerning fundamental rights.[20] For the global reach of previous legislation, one of the main concerns with the AI Act is whether it will replicate the GDPR's Brussels Effect. This 'competition' was pursued by the President of the European Commission, who in 2019 called for the creation of a GDPR for AI.[21] There are numerous analogies between the two regulations: most of the rules will both apply to the same type of companies,[22] and they both adopt a risk-based approach.[23] However, it is unclear whether this offers transferable insights for (other) AI regulation since the Brussels Effect of data protection regulation may have been due to unique features of this regulatory target and design.

Moreover, the EU is not the only one trying to establish a standard on AI: the Council of Europe (CoE) issued legal texts addressing AI regulation and has been actively engaged in developing guidelines for ethical AI governance, aligning with its mandate to uphold human rights across its Member States;[24] the United Nations also made strides in AI regulation with a groundbreaking resolution aiming to safeguard human rights in the context of AI technologies.[25]

The Brussels Effect thus represents more than just regulatory control; it signifies a comprehensive integration of internal policies with external market dynamics. By setting high standards and effectively exporting them, the EU not only enhances its own regulatory environment but also exerts significant influence on global norms and practices. However, given the delicate phase of transition from the regulatory design to enforcement, it is challenging to predict the future of the AI Act, especially beyond the EU. Instead, it is examined for its internal impact. Specifically, it explores how its standards for regulating biometric tools could influence other sectors within the single market. Similar to how the GDPR has become a regulatory

[19]This is, for example, demonstrated by the adoption by other states of regulations 'similar' to the GDPR, as in the case of the California Consumer Privacy Act (CCPA), as demonstrated by Gunst and Ville (2021).

[20]Bradford (2023a, b).

[21]Directorate-General for Neighbourhood and Enlargement Negotiations (2019) Speech by President-Elect von Der Leyen.

[22]Siegmann and Anderljung (2022).

[23]Dunn and Gregorio (2022).

[24]Council of Europe (CoE) (2024) Committee of Ministers, Draft Framework Convention on artificial intelligence, human rights, democracy, and the rule of law and draft explanatory report by the CAI, CM(2024)52-addprov.

[25]United Nations Educational Scientific and Cultural Organization (UNESCO) (2021) Recommendation on the Ethics of Artificial Intelligence, available at https://unesdoc.unesco.org/ark:/48223/pf0000380455, last accessed 30.03.2024.

model within the EU,[26] the AI Act is likely to set a protective standard for biometrics and identification tools, as seen in the case of the Digital Identity Wallet. Thus, this analysis focuses on the internal implications of the Brussels Effect, affecting both EU regulatory production and Member States tasked with implementing these standards.

3 The Regulation of Facial Recognition Systems: A Fight for Democracy

The regulation of facial recognition systems has undergone concrete and significant turns. As anticipated, the AI Act is imposing dedicated norms that will not just complement the applicability of the previous ones but will stand over them.[27] Therefore, while providing that the rules in question must 'continue to comply with all requirements resulting from Article 9(1) of GDPR, Article 10(1) of Regulation (EU) 2018/1725[28] and Article 10 of Directive (EU) 2016/680 (also, LED),[29] as applicable' (rec. 39), the AI Act is strictly mandating the conditions upon which FRT can be placed in the market and put into service.

Given the potential for significant backlash regarding the protection of fundamental rights, particularly the rights to privacy and data protection under the CFEU, FRT is categorized under the highest level of risk. Specifically, the AI Act outlines four risk categories, with biometric systems classified based on their use. FRT in real-time conditions is prohibited, with limited exceptions, while *ex-post facto* uses are categorized as high-risk. Article 5 and its provisions focus heavily on prohibitions and regulations concerning the deployment of biometric categorization systems and real-time remote biometric identification systems in publicly accessible spaces for law enforcement. These systems are only allowed under narrowly defined circumstances, adhering to the principles of necessity, proportionality, and respect for individual rights and freedoms.[30] This emphasis on proportionality is a hallmark of the EU's approach, balancing innovation and rights protection, though it remains imperfect and in need of refinement in certain areas.

---

[26] Hert (2023).

[27] Recital 3 of the AI Act.

[28] Regulation (EU) 2018/1725 of the European Parliament and of the Council of 23 October 2018 on the protection of natural persons with regard to the processing of personal data by the Union institutions, bodies, offices and agencies and on the free movement of such data, and repealing Regulation (EC) No 45/2001 and Decision No 1247/2002/EC.

[29] Directive (EU) 2016/680 of the European Parliament and of the Council of 27 April 2016 on the protection of natural persons with regard to the processing of personal data by competent authorities for the purposes of the prevention, investigation, detection or prosecution of criminal offences or the execution of criminal penalties, and on the free movement of such data, and repealing Council Framework Decision 2008/977/JHA.

[30] Menéndez González (2022) id. note no. 2.

Henceforth, the proportionality framework is critical in maintaining public trust in the deployment of FRT, particularly as citizens fear the potential for mass surveillance and its chilling effects on democratic engagement.[31] As a matter of fact, when FRT is used excessively or inappropriately, it threatens to erode this trust between the public authority and the people, and to be in a democracy is essential to maintain it. Nonetheless, the potential for abuse is particularly concerning in cases where FRT becomes a tool for state surveillance, potentially deterring people from engaging in democratic activities. This is not a hypothetical risk but a reality that has manifested in various contexts, particularly in authoritarian regimes.[32]

In regimes where democratic safeguards are weak, FRT and other biometric technologies have been weaponized to exert control over society, leading to (digital) authoritarianism. For example, in Russia, as also demonstrated by the jurisprudence of the European Court of Human Rights,[33] cases such as *Glukhin v. Russia,*[34] raised serious concerns about the invasive nature of FRT, highlighting how its deployment could infringe on fundamental rights such as privacy and freedom of assembly. Similarly, in Venezuela, the government has integrated FRT into broader digital identification systems, using these tools to monitor and suppress political opposition.[35] These instances demonstrate how FRT, without adequate legal and procedural safeguards, can evolve from a security tool into a mechanism of state control and oppression. Moreover, in Uganda, FRT-enhanced surveillance systems provided by Chinese technology firms have been used to track and arrest political dissidents, underscoring the risk that FRT can stifle political participation and dissent.[36] The erosion of public trust and political autonomy as a result of mass surveillance has further-reaching consequences. The pervasive use of FRT in public spaces, even in democracies, can have a chilling effect on political participation by making individuals fear potential reprisals for their actions. As seen in these examples, FRT is often part of broader AI surveillance systems, designed to monitor entire populations and classify individuals by their perceived threat level, exacerbating concerns about racial profiling and function creep. When citizens fear that their actions are constantly monitored, they are less likely to participate in public discourse or engage in protest, key components of a vibrant democracy.

In contrast, the European Union's approach, as outlined in the AI Act, underscores the importance of transparency, accountability, and proportionality in the deployment of FRT. By emphasising these principles, the EU aims to prevent the

---

[31] 'According to Article 52(1) of the Charter, any limitation to the exercise of fundamental rights and freedoms must be provided for by law and respect the essence of those rights and freedoms. Subject to the principle of proportionality, limitations may be made only if they are necessary and genuinely meet objectives of general interest recognised by the European Union or the need to protect the rights and freedoms of others', EDPB (2022) id. note no. 12.

[32] Katrak and Chakrabarty (2023).

[33] Kosta (2022).

[34] ECHR [III Sec.], *Glukhin v. Russia,* no. 11519/20, 2023.

[35] Al Sur (2021); Derechos Digitales (2024).

[36] Katrak and Chakrabarty (2023) id.

kind of authoritarian misuse seen in other parts of the world. This regulatory framework seeks to balance innovation with the protection of democratic rights, setting a global standard for how advanced surveillance technologies should be governed.

As a matter of fact, the desire to strengthen the protection of critical AI systems is also symbolised by the great effort that institutions have invested in regulating facial recognition. Indeed, initially, the European Commission classified biometric identification systems as particularly intrusive, establishing strict exceptions (Rec. 18),[37] akin to GDPR provisions on the processing of special categories of personal data under Article 9.[38] The Council later introduced distinctions between real-time and remote biometric identification systems, extending the list of justifiable law enforcement objectives for real-time systems. The European Parliament[39] then sought to further harmonize these provisions while acknowledging the risks inherent in biometric identification systems.[40]

As anticipated, not all the uses of biometric recognition are classified as 'prohibited risk' under the AI Act: the AI Act distinguishes between *real-time* and *ex-post* application of biometric data. Real-time applications of biometric recognition are generally prohibited, while post-uses are considered high-risk. Specifically, real-time biometric identification systems by law enforcement in publicly accessible spaces are prohibited, with exceptions listed in Article 5, paragraph 1, letter h). *Ex-post* biometric identification systems are labelled as high-risk AI systems under Article 6, paragraph 2. This classification also includes biometric categorisation and emotional recognition systems. Interpreting this rule alongside Article 26 of the AI Act and Annex III is crucial since it outlines the crimes occurring in which it is possible to authorise the use of biometric systems.

However, some complexities remain. The Act's distinction between 'remote' and 'real-time' biometric identification systems (Articles 3, paras 36 and 37) has been critiqued for creating confusion rather than clarity.[41] Furthermore, the Act does not cover the use of remote biometric identification for non-law enforcement purposes, which remains under GDPR regulation. This indicates two key issues: first, the AI Act does not explicitly define when AI poses unacceptable risks; instead, it assumes risk based on its application.[42]

Second, expanding the scope of prohibited uses under Article 5 will require an amendment to the Act: the Regulation does not list criteria for when AI poses

---

[37] European Commission (2021) Proposal. See note no. 9.

[38] Kindt (2013a).

[39] European Parliament (2023) Amendments adopted by the European Parliament on 14 June 2023 on the proposal for a regulation of the European Parliament and of the Council on laying down harmonised rules on artificial intelligence (Artificial Intelligence Act) and amending certain Union legislative acts (COM(2021)0206 – C9-0146/2021 – 2021/0106(COD)).

[40] European Parliament Resolution (2020) on a framework of ethical aspects of AI, robotics and related technologies, in part. point 66.

[41] Veale and Borgesius (2022), pp. 97–112.

[42] Schoder (2022).

unacceptable risks to society and individuals; it just states the presumption of risk.[43] This also implies that besides the listed prohibited uses, further expansion of Art. 5 scope of application will amount to an amendment of the Act. Notably, the final articles dedicated to this aspect underscore the significant role of the European Commission in conducting bi-annual assessments in collaboration with the AI Board, as per Article 66(1)(e)(vii).[44] Although the mechanism was already provided for in the GDPR,[45] with the AI Act, it would broaden the scope of the Commission's action to also include the assessment of the material application of the standard with respect to high-risk profiles and annexes-aspects that are outside the certifying mechanisms in the GDPR.

Despite these potential deficiencies, the AI Act is poised to become paramount for regulating biometric systems across the EU market. Its provisions on FRT will likely influence broader applications of biometric technologies, not only in law enforcement but also in areas such as digital identity systems, which raise similar concerns about privacy, surveillance, and democratic accountability. As the EU's regulatory standards often influence global markets through the Brussels Effect, the AI Act could serve as a model for other regions, setting global benchmarks for the responsible use of FRT while safeguarding fundamental rights. In what follows, therefore, it will be analysed whether and how the way in which the AI Act has approached the use of biometrics and advanced technological systems can be traced back to other areas that also benefit from this type of tools and data, as is the case with the identification of individuals and the use of the so-called Wallets.

4 The Internal Point of View: The Evolving Discourse on FRT and Digital Identity in the EU

Facial recognition and the use of biometric technologies are most perceived as threats to privacy and data protection.[46] However, the deployment of these technologies might also create deleterious effects on democracy and civil liberties, as mentioned *supra*. In between 'commercial pressures of the data-driven surveillance economy, the security imperatives of law enforcement, and civic values of freedom of expression, movement, and personal autonomy',[47] biometrics might also represent a tool for faster bureaucracy and digitalise processes.

---

[43] Edwards (2022).

[44] Court of Justice of the European Union (CJEU), Joined Cases C-124&125/13, Parliament and Commission v. Council, §73.

[45] Rec. 166 of the AI Act.

[46] Hartzog et al. (2023).

[47] Selwyn et al. (2024), pp. 11–28.

The rapid digitalisation of services that occurred in the aftermath of the COVID-19 pandemic,[48] driven by the need to provide vital services such as healthcare online, has led to an increased demand for digital credentials for identification and authentication purposes. This demand arises from both governments and businesses striving to adapt to digital service delivery models to better serve customers and citizens. In sectors like healthcare and finance, secure identification and authentication systems are crucial not only to comply with legal mandates but also to ensure high levels of security and trustworthiness, particularly concerning data protection. For these reasons, the EU aims to amplify the use of digital identification methods via the review of the European Electronic Identification and Trust Services (eIDAS) Regulation of 2014.[49] Alongside the demand described above, there is a growing threat of online fraud, including identity theft, which poses significant challenges to cybersecurity and law enforcement efforts. Every MS had to adopt on a voluntary basis a scheme which is defined in the Regulation as a system for electronic identification under which electronic identification means are issued.[50] Hence, the shortcomings of the eIDAS Regulation mainly stem from limitations predominantly within the public sector, complexities faced by private providers in system connectivity, and inadequate availability of notified eID solutions across Member States.[51] In response to these challenges, a proposal has been put forth for a European Digital Identity framework aimed at ensuring that at least 80% of citizens can access key public services digitally by 2030.[52] This framework seeks to instil confidence in citizens by offering security and control over their digital identity, including the ability to manage access to their data, while fostering the need for a harmonised European approach to digital identity.

On the operational and technical aspects of such a project, the text resulting from the negotiations between the European Parliament and the Council of the European Union provides that users are going to be identified through a 'reference to a minimum set of person identification data necessary to uniquely represent a natural or legal person [...]' (Art. 12, para 4).[53] Saying it differently, since the data collection should not go further than a minimum set of data—otherwise, the user

---

[48] Selwyn, id.

[49] Proposal for a Regulation of the European Parliament and of the Council Amending Regulation (Eu) No 910/2014 as regards establishing a framework for a European Digital Identity COM/2021/281 final.

[50] For a comment on the Directive refer to Finocchiaro (2016), pp. 5–19.

[51] European Parliament (2024) Briefing Updating the European digital identity framework; Explanatory Memorandum of the Proposal for a Regulation of the European Parliament and of the Council Amending Regulation (Eu) No 910/2014, id. note no. 41. Finocchiaro, id.; Finocchiaro (2022), pp. 441–460; Baldini (2024), pp. 297–317.

[52] Explanatory memorandum, id.

[53] Regulation (EU) 2024/1183 of the European Parliament and of the Council of 11 April 2024 amending Regulation (EU) No 910/2014 as regards establishing the European Digital Identity Framework.

consents. Hence, the minimum threshold of the data set is composed of the first and the last names of a person, their date of birth and a unique identifier, namely a number via which any individual would be able to uniquely and persistently be identified.

The cautious approach taken by EU institutions within the AI Act mirrors the design of the new identity framework, where the collection of biometric data is approached with careful consideration. According to Article 9 of the General Data Protection Regulation (GDPR), biometric data is defined as a minimum threshold for uniquely identifying a natural person. However, in alignment with the GDPR's principle of data minimisation (Art. 5, para. 1, letter c), the EU legislator has opted to limit the collection of biometric data within the context of the new identity framework. Despite the undeniable potential of biometric data for unambiguous identification, this decision aims to prevent excessive and disproportionate intrusions into individuals' privacy spheres. Moreover, the regulation underscores the importance of maintaining a clear separation between personal data associated with the European Digital Identity Wallets and any other data held by service providers. This emphasis on data segregation serves to mitigate the risks of unauthorised access or misuse of personal information, as outlined in Rec. 12. By establishing this framework, the EU aims to uphold the principles of data protection and privacy while facilitating the adoption of digital identity solutions. The incorporation of the principle of proportionality into both the AI Act and the European Digital Identity Regulation reflects the legacy of the Court of Justice of the European Union (CJEU).[54] This principle serves as a cornerstone of the 'Brussels effect,' balancing the costs and benefits of technology deployment while safeguarding fundamental rights.[55] By striking a balance between data privacy and societal imperatives, such as national security and law enforcement, the EU continues to assert its leadership in shaping global standards for digital governance. In essence, the EU's approach underscores its commitment to fostering innovation while ensuring the responsible and ethical use of technology. By embedding principles of proportionality and data minimisation into its regulatory frameworks, the EU seeks to build trust among citizens and stakeholders while navigating the complexities of the digital age.

This general precautionary approach to the processing of biometric data was, among other things, also recently reaffirmed by the CJEU,[56] which ruled that the obligation to insert fingerprints in identity cards does not constitute a restriction to the exercise of fundamental rights to respect for private life and protection of personal data, which the Charter of Fundamental Rights guarantees. Nevertheless,

---

[54] Defined by Art. 3 no. 42 as 'an electronic identification means which allows the user to securely store, manage and validate person identification data and electronic attestations of attributes for the purpose of providing them to relying parties and other users of European Digital Identity Wallets, and to sign by means of qualified electronic signatures or to seal by means of qualified electronic seals'.

[55] Bradford (2023a, b), note no. 20:113. Art. 52, Charter of Fundamental Rights of the European Union. For a comment, Kindt (2013b), pp. 403–567.

[56] CJEU, *RU v Landeshauptstadt Wiesbaden*, no. C-61/2022.

the Court confirmed that such restriction is justified by the objectives of the general interest of combatting the production of false identity cards.[57] Therefore, in this case, the interference with fundamental rights resulting from the inclusion of two fingerprints in the storage medium of identity cards did not appear to be 'of a seriousness which is disproportionate when compared with the significance of the various objectives pursued by that measure' (§123). The purpose of uniquely identifying a natural person, particularly in cross-border situations, has been deemed to be a 'fair balance' (id.) with the fundamental rights involved. Hence, the essence of the fundamental rights enshrined in Articles 7 and 8 of the Charter (§81).

The proposed European Digital Identity framework aims to improve access to public services while ensuring data security and privacy, reflecting the EU's commitment to unified digital governance. Regulatory provisions, like cautious biometric data collection, demonstrate a balanced approach between innovation and rights protection.

5 The Member States Perspective: Effective Protection of Fundamental Rights Within the AI Act?

Recognising the inherent sensitivity of employing such systems, especially in fields where fundamental rights are at stake, the European Union (EU) legislator has expressed apprehensions and advocated for stringent regulations. In this regard, the EU emphasises the necessity of restricting the use of biometric recognition systems to narrowly defined situations where their deployment is deemed strictly necessary to serve substantial public interests. This introduction sets the stage for exploring the complexities surrounding the use of biometric recognition systems within the EU regulatory framework, with a particular focus on balancing public security concerns with the imperative of safeguarding individual rights and freedoms. Therefore, precisely because of the sensitivity of using an instrument like this in the field of law enforcement[58] and the possible consequences for the protection of rights, the uses of face recognition can be allowed excerpt for specific conditions detailed by the AI Act itself. As mentioned above, real-time biometric identification systems by law enforcement in publicly accessible spaces are prohibited, with exceptions listed in Article 5, paragraph 1, letter h). Meanwhile, ex-post biometric identification systems are categorised as high-risk AI systems per Article 6, paragraph 2. This classification also includes biometric categorisation and emotional recognition systems. Interpreting this rule alongside Article 26 of the AI Act and Annex III is crucial. Importantly, such usage is contingent upon authorisation from a judicial or administrative authority but is limited to 'targeted' cases. This implies that

[57] Nonetheless, the Court affirmed that Regulation (EU) 2019/1157 in question was adopted on an incorrect legal basis.

[58] Hert and Bouchagiar (2024), pp. 139–154.

there is no authorisation for widespread and indiscriminate use unless it is directly linked to a criminal threat, ongoing criminal proceedings, or the search for a missing person.

Nonetheless, the described legal framework presents a series of technical and legal issues. On the first aspect, as already pointed out by the Joint Opinion of the European Data Protection Board (EDPB) and the European Data Protection Supervisor (EDPS) (5/2021),[59] the distinction between the real-time and ex-post application of biometric recognition is futile from a fundamental rights perspective. The intrusiveness of the processing does not always depend on when the identification or the recognition is performed. The difference is purely technical[60] and consists of two different moments of the identification process, but it entails the same consequences for the surveillance of citizens. Particularly, the biometric system is mostly the same, trained with a biometric data set, and it is used in two modalities: e.g., live while the crime is happening or after *ex-post.*

On the legal aspects, the applicability of this distinction in practice remains to be seen, as does the feasibility of compliance by law enforcement authorities, harnessing the safeguard of fundamental rights that this provision tends to achieve. Moreover, and of greater significance, such applications hinge upon authorisation from a judicial or administrative body, albeit confined to 'targeted' scenarios. This signifies that broad and indiscriminate usage lacks authorisation unless directly tied to a criminal threat, ongoing legal proceedings, or locating a missing individual. Additionally, Article 5(3) of the AI Act stipulates that any deployment of 'real-time' remote biometric identification systems for law enforcement necessitates prior approval from a judicial or administrative entity. These measures aim to ensure oversight and accountability in the utilisation of such technologies. Undoubtedly, this requirement underscores the pivotal role of procedural equity and legal scrutiny in mitigating potential abuses of authority. However, the manner in which this objective is to be achieved remains somewhat perplexing.

In the area of police and law enforcement powers, it is crucial to find 'the right balance between due process requirements and efficiency concerns',[61] meaning that it is of utmost importance to proportionately ascertain the use of technological support by the public authorities due to the possible implications on fundamental rights. Similarly, the application of AI in this specific sector needs to be carefully considered with respect to the police's procedural authorisation of the use of biometrics.

In this regard, the second and main concern with the regulation of biometrics in the law enforcement sector relates to the broad freedom granted to Member States to define the modalities of using biometric systems, especially concerning the authorisation procedure, as stipulated in Article 5, paragraph 2. While the Regulation

---

[59]EDPB-EDPS (2021) Joint Opinion 5/2021 on the proposal for a Regulation of the European Parliament and of the Council laying down harmonised rules on artificial intelligence.

[60]Veale and Borgesius, id.

[61]Hert (2023) note no. 27.

identifies the margins within which the use of these systems must occur, it also contains several grey areas. For example, Member States are left to determine which authority should authorise the use of biometric recognition: judicial authority or independent administrative authority. This aspect is highly dangerous for individuals' protection, as it allows non-judicial authorities to allow the use of facial recognition—a technology that inherently carries various levels of risk. The choice between the two options is by no means neutral.

First of all, ensuring that the judicial authority can be the only one to authorise such uses of AI represents an important guarantee for the protection of individuals, not only with regard to the massive uses of biometric recognition but also for a formal control, which, on closer inspection, has several substantive consequences, which the judicial authority, by its very nature, is and must be able to guarantee.

Secondly, judicial authorities can grant independence and transparency of a decision that has a high impact on the individual's rights, as the CJEU has clarified in *Corbiau*, C-24/92 (i.*e.* par. 15).[62] In this decision, the Court placed significant importance on the idea of independence in defining whether a body constitutes a court or tribunal. This emphasis is not surprising given that the core principle of the rule of law hinges on the reviewability of decisions made by public authorities through independent courts. Thus, the criterion of independence is widely regarded as the most crucial factor distinguishing national courts from administrative authorities.

This choice is not without consequences since it might provoke a clash with respect to the jurisprudence of the European Court of Human Rights, to which the MS refer. In this respect, the ECtHR elaborated a three-tiered 'quality of law' requirement to ascertain the justification for the interference of law enforcement on individuals' privacy.[63] Thus, according to established jurisprudence, any interference must adhere to stringent standards of legal quality, necessitating that domestic legislation be clear, foreseeable, and readily accessible. Specifically, the Court emphasised that domestic law must provide robust measures to prevent any misuse of personal data that could violate these guarantees. This need for safeguards is particularly pronounced when it comes to using personal data for police purposes, especially given the increasingly sophisticated technology available, as in the case of AI and biometric technologies. For this very purpose, the application of such systems should happen with adequate care for individuals' rights, striking a careful balance between the benefits of technology and the protection of fundamental rights,[64] which is to be ensured via stringent justifications.[65] Moreover, the Court, in the case of *Big Brother Watch and Others v. UK,* established that, especially in cases of criminal investigation, without individual knowledge, 'in a field where abuse in individual cases is potentially so easy and could have such harmful

[62] CJEU, *Pierre Corbiau v Administration des Contributions*, no. C-24/92.

[63] Slosser (2018), pp. 1–26.

[64] ECHR, *S and Marper v. the United Kingdom* [GC], nos. 30562/04 and 30566/04, § 67, 2006.

[65] ECHR, *Podchasov v. Russia* [III Sec.], no.33696/19, §60–65, 2024.

consequences for a democratic society as a whole', it is desirable to entrust supervisory control to a judge, judicial control offering the best guarantees of independence, impartiality and a proper procedure'.[66]

Thus, any infringement upon individuals' right to privacy, and thus any utilisation of biometric technology, must adhere to the principle of 'quality of law', guaranteeing thorough oversight by the judicial authority over the reasoned implementation of such tools. Furthermore, legislation should clearly define the scope of discretion granted to competent authorities and specify how it should be exercised with precision to ensure individuals are adequately shielded from arbitrary encroachments.[67]

The quality of law, the effective protection of fundamental rights, as well as the role of the judiciary are all general principles of law that together form a concrete expression of the rule of law principle.[68] Hence, as a core element of the European Union, under the interpretation of the Court of Justice of the European Union, Article 19 of the Treaty on European Union (TEU) has been commonly interpreted alongside Article 2 TEU, which asserts the rule of law as a foundational value of the Union. In this context, it functions as a fundamental structural element, significantly impacting the overall constitutional framework of the EU.[69] This influence extends to the interactions between the Union and its Member States, as well as between the Court of Justice and national judicial bodies. In this capacity, the principle holds relevance at both the EU and national levels and should orient the interpretation and application of any relevant provision at the European and MS levels. In this respect, following the analysis of the ECtHR, the rule of law principle should be reinstated under the implementation of the AI Act not only on the substantial merit of the alternative between a national or a judicial body authorising the use of biometric systems but, moreover, is reflected on a formalistic and procedural level. As previously mentioned, the selection between the two options is not impartial, and while it may seem like a technical detail, it also plays a role in ensuring decisions uphold individual rights. The principle of the rule of law, as a fundamental principle, serves as a valuable tool to supplement the interpretation of Article 47 of the Charter, particularly in a rights-oriented approach to the AI Act. Despite the Act primarily aiming at product-based regulation, its enforcement phase will nonetheless, due to the aforementioned reasons, affect the rights of individuals.

Therefore, when applying this analysis to the case at hand, it becomes evident that a law in an MS lacking a proper authorisation procedure evaluated by a judicial authority fails to uphold the aforementioned quality standards and safeguards. In essence, the assurance of judicial independence can be considered to suffice the highest level of justification criterion, and without prejudice to the principle of

[66] ECHR, *Big Brother Watch and Others v. the United Kingdom* [GC], nos. 58170/13 and 2 others, 2021.

[67] ECHR, *Glukhin v. Russia,* id.. For a case commentary, Palmiotto and González (2023).

[68] CJEU, *Associaio Sindical dos Juizes Portugueses* [GC], no. 64/2016 §32, 2018.

[69] Bonelli (2019), pp. 35–62.

procedural independence, the Member States need to determine that judicial authority is going to be the only one in charge of such an authorisation in order not to undermine rights and grant procedural fairness.

Furthermore, focusing on judicial and administrative authority in authorising and regulating FRT not only ensures the protection of fundamental rights but also aligns with the EU's ambition to create a global standard. Embedding this robust oversight mechanism into the AI Act strengthens the EU's ability to set international norms through the 'Brussels Effect.' By demonstrating the importance of judicial safeguards, the EU's regulatory model on FRT has the potential, and becomes then desirable, to influence other countries and ensure that the deployment of AI technologies globally adheres to high standards of transparency, accountability, and democratic protection.

6 Conclusion

The regulatory landscape surrounding the use of facial recognition systems within law enforcement highlights a delicate balance between security imperatives and individual rights. The EU recognises the sensitivity of deploying such systems and advocates for stringent regulations to mitigate potential risks. By emphasising the need to restrict biometric recognition to narrowly defined situations serving substantial public interests, the EU aims to safeguard individual rights and freedoms within its regulatory framework.

The analysis delves into the challenge of predicting the 'Brussels Effect' of the AI Act and its future impact. Thus, it examines its internal influence within the EU, particularly in regulating biometric tools. Similar to the GDPR's narrative, the AI Act is expected to establish a protective standard for biometrics and identification tools, reflecting the EU's commitment to proportionally balancing innovation with regulation, exemplified in the Digital Identity Wallet.

However, the EU appears to overlook the risks related to enforcing the rule. Particularly, the AI Act faces technical and legal challenges, notably concerning the distinction between real-time and ex-post application of biometric recognition and the authorisation procedure. The AI Act seeks to address these challenges by requiring prior approval from a judicial or administrative entity for real-time biometric identification systems. Yet, the choice between judicial and administrative authorisation remains contentious, with significant implications for individual rights protection. Ensuring judicial oversight is crucial to upholding the rule of law and preventing arbitrary encroachments on privacy rights, as reaffirmed by the ECtHR's jurisprudence, which is of crucial importance for the MS.

On their side, Member States must carefully consider the balance between security concerns and individual protections in implementing biometric recognition systems, especially since they must adopt an internal law that establishes the procedure for using FRT, as clarified by the European Commission in the Guidelines on Prohibited Practices, released in February 2025. Therefore, respecting principles of procedural fairness and judicial independence as well as prioritising the quality of law and robust safeguards will be all not negotiable imperatives.

While acknowledging the AI Act's achievements, such as the inclusion of the Fundamental Rights Impact Assessment framework and procedural rights exercise, concerns persist regarding inconsistencies in biometric surveillance and potential inefficiencies in fundamental rights protection mechanisms. The imbalance of power between public authorities and individuals, along with the inherent risks of collecting data on vulnerable populations, underscores the necessity of judicial oversight. In the realm of AI, preserving judicial authority as a guardian of rights, particularly in authorizing and monitoring the implementation of AI, is crucial to ensuring that the European standard on FRT becomes paramount not only in digital regulation but also in the protection of democracy.

References

Al Sur (2021) Facial recognition in Latin America: trends in the implementation of a perverse technology. 7

Baldini D (2024) The impact of the right to personal data protection on the design of the European Digital Identity Wallet. Ital J Public Law 16:297–317

Bonelli M (2019) Effective judicial protection in EU law: an evolving principle of a constitutional nature. REALaw 12:35–62

Bradford A (2020) The Brussels Effect: how the European Union rules the world. Faculty Books:25

Bradford A (2023a) Digital empires: the global battle to regulate technology. Oxford University Press, pp 114–115

Bradford A (2023b) Europe's digital constitution. Verfassungsblog

Bradford A (2024 - *forthcoming*) The false choice between digital regulation and innovation: 1–56

Christakis T et al (2022) Mapping the use of facial recognition in public spaces in Europe – Part 1: a quest for clarity: Unpicking the 'Catch-All' Term

Council of Europe (CoE) (2024) Committee of Ministers, Draft Framework Convention on artificial intelligence, human rights, democracy, and the rule of law and draft explanatory report by the CAI, CM(2024)52-addprov

Council of the European Union (2022) Proposal for a Regulation of the European Parliament and of the Council laying down harmonised rules on artificial intelligence (Artificial Intelligence Act) and amending certain Union legislative acts - General approach, 2021/0106(COD)

Derechos Digitales (2024) Gender impacts and other inequalities. Identity systems and social protection in Venezuela and Bolivia: 1–46

Directorate-General for Neighbourhood and Enlargement Negotiations (2019) Speech by President-Elect von Der Leyen

Dunn P, Gregorio GD (2022) The European risk-based approaches: connecting constitutional dots in the digital age. Common Mark Law Rev 59

EDPB (2022) Guidelines 05/2022 on the use of facial recognition technology in the area of law enforcement

EDPB-EDPS (2021) Joint Opinion 5/2021 on the proposal for a Regulation of the European Parliament and of the Council laying down harmonised rules on artificial intelligence

Edwards L (2022) Expert opinion: regulating AI in Europe. Ada Lovelace Institute. https://www.adalovelaceinstitute.org/report/regulating-ai-in-europe/. Accessed 3 Apr 2024

European Parliament (2023) Amendments adopted by the European Parliament on 14 June 2023 on the proposal for a regulation of the European Parliament and of the Council on laying down

harmonised rules on artificial intelligence (Artificial Intelligence Act) and amending certain Union legislative acts (COM(2021)0206 – C9-0146/2021 – 2021/0106(COD))
European Parliament Resolution (2020) On a framework of ethical aspects of AI, robotics and related technologies, in part. point 66
Finocchiaro G (2016) The European e-IDAS Regulation. Diritto Mercato e Tecnologia:5–19
Finocchiaro G (2022) Il contratto nell'era dell'Intelligenza Artificiale. Rivista Trimestrale di Diritto e Procedura Civile 2:441–460
Gunst S, Ville FD (2021) The Brussels Effect: how the GDPR conquered Silicon Valley. Eur Foreign Aff Rev 26
Hartzog W et al (2023) Privacy Nicks: how the law normalizes surveillance. SSRN
Hert PD (2023) C4Post-GDPR lawmaking in the digital data society: mimesis without integration. Topological understandings of twisted boundary setting in EU Data Protection Law. In: Curtin D, Catanzariti M (eds) Data at the boundaries of European law. Oxford University Press
Hert PD, Bouchagiar G (2024) European biometric surveillance, concrete rules, and uniform enforcement: beyond regulatory abstraction and local enforcement. In: Zalnieriute M, Matulionyte R (eds) The Cambridge handbook of facial recognition in the modern state. Cambridge University Press, Cambridge, pp 139–154
Information Commission Officer (ICO) Order against Serco Limited UK, 23 February 2024
Italian Data Protection Authority (DPA) decision no. 65, 11 January 2024
Italian DPA, Italian Data Protection Authority (DPA), decisions nn. 105, 106, 107, 108 and 109, 22 February 2024
Katrak M, Chakrabarty I (2023) Privacy, political participation, and dissent: facial recognition technologies and the risk of digital authoritarianism in the global south. In: Temperman J, Quintavalla A (eds) Artificial intelligence and human rights. Oxford University Press
Kindt EJ (2013a) Biometric data, data protection and the right to privacy. In: Kindt EJ (ed) Privacy and data protection issues of biometric applications: a comparative legal analysis. Springer, Netherlands, Dordrecht, pp 87–272
Kindt EJ (2013b) The proportionality principle as a general principle of law applied to biometric data processing. In: Kindt EJ (ed) Privacy and data protection issues of biometric applications: a comparative legal analysis. Springer, Netherlands, Dordrecht, pp 403–567
Kosta E (2022) Algorithmic state surveillance: challenging the notion of agency in human rights. Regul Gov 16:212–224. https://doi.org/10.1111/rego.12331
Menéndez González N (2022) The impact of facial recognition technology empowered by artificial intelligence on the right to privacy. In: Bielicki DM (ed) Regulating artificial intelligence in industry, Abingdon. Routledge, New York, pp 21–35
Mobilio G (2023) Your face is not new to me – regulating the surveillance power of facial recognition technologies. Internet Policy Rev 12
Novelli C, Casolari F, Rotolo A et al (2024) AI risk assessment: a scenario-based, proportional methodology for the AI Act. DISO 3:13
Palmiotto F, González NM (2023) Facial recognition technology, democracy and human rights. Comput Law Secur Rev 50
Proposal for a Regulation of the European Parliament and of the Council Amending Regulation (Eu) No 910/2014 as regards establishing a framework for a European Digital Identity COM/2021/281 final
Rezende IN (2020) Facial recognition in police hands: assessing the 'Clearview case' from a European perspective. New J Eur Crim Law 11:375–389
Schoder A (2022) 'Real-time' versus 'post' remote biometric identification systems under the AI Act. In: ALTI Amsterdam. https://alti.amsterdam/schroder-biometric/. Accessed 6 Apr 2024
Selwyn N, Andrejevic M, O'Neill C et al (2024) Facial recognition technology: key issues and emerging concerns. In: Zalnieriute M, Matulionyte R (eds) The Cambridge handbook of facial recognition in the modern state. Cambridge University Press, Cambridge, pp 11–28
Siegmann C, Anderljung M (2022) The Brussels Effect and Artificial Intelligence: how EU regulation will impact the global AI market

Slosser JL (2018) Interpreting the 'Quality of Law' at the European Court of Human Rights: metaphorical framing and evaluative judgment. iCourts Working Paper Series 143:126

Svantesson D (2022) The European Union Artificial Intelligence Act: potential implications for Australia. Altern Law J 47:4–9

United Nations Educational Scientific and Cultural Organization (UNESCO) (2021) Recommendation on the Ethics of Artificial Intelligence, available at https://unesdoc.unesco.org/ark:/48223/pf0000380455. Accessed 30 Mar 2024

Veale M, Borgesius FZ (2022) Demystifying the Draft EU Artificial Intelligence Act. Comput Law Rev Int 4:97–112

Wharton E (2021) The age of innocence. Phoemixx Classics Ebooks

Biometric Data and Facial Recognition Technology in the EU

The Interplay Between Data Protection and Cybersecurity

Theodoros Karathanasis

Abstract In the European Union (EU), where privacy, data protection and human rights are at the very heart of the European integration project, there is an important debate going on about the "red lines" that should be set by regulators to prevent people's freedoms being endangered. One emblematic example lies in the regulation of the use of facial recognition technology (FRT). Drawing on the requirements imposed by the GDPR on the controller and the processor to carry out appropriate technical and organisational measures to ensure a level of security appropriate to the risk involved, the present article highlights the links between facial image data protection and the cybersecure deployment of FRTs. The results of this analysis seem to point to a double-layered risk approach to the security of processed, stored and transmitted facial image biometric data in the EU, by means of the privacy and cybersecurity legal frameworks.

Keywords Biometric · Cybersecurity · Data · EU · GDPR · Large-scale processing

1 Introduction

Facial (or face) recognition technology refers to a specific set of systems that are used for different purposes, ranging from the simple detection of the presence of a face in an image, to more complex verification, identification, and categorisation or classification of individuals.[1] The use of FRT in cyberspace (i.e. the web) is becoming more and more popular in critical sectors and processes such as banking

[1] FRA (2019).

T. Karathanasis (✉)
University of Grenoble Alpes (UGA), Chair on Legal and Regulatory Implications of AI (MIAI) Grenoble, Grenoble, France
e-mail: theodoros.karathanasis@univ-grenoble-alpes.fr

N. Menéndez González, G. Mobilio (eds.), *Next Democratic Frontiers for Facial Recognition Technology (FRT)*, Law, Governance and Technology Series 74,
https://doi.org/10.1007/978-3-031-89794-8_6

(e.g., e-banking face authentication[2]), transport (e.g., facial recognition ticketing systems), health (e.g., patient screening) and even elections (e.g., e-voting). Data breaches and leaks are also on the rise. Over the past three years, the European Union (EU) has tightened cyber security rules for member states by adopting the Cyber Security Act[3] and the NIS 2 Directive[4] to address cyber threats. New cybersecurity rules should come to the fore, because of the Commission's proposal to introduce a Cyber Resilience Act (CRA)[5] and a Cyber Solidarity Act.[6]

A robust cybersecurity policy protects critical or sensitive data by preventing it from falling into the hands of malicious third parties. Adopting the cybersecurity measures set out in the NIS 2 Directive enhances the risk-based approach required by the GDPR, particularly when it comes to the use of FRT and the processing, storage and transmission of facial image biometric data. In order to demonstrate compliance with the NIS 2 Directive, significant and important entities may be required to 'use certain ICT products, ICT services and ICT processes developed by the significant or important entity or procured from third parties that are certified under European cybersecurity certification schemes'.[7] The security objectives of these certification schemes will further enhance the security of biometric data.

In addition, the EU's cyber security framework will be further strengthened by another piece of legislation, the Cyber Resilience Act, which is currently in the middle of the legislative process in Brussels. The Cyber Resilience Act is broad in scope and includes the Commission's proposal to establish common rules for all products with digital elements. For example, products used in facial recognition ticketing systems or mobile phones that access facial recognition applications will have to comply with the CRA's essential cyber security requirements.[8] Protection against unauthorised access, the use of appropriate control mechanisms or maintaining the confidentiality of stored, transmitted or otherwise processed data, personal or otherwise, are all requirements that will have to be met by manufacturers.

The purpose of this paper is therefore to highlight the interplay between the protection of biometric data, in particular facial image data, collected with FRT, and their cybersecure transmission, processing and storage. The following developments go through an analysis of the EU's approach to defining 'facial recognition

[2] Agarwal et al. (2021).

[3] Regulation (EU) 2019/881 of the European Parliament and of the Council of 17 April 2019 on ENISA (the European Union Agency for Cybersecurity) and on information and communications technology cybersecurity certification and repealing Regulation (EU) No 526/2013 (Cybersecurity Act), (OJ L151/2019, p. 15).

[4] Directive (EU) 2022/2555 of the European Parliament and of the Council of 14 December 2022 on measures for a high common level of cybersecurity across the Union, amending Regulation (EU) No 910/2014 and Directive (EU) 2018/1972, and repealing Directive (EU) 2016/1148 (NIS 2 Directive), PE/32/2022/REV/2, (OJ L333/2022, p. 80).

[5] European Commission (2022).

[6] European Commission (2023).

[7] Article 24 NIS 2 Directive.

[8] Annex 1 CRA.

technology', focusing on the position of FRT and the processing of biometric data in the EU legal framework (Sect. 2), as well as of how security breaches of facial image data are impacting FRT (Sect. 3); before to assess whether the EU's cyber security legal framework adds value to the protection of biometric data (Sect. 4).

2 The Position of FRT and Biometric Data Processing in the EU's Legal Framework

Facial recognition by definition raises concerns about balancing personal data protection, mass surveillance, commercial interests and national security—issues that societies must thoughtfully evaluate. While technology is often remarkable, impressive, and efficient, this should not be mistaken for it being essential, advantageous, or beneficial to society.

Even if it is possible to find a definition for biometric data in Article 4(14) of the GDPR,[9] the term "facial recognition" has not been defined in any EU data protection law instrument. Neither the GDPR, nor the Law Enforcement Directive (LED),[10] nor any other binding instrument has proposed a definition for this term. The Regulation (EU) 2024/1689 of the European Parliament and of the Council of 13 June 2024 laying down harmonised rules on artificial intelligence (AI Act)[11] also does not define what "facial recognition" is. Instead, it is expected to focus on the term "remote biometric identification" (RBI), which is broader than "facial recognition", as it potentially includes systems that process elements other than faces, such as a person's gait or voice. Therefore, a non-binding definition of facial recognition should be sought in other areas of the EU legal framework. For example, recent guidance from the European Data Protection Board (EDPB) defines facial recognition as "a probabilistic technology that can automatically recognise individuals based on their face for the purpose of authentication or identification" and therefore "FRT falls within the broader category of biometric technology".[12] The link between

---

[9] 'Biometric data' means personal data resulting from specific technical processing relating to the physical, physiological or behavioral characteristics of a natural person, which allow or confirm the unique identification of that natural person, such as facial images or dactyloscopic data.

[10] European Parliament and of the Council (2016), Directive (EU) 2016/680 of 27 April 2016 on the protection of natural persons with regard to the processing of personal data by competent authorities for the purpose of preventing, investigating, detecting or prosecuting criminal offences or executing criminal penalties, and the free movement of such data, and repealing Council Framework Decision 2008/977/JHA (OJ L119/2016, p. 89).

[11] Regulation (EU) 2024/1689 of the European Parliament and of the Council of 13 June 2024 laying down harmonised rules on artificial intelligence and amending Regulations (EC) No 300/2008, (EU) No 167/2013, (EU) No 168/2013, (EU) 2018/858, (EU) 2018/1139 and (EU) 2019/2144 and Directives 2014/90/EU, (EU) 2016/797 and (EU) 2020/1828 (Artificial Intelligence Act), PE/24/2024/REV/1, *OJ L, 2024/1689, 12.7.2024.*

[12] EDPB (2023), p. 9.

"facial recognition" and "biometric data" is very important because it is not only the GDPR that defines "biometric data" in the same way, but all existing European data protection instruments, as well as the proposed EU AI Act.[13] Therefore, when facial images are prepared for facial matching, which enables the "unique identification"[14] of a natural person, biometric processing takes place, the result of which is the creation of "biometric data".

It should be stressed that contrary to the EU, Facial Recognition Technology is generally defined across various U.S. state laws and proposed federal legislation. The Revised Code of Washington (RCW) defines for example FRTs as a "technology that analyzes facial features and is used by a state or local government agency for the identification, verification, or persistent tracking of individuals in still or video images".[15] The proposed Commercial Facial Recognition Privacy Act of March 2019,[16] which would generally prohibit organizations from using facial recognition technology to collect facial recognition data without providing notice and obtaining their consent; defines also FRTs as "technology that—(A) analyzes facial features in still or video images; and (B) (i) is used to assign a unique, persistent identifier; or (ii) is used for the unique personal identification of a specific individual".[17] The Illinois Biometric Information Privacy Act (BIPA), which is one of the most notable state laws that defines biometric data, including facial recognition, does not explicitly define facial recognition technology, but refers to facial geometry as a biometric identifier.[18]

Facial recognition can be therefore used for a variety of purposes, in both the commercial world and public security and law enforcement. It can be used in many different contexts (e.g. to monitor entry to a specific location) and on any kind of data subject (e.g. a customer at a business). However, the processing of biometric data for the purpose of uniquely identifying a natural person is prohibited by the GDPR, unless one of the exceptions listed in Article 9§1 GDPR applies. In such a situation, Article 32 GDPR, which imposes data security obligations on both data controllers and data processors by requiring them to implement technical and organisational measures appropriate to the risks of the data processing, would need to be considered by entities that use FRT.[19] Consequently, facial recognition raises even more concerns, such as the level of security.

---

[13] Recital 14 and Article. 3(34) AI Act.

[14] Article 9§1 GDPR.

[15] RCW 43.386.010 (3)(a).

[16] See US Congress, S.847

[17] Sec. 2. Definitions, (5).

[18] (740 ILCS 14/).

[19] It should be noted here that according to Article 9(4), Member States may maintain or introduce further conditions, including those that impose limitations, with regard to the processing of genetic data, biometric data or data concerning health. According to the Commission's Report on the implementation of specific provisions of Regulation (EU) 2016/679, BE, BG, DE, EE, FI, FR, HR, HU, IE, LU, LV, MT, NL, PL, PT and RO impose conditions/limitations in relation to genetic data, biometric data and data concerning health. For instance, in the Netherlands, according to Article 29 of the Dutch GDPR Implementation Act, the processing of biometric data for the purpose of uniquely identifying a person is allowed, but it can only be conducted if it involves identity verification or is needed for security purposes.

3 Security Breaches and FRT

With facial recognition technologies—whether AI enabled or not—the collected biometric information is matched to information found in databases. Facial recognition data storage is however a source of worry due to the vulnerability of such databases. Data breaches involving facial recognition data increase indeed the potential for identity theft, stalking, and harassment. Hackers may access databases containing facial scans collected by banks, police departments, and defense companies. If threat actors obtained facial data linked to a victim's phone or banking information, they could escalate the breach and gain access to even more sensitive data.[20]

Data breaches involving FRT compromise not only individual security but also create conditions for mass surveillance and state overreach, which can chill political participation and deepen social inequality. As FRT evolves, new anti-spoofing and anti-attack techniques have also emerged (e.g. 3D capture scanners). According to the Article 29 Data Protection Working Party,[21] security breaches are likely to occur during data transmission in the case of online and mobile FRT, and during data storage in the case of identification and authentication/verification. Therefore, implementing appropriate measures and ensuring a level of security appropriate to the risk are crucial measures that need to be taken in order for Article 32 GDPR to be adopted appropriately.

Article 32 GDPR requires that controllers and processors implement technical and organisational measures appropriate to the risks posed by the data processing (e.g., pseudonymisation and encryption of personal data). These measures should be carried out when the processing is initiated, which is when the biometric data is converted into templates or images (i.e. feature extraction). It is crucial that data controllers acknowledge that "any loss of the integrity, confidentiality and availability features (...) would be clearly prejudicial to all future applications (...), as well as causing irretrievable damage to data subjects".[22]

Security measures should be assessed according to whether they are reasonably likely to achieve their objectives, and whether there are any conflicts of interest.[23] This assessment stems from the general principle of proportionality written into EU law, which requires that EU measures must be (a) suitable to achieve the desired end; (b) necessary to achieve the desired end; and (c) must not impose a burden on the individual that is excessive in relation to the objective sought.[24] Indeed, the GDPR does not require the use of any particular technology or technical standard with respect to data security. However, Article 32(1) lists four—non-mandatory—types of security measures that controllers and processors are advised to implement 'where

[20] See Cifaldi (2022).

[21] Article 29 Data Protection Working Party (2012).

[22] Article 29 Data Protection Working Party (2003), p. 9.

[23] Under the general principle of proportionality enshrined in EU law.

[24] See Bjorge and Zglinski (2022); Sauter (2017).

appropriate', namely: the pseudonymisation and encryption of personal data; ensuring that the confidentiality, integrity, availability and resilience of processing systems is maintained; restoring availability and access to personal data in a timely manner in the event of an incident; and regularly testing, assessing and evaluating the effectiveness of security measures.

GDPR security applies equally to confidentiality, integrity and availability, and should be seen as adhering to a risk-based approach: the higher the risk (to the rights and freedoms of data subjects), the more stringent the measures that the controller or processor must take.[25] Most of the ways in which FRT is used and deployed inherently poses a high level of risk to the rights and freedoms of data subjects,[26] and in such cases the processing of biometric data on a large scale will always require a Data Protection Impact Assessment (DPIA) to be carried out.[27]

Examples of large-scale processing operations include the storing of patient medical records at a hospital, or the travel data of individuals using a city's public transport system. However, the term 'large-scale' is not defined in the GDPR, and while the Article 29 Working Party has provided some guidance on what does and does not qualify as large-scale,[28] it has stopped short of providing a specific numerical threshold.[29] Despite the efforts of Estonia, the Czech Republic and Greece to provide their own numerical interpretation, the EDPB requested, in its 2018 opinion, that the supervisory authorities of these countries "amend" their list of processing activities requiring a DPIA by deleting any numerical threshold regarding what constitutes large scale processing.[30]

Specifying a numerical threshold for large-scale processing operations is important, as more and more cloud environments are being used to handle FRT over the web. There are more than 20 different types of biometric data, including fingerprints, face and voice. Each type of biometric data can be compromised in different ways. As the result of a biometric spoofing attack, hackers can compromise a secure system by using selfies, photos and videos drawn from social media profiles to create fake identifiers in the form of faces, voices or even fingerprints. According to a 2023 research study,[31] insecure data transmission in cloud environments has been identified as a potential breach risk. In addition, individual error, data management and legal oversight are the three main factors associated with data breaches, with data management being the most problematic. The role of cyber security is to provide the

---

[25] ENISA (2017).

[26] EDPB (2022).

[27] Article 35(1) GDPR.

[28] The number of data subjects concerned—either as a specific number or as a proportion of the relevant population; The volume of data and/or the range of different data items being processed; The duration, or permanence, of the data processing activity; The geographical extent of the processing activity.

[29] Article 29 Data Protection Working Party (2017a), pp. 7–8.

[30] EDPB (2018), p. 7.

[31] Meng et al. (2023).

necessary protection for the user's data by preventing it from being stolen or corrupted.

Given the likelihood of facial data being gathered whenever FRT is used, the next section tries to assess the EU's cyber security legal framework in relation to data breaches.

4 Does the EU's Cyber Security Legal Framework Add Value in Terms of Protecting Biometric Data?

A robust cyber security policy protects critical or sensitive data and prevents it from falling into the hands of malicious third parties. The EU's cyber security legal framework is based on the Cybersecurity Act[32] and the NIS 2 Directive,[33] and two further legal instruments are due in the shape of the Cyber Resilience Act[34] and the Cyber Solidarity Act proposals.[35]

In order to enable a thorough understanding of the added value provided by the EU's cyber security legal framework, but also of the complexity of the interplay between data protection and cyber security policies, which is shifting from complementarity to hierarchy in nature, four key cases are analysed: the interplay between the NIS 2 Directive and the Cybersecurity Act, and FRT (Sect. 4.1); the large-scale processing of biometric data in relation to law enforcement (Sect. 4.2); the GDPR's data protection impact assessment and the large-scale processing of facial image data by the essential and important entities (Sect. 4.3); and the 'hierarchy' that exists between data privacy and cyber security administrative penalties (Sect. 4.4). The selected cases provide a comprehensive examination of the regulatory landscape and potential conflicts that arise at the intersection of data privacy regulations like the GDPR, the NIS 2 Directive and the Cybersecurity Act, and emerging technology such as FRT, emphasising the crucial balance between safeguarding individual privacy rights and ensuring effective cyber security measures.

4.1 The Interplay Between the NIS 2 Directive and the Cybersecurity Act, and FRT

The EU Cybersecurity Act (CSA) dates back to 2017, when the European Commission, in light of the lack of recognised cyber security certification schemes across the EU, proposed a series of measures aimed at ensuring a high common level of cyber

[32] Op. cit. 4.

[33] Op. cit. 5.

[34] European Commission (2022).

[35] European Commission (2023).

security across the Union.[36] As "Cyber-attacks can be more dangerous to the stability of democracies and economies than guns and tanks".[37] The core objective of this regulation is therefore to enhance the EU's overall cyber security position by strengthening the mandate of the European Union Agency for Cybersecurity (ENISA); and by establishing an EU-wide cyber security certification framework.

On the other hand, the NIS2 Directive[38] has evolved since the original NIS Directive.[39] Both Directives are key pieces of legislation in the European Union's cyber security strategy. However, the NIS2 Directive represents a significant evolution compared to its previous version. The main changes to the new NIS2 directive are the addition of "important entities" which must comply with the obligations laid out by the directive and provide reports;[40] the attribution of personal liability for incidents to company executives; more streamlined cooperation between member states; the implementation of prescriptive cyber risk management measures; mandatory staff training and audits; and fines and penalties in the event of non-compliance.

Both the Cybersecurity Act and the NIS 2 Directive have introduced, among others,[41] requirements in relation to data security, that 'protect the availability, authenticity, integrity or confidentiality of stored, transmitted or processed data'.[42] The link with the GDPR's data protection requirements can be found under recital 49 of the GDPR, which defines network and information security as 'the ability of a network or an information system to resist, at a given level of confidence, accidental events or unlawful or malicious actions that compromise the availability, authenticity, integrity and confidentiality of stored or transmitted personal data (...)'.

The terms "confidentiality", "integrity" and "availability" are collectively known as the "CIA triad", and they are well established information security concepts.[43]

---

[36] European Commission (2017).

[37] Statement of the President of the European Commission, Jean-Claude Juncker, at the State of the Union address in September 13, 2017.

[38] The NIS 2 Directive entered into force on 16 January 2023. By 17 October 2024, the Member States of the EU will have to have successfully transposed the European directive into national law. If a Member State fails to notify the Commission that it has implemented the measures within the deadline, the Commission may require that the Member State pay a penalty (Article 258 TFEU – Infringement Procedure).

[39] Directive (EU) 2016/1148 of the European Parliament and of the Council of 6 July 2016 concerning measures for a high common level of security of network and information systems across the Union (OJ L194/2016, p. 1).

[40] These cover wastewater processing, public administration, space, postal and courier services, waste management, chemicals, food, manufacturing, and various IT data centre and digital service providers.

[41] Protection against accidental or unauthorised storage, processing, access, disclosure, loss, alteration or lack of availability of processed data during the entire life cycle of the ICT product, service or process.

[42] Article 46 Cybersecurity Act and Article 6(2) NIS 2 Directive.

[43] ISO/IEC 27000:2018, Information technology—Security techniques—Information security management systems—Overview and vocabulary.

Confidentiality measures protect information from unauthorised access and misuse by individuals, entities or processes, while integrity measures protect information from unauthorised modification. The level of security required to protect data in transit is proportional to the impact that the loss of confidentiality or integrity may have on the organisation. Availability measures protect timely and uninterrupted access to the information system. The CSA and the NIS 2 Directive add "authenticity" to the three commonly known attributes of the CIA triad.[44]

The terms "authenticity" and "integrity" represent two core concepts in information security. According to the Parkerian hexad,[45] which expands on the three classic security attributes of the CIA triad, authenticity refers to the veracity of the claim of origin or authorship of the information (e.g., the digital signature). The differences between them lie in whether the data is stored, transmitted or otherwise processed. When stored data are processed, it becomes vital to ensure that data have not been modified in an improper manner (integrity). On the other hand, the authenticity of the transmitted data refers to whether the sender's origin has been verified (authentication).[46] Indeed, information may be false or inauthentic but have integrity, or it may be true and authentic but lack integrity. The development of telecommunications services makes it essential to protect the authenticity of the data transmitted. Protecting the integrity (data, algorithms and documents) of the participants during data transmission is a fundamental requirement for trustworthy usage of FRT over network systems.

4.2 *Large-Scale Processing of Biometric Data in Law Enforcement*

Advanced biometric systems responsible for the storage and comparison of facial image data are crucial components of many large-scale IT systems used in law enforcement. The use of FRT for identification purposes[47] within law enforcement has come 'under attack from all sides',[48] as FRT processes biometric data. The confidentiality of big data[49] is usually the main concern, making encryption and access control techniques the main research areas when it comes to big data security.

[44] Recital 49 of the GDPR is the only part of the regulation in which the term "authenticity" is employed.

[45] Parker (1998).

[46] It should be stressed that recital 49 GDPR also makes reference to the concept of authenticity. However, it continues to be associated with network and information security (cyber security).

[47] Use of FRT to identify individuals using photos and/or facial recognition cameras, whether in real-time or not. See Christakis et al. (2022).

[48] Raposo (2022), p. 515.

[49] Big Data Analytics (BDA) is the term coined by researchers to describe the art of processing, storing and gathering large amounts of data for future examination. Data is being produced at an alarming rate.

The large-scale processing of biometric data in law enforcement poses several risks to democratic values, including civil liberties, privacy, and human rights. These risks stem from the potential for abuse, discrimination, and overreach by government authorities, as well as broader societal implications of widespread surveillance. Although the EU has the competence to regulate many issues concerning big data, 'the protection of national security remains, inter alia, the competence of the national member states and, despite Title V of the TFEU, most law enforcement activities and criminal justice in general are regulated by the national states'.[50]

The NIS 2 Directive excludes from its scope public administrations that 'carry out their activities in the fields of national security, public security, defense or law enforcement, including the prevention, investigation, detection and prosecution of criminal offences'.[51] In addition, EU Member States reserve the right to exempt 'specific entities' that carry out activity in these areas from the NIS 2 Directive's obligations regarding cybersecurity risk management measures and reporting requirements.[52] That said, cybercrime analysts believe that regardless of how well they are protected, all databases can eventually be hacked.[53] It is worth noting that the United States of America recognizes that the privacy and security of its citizens are at risk when personal data is collected on a broad scale.[54]

The NIS 2 Directive has a transposition deadline of 18 October 2024. At the time of writing, most national legislators in EU member states are either in the consultation phase[55] or there are no developments at all, except for Hungary, which has already transposed the Directive into its national legislation. To transpose the provisions of the NIS2 Directive into Hungarian law, the Parliament enacted Act XXIII of 2023 on Cybersecurity Certification and Supervision ("Cybersecurity Certification Act"), which entered into force on 2 January 2024.[56] Section 18 states that the provisions of Chapter III of the Hungarian transposition act do not apply to, *inter alia*, "local government bodies". Other Member States, such as Belgium, Croatia and Finland, have already published draft NIS2 transposition laws. The Belgian draft transposition law also states that the provision it contains will not apply to, inter alia, the police and judicial authorities.[57]

It should be noted that the Council and the Parliament reached an agreement on 20 November 2023 to advance police cooperation in Europe. The forthcoming regulation on automated data exchange for police cooperation (Prüm II) will

---

[50] Raposo (2022), p. 517.

[51] Article 2(7) NIS 2 Directive.

[52] Article 2(8) NIS 2 Directive.

[53] *Ibid.*

[54] O'Connor (2018).

[55] Such as Austria, France and Germany.

[56] Hungarian National Legislation Archive, Act XXIII of 2023 on cybersecurity certification and cybersecurity supervision (as in force on 2 January 2024).

[57] Belgium Center for Cybersecurity, Article 5§4 de l'avant-projet de loi établissant un cadre pour la cybersécurité des réseaux et des systèmes d'information d'intérêt général pour la sécurité publique.

modernize the technical infrastructure that underpins the exchange of information.[58] This modernization should allow national police forces in the EU to carry out quick searches, including facial image searches, via law enforcement databases across Europe. According to the Commission, eleven EU countries currently have national databases that contain facial images.[59] Half of these have provided information on the number of people stored in the databases, resulting in the fact that 60 million facial images would be accessible under Prüm II. Prüm II significantly expands therefore the type and amount of biometric data shared across borders, especially facial images. While this increases the scope for mass surveillance not just by individual countries but across the EU, it also highlights the need to apply high technical security standards to the automated exchange of data to prevent it falling into the "malicious" hands.

In general, automated data exchange should be accompanied by high technical standards, including privacy by design and data protection safeguards. Centralized or widely accessible biometric databases, such as those envisioned under Prüm II, become indeed high-value targets for cyberattacks. If facial image databases are hacked or leaked, this would not only compromise sensitive personal data but also raise the risk of identity theft or other forms of fraud. While Prüm II applies to EU member states, if data-sharing practices expand or data is shared with non-EU countries, there's a risk that biometric data could be accessed or misused by governments that do not uphold the same democratic standards or human rights protections.

The fact that the Prüm framework already covers the exchange of (special categories of) personal data facilitates the introduction of additional categories of data, as standards already exist. However, the introduction of a category such as facial images may require additional safeguards. According to Article 23a of the Prüm II proposal, which sets out the principles for the exchange and automated comparison of facial images, 'the transmission of facial images to other Member States or Europol shall be carried out in accordance with European or international standards'. The Commission will be empowered to adopt 'implementing acts specifying the relevant European or international standards for the exchange of facial images to be used by Member States and Europol' throughout the procedure referred to in Article 76(2) of the proposal. However, even though it is preferable to adopt existing internationally accepted standards, Member States 'tend to follow national requirements and standards, such as the ISKE standard in Estonia'.[60] As far as cyber security schemes are concerned, the Cybersecurity Act does not make any reference to law enforcement. It neither excludes nor includes it. This means that these national authorities are free to decide which standards they wish to adopt. However, such a situation may lead to a fragmented approach to the cyber security of large-scale IT

[58] European Commission (2021a).

[59] European Commission (2021b).

[60] Järvsoo et al. (2018), p. 150.

systems used in law enforcement for the automated processing, exchange and comparison of facial image data.

It should also be stressed that Article 40 of the Prüm II proposal provides that the European Union Agency for the Operational Management of Large-Scale IT Systems in the Area of Freedom, Security and Justice (EU-LISA) will have "supervisory powers" over national law enforcement authorities in relation to data security and integrity,[61] throughout the analysis of the logs of data processing operations held in the Prüm II and EPRIS central routers.[62] The European Agency for the operational management of large-scale IT systems in the area of freedom, security and justice (eu-LISA)[63] is not mentioned in the NIS 2 Directive. Nevertheless, eu-LISA's Consolidated Annual Activity Report 2022 states that 'although the NIS 2 Directive does not directly affect eu-LISA's core activities, it will enhance cybersecurity in the EU (…)'.[64] This means that NIS 2 may indirectly affect eu-LISA's core activities, which is welcome given the sensitivity of facial image data. Indeed, the Explanatory Memorandum that was published following the Prüm II proposal states that Chapter 6 on data protection contains, inter alia, provisions that set out 'the measures required by eu-LISA (…) to ensure the security of data processing, the appropriate handling of security incidents and the monitoring of compliance with the measures in this Regulation [Prüm II]'.

The link with the NIS 2 Directive can be found in the term "incident". Indeed, Article 3(24) of Prüm II refers to the definition contained in the NIS 2 Directive, which defines it as 'an event that compromises the availability, authenticity, integrity or confidentiality of stored, transmitted or processed data or of the services offered by, or accessible via, network and information systems'. As can be seen, the principles of availability, authenticity, integrity and confidentiality remain at the core of not only the NIS 2 Directive, but also the Prüm II Directive, and therefore concern the large-scale processing of facial image data in law enforcement.

---

[61] Article 40§3 Prüm II proposal.

[62] The proposal envisages the creation of central routers (the Prüm II router and EPRIS) that would each act as a connecting point between Member States. These routers would serve as message brokers, forwarding search transactions and replies to national systems, without creating new data processes, enlarging access rights or replacing national databases.

[63] Established by the by Regulation (EU) No 1077/2011 of the European Parliament and of the Council of 25 October 2011 establishing a European Agency for the operational management of large-scale IT systems in the area of freedom, security and justice (OJ L286/2011, p. 1). And repealed by Regulation (EU) 2018/1726 of the European Parliament and of the Council of 14 November 2018 on the European Union Agency for the Operational Management of Large-Scale IT Systems in the Area of Freedom, Security and Justice (eu-LISA), and amending Regulation (EC) No 1987/2006 and Council Decision 2007/533/JHA and repealing Regulation (EU) No 1077/2011 (OJ L295/2018, p. 99).

[64] EU-LISA (2023).

4.3 *The GDPR's Data Protection Impact Assessment and the Large-Scale Processing of Facial Images Data by Essential and Important Entities*

So far, we have seen that the NIS 2 Directive does not apply to the law enforcement sector. With regard to the other sectors (e.g. energy and banking), the extension of the scope of the NIS 2 Directive is a welcome development. However, the lack of a clearly defined threshold that applies to the large-scale processing of special categories of data,[65] may hamper the protection of facial image data.

It should be recalled that to ensure that all Member States follow a common approach to the identification of the operator of essential services (OES)[66] under the NIS Directive, Annex II of the Directive provided a list of sectors and subsectors that serve as a roadmap for the identification process. However, Member States have been left free to come to a decision on 'the national measures allowing for the identification of operators of essential services (…)'[67] and 'the thresholds established to determine the level of supply by reference to the number of users relying on the service or to the importance of the particular OES'.[68] The criteria deemed necessary to identify the operators of essential services referred to in Article 5(2) are as follows: (a) the entity provides a service which is essential for the maintenance of critical societal and/or economic activities; (b) the provision of that service depends on network and information systems; and (c) an incident occurs which would have a significantly disruptive impact on the provision of that service. However, the regulatory leeway given to Member States in setting the identification thresholds has resulted in a fragmented approach to the entities falling within the scope of the NIS Directive.

In the proposal to revise the NIS Directive published by the Commission at the end of 2020, it was considered necessary to change the approach to the identification of covered entities.[69] The explanatory memorandum to the NIS2 proposal acknowledges that 'cybersecurity requirements imposed on entities providing services or economically relevant activities' vary considerably across Member States in terms of the nature of the requirements, the level of detail and the method of supervision. It is also recognised that one of the reasons for this fragmentation is the unclear definition

[65] Special categories of data are regulated under Article 35§3, point b, of the GDPR.

[66] The terms 'Operators of Essential Services' and 'Digital Service Provider' are used in the original NIS Directive. In the revised version of this NIS Directive, the terms used now are 'Essential' and 'Important' entities.

[67] Article 5 §7 (a) of Directive 2016/1148.

[68] Article 5 §7 (d) of Directive 2016/1148.

[69] Proposal for a Directive of the European Parliament and of the Council on measures for a high common level of cybersecurity across the Union, repealing Directive (EU) 2016/114, COM(2020) 823 final, 2020/0359 (COD), Brussels, 16.12.2020.

of the scope of the NIS Directive, which was largely left to the discretion of Member States.[70]

The scope of organisations covered by the NIS 2 Directive is now wider than its predecessor. Although there are specific exceptions, in general all large and medium-sized organisations[71] in the selected sectors, whether public or private, are covered by the legislation.[72] Therefore, the criteria concerning the number of users that rely on such a service has been replaced by the number of employees and the annual turnover. However, the interplay between the GDPR and the NIS 2 Directive remains blurred by the lack of clearly defined threshold criteria concerning when large-scale processing takes place, which is somewhat questionable in terms of the DPIA requirement, especially in relation to FRTs and biometric data. But let's make this argument clearer.

The GDPR does not define what constitutes large-scale processing. However, the WP29 DPIA Guidelines,[73] which set out nine criteria that should be taken into account when determining whether a data processing operation is 'likely to give rise to high risk', refer to 'data processed on a large scale, which can be determined on the basis of the following factors: (a) the number of data subjects concerned, either as a specific number or as a proportion of the relevant population; (b) the volume of data and/or the range of different data items processed; (c) the duration or permanence of the data processing activity; (d) the geographical extent of the processing activity'. The first observation to keep in mind is the criteria concerning the number of data subjects identified by the WP29, which is like the NIS Directive criteria concerning the number of users that rely on an essential service.

The WP29 DPIA Guidelines refer to certain examples of large-scale processing, such as the processing of patient data by a hospital, or the processing of content, traffic or location data by telephone or internet service providers. The French data protection authority (CNIL)[74] has provided a more precise example of the large-scale criteria cited in Article 35(3) GDPR, stating that 'a small family business active in the distribution of household appliances in a single town uses the services of a processor whose core activity is to provide website analysis services and assistance with targeted advertising and marketing. The activities of the family business and its customers do not lead to the processing of data on a "large scale", given the small number of customers and the relatively limited activities. However, the activities of the processor, who has many customers like this small business, taken together, do constitute large-scale processing'.[75] Let's now look at how the DPIA interacts with the NIS 2 Directive.

---

[70] *Ibid*, p. 13 recital 4.

[71] Companies having more than 50 employees and an annual turnover greater than 10 million euros.

[72] Article 2 NIS 2 Directive.

[73] Article 29 Data Protection Working Party (2017b), p. 10; Article 29 Data Protection Working Party (2017a), p. 21.

[74] Commission Nationale de l'Informatique et des Libertés, French Data Protection Authority.

[75] CNIL (2017).

For example, a medium-sized food company engaged in wholesale distribution is considered an essential entity under Article 2§1 of the NIS 2 Directive. It is therefore subject to enhanced cybersecurity measures. The company decides to use FRT for allowing large corporate clients to create their account and have access to online services. The food company is considered a major wholesaler, and the processing of facial image data is carried out in this context. Taking into account the CNIL's reasoning above, as well as the company's large customer base and commercial activity, the company would be required to carry out a DPIA. As a result, it is subject not only to enhanced cyber security measures, but also to data protection measures. Suppose the food business now uses the services of a processor whose core business is to provide facial recognition solutions. The food business remains subject to the measures of the NIS 2 Directive, but the DPIA obligation under the GDPR now falls to the external processor. In such a situation, the question arises as to whether the external processor is subject to enhanced cyber security measures.

However, in both cases the threshold above which the processing of facial images should be considered large-scale remains unknown. This adds to the complexity of the issue. Is the external processor providing a facial recognition solution subject to NIS 2? Is there a company that provides FRT solutions that is not covered by the NIS 2 Directive? And if so, which category does this involve? A cloud computing service provider? A data centre service provider?

It is also possible to observe a kind of 'hierarchy' between privacy and cyber security policies throughout the NIS 2 Directive. The next section examines this hierarchy in reference to administrative penalties.

4.4 The 'Hierarchy' Between Data Privacy and Cyber Security Administrative Penalties

Article 35§1 of the NIS 2 Directive states that 'where the competent authorities become aware in the course of supervision or enforcement that the infringement by an essential or important entity of the obligations laid down in Articles 21 and 23 of this Directive can entail a personal data breach' under the GDPR, their national Data Protection Authority (DPA) must be informed without undue delay.

The obligations set out in Articles 21 and 23 of the NIS 2 Directive relate to cyber security risk management measures and reporting obligations. The purpose of both articles is to (a) manage the risks to the security of network and information systems, (b) prevent or minimise the impact of cyber security incidents, and (c) deal promptly with any incident that has a significant impact on the provision of services by essential and important entities. The common denominator is the notion of an incident having a significant impact. According to Article 23 of the NIS 2 Directive, 'an incident shall be considered significant if (a) it has caused, or is likely to cause, serious disruption of services or financial loss to the entity concerned; (b) it has affected, or is likely to affect, other natural or legal persons by causing significant material or non-material damage'. In the light of these criteria, one might wonder whether the term "non-pecuniary damage" includes damage caused to a natural person.

The NIS 2 Directive, as well as the documents that were published following the proposal, do not provide any information on how the term "non-material" should be understood.[76] However, it is possible to find certain clues in the GDPR. For example, Article 4(12) of the GDPR defines "personal data breach", as 'a breach of security leading to the accidental or unlawful destruction, loss, alteration, unauthorised disclosure of, or access to, personal data transmitted, stored or otherwise processed'. Failure to remedy such a breach in an appropriate and timely manner may result, inter alia, in non-material damage to individuals.[77] However, recital 86 of the same Regulation states that 'the controller should notify the data subject without undue delay of a personal data breach where that personal data breach is likely to result in a high risk to the rights and freedoms of natural persons, in order to allow the data subject to take the necessary precautions'. It is therefore reasonable to assume that, when it comes to the GDPR or the NIS 2 Directive, the term "non-material damage" should be understood as damage to the rights and freedoms of a natural person. And if we take our research further, it is possible to discern that both Article 23 of the NIS 2 Directive and Article 33 of the GDPR, under the umbrella of the notification/reporting obligation, provide for an undue delay in responding to any personal data breach or cybersecurity incident.

Nevertheless, it should be noted that whenever the supervisory authorities of the GDPR impose an administrative fine on an essential or important entity under the provisions of the GDPR for an infringement involving a personal data breach, the competent authorities of the NIS 2 Directive may not impose an administrative fine under Article 34 of the NIS 2 Directive for such an infringement.[78] In other words, if the failure to comply with the cybersecurity risk management measures set out in Article 21 of the NIS 2 Directive or the failure to notify an incident with a significant impact by an essential or important entity subject to the NIS 2 Directive results in a personal data breach, the national DPA remains responsible for imposing the relevant sanction under the GDPR.

The NIS 2 national competent authority reserves the right to enforce the administrative fine through the enforcement measures provided for in the NIS 2 Directive.[79] Given the sensitivity of facial image data, such an approach is welcome. After all, sanctions concerning personal data breaches will continue to be imposed in accordance with the GDPR. However, the question arises as to how "jurisdiction" is

---

[76]It should be specified that the term 'non-material damage' was not figuring at all in the NIS Directive.

[77]Recital 85 GDPR.

[78]Article 35§2 NIS 2 Directive

[79]Article 35§2 NIS 2 Directive: 'The competent authorities may, however, impose the enforcement measures provided for in Article 32(4), points (a) to (h), Article 32(5) and Article 33(4), points (a) to (g), of this Directive'.

separated between the data protection authority and the national competent authority in terms of the enforcement of NIS 2, as well as the ability of the data protection authorities to carry out a cyber security assessment in relation to the penalties imposed for the cyber security breach that led to the data breach. Given the wording of Article 35(2) of the NIS 2 Directive, let us assume that any penalty that concerns a cyber security breach will be assessed by the DPA.

Regarding the Cybersecurity Act, as well as the Cyber Resilience Act and the Cyber Solidarity Act proposals, there is no mention of personal data breaches in the body of these documents.

5 Conclusion

The analysis of the interplay between facial recognition technology (FRT), data protection regulations such as the GDPR, and cybersecurity frameworks revealed several critical issues and complexities, since the evolution of FRT has brought about significant challenges, particularly concerning security breaches, data integrity, and privacy infringements.

The implementation of appropriate security measures is crucial to mitigate the risks associated with FRT, especially during data transmission and storage. However, the lack of a clear definition of 'large-scale processing' complicates compliance, particularly when it comes to the deployment of FRT. Furthermore, the interaction between data protection and cyber security policies, as highlighted by the NIS 2 Directive and the GDPR, adds layers of complexity. The absence of defined thresholds for large-scale processing under the GDPR and the fragmented approach to identifying covered entities in the NIS 2 Directive exacerbate uncertainty and compliance challenges. Last but not least, the 'hierarchy' between data privacy and cyber security administrative penalties, as outlined in the NIS 2 Directive, raises questions about jurisdiction and enforcement mechanisms. The delineation of responsibilities between data protection authorities and national competent authorities underlines the need for clarity and coordination in addressing cyber security breaches involving personal data.

While efforts are being made to enhance cyber security frameworks such as the Cybersecurity Act and the NIS 2 Directive, the intricate interplay between data protection and cyber security remains a significant challenge. Addressing these complexities requires comprehensive measures that prioritize the protection of individual privacy rights while ensuring that there is a robust approach to cyber security as FRT evolves.

First, it should be ensured that privacy is embedded into the development lifecycle of FRT and other technologies (e.g., AI-enabled). This requires entities to minimize data collection to the bare minimum (data minimization) or even use anonymization or pseudonymization techniques where possible. This is because incorporating privacy and security considerations from the outset reduces the risk of breaches and ensures compliance with data protection regulations, such as GDPR, without compromising security.

Second, policymakers should build on existing frameworks, such as the NIS 2 Directive and the Cybersecurity Act, by incorporating FRT-specific guidelines to ensure (a) clear responsibilities for data processors and controllers using FRT, and (b) compliance with both cybersecurity standards and data protection laws, such as the GDPR. Introducing a regulatory 'sandbox', like the one established under Article 57 of the EU AI Act, to test new security technologies and policies in a controlled environment. A well-defined regulatory landscape provides organizations with clear expectations and accountability measures, ensuring compliance without stifling innovation.

Third, the protection of critical infrastructures, especially those using advanced technologies such as FRT, should be prioritized by mandating regular cyber resilience audits and conducting vulnerability assessments and penetration tests to identify weaknesses. This is because ensuring that critical infrastructure has a robust cybersecurity framework in place reduces the risk of large-scale breaches and maintains public confidence in technological advances such as FRT.

Finally, more transparent and granular user consent mechanisms, especially for FRT, should be put in place to give users control over how their biometric data is used (e.g. ensuring clear and easy to understand privacy policies detailing how data is collected, processed and stored). Balancing cybersecurity and privacy require gaining the trust of individuals. Transparent consent processes are the cornerstone of a democratic society and should be developed to reassure users that their data will be handled responsibly and securely.

Competing Interests This study was funded by the Interdisciplinary Project on Privacy (IPoP) overseen by Cybersecurity PEPR (ANR 22-PECY-0002 IPOP).

References

Agarwal A, Singhal C, Thomas R (2021 March 23) AI-powered decision making for the bank of the future. McKinsey and Company. https://www.mckinsey.com/industries/financial-services/our-insights/ai-powered-decision-making-for-the-bank-of-the-future. Accessed 19 Feb 2024

Article 29 Data Protection Working Party (2003 August 1) Working documents on biometrics. 12168/02/EN WP80

Article 29 Data Protection Working Party (2012 March 22) Opinion 2/2012 on facial recognition in online and mobile devices. 00727/12/EN WP192

Article 29 Data Protection Working Party (2017a October 4) Guidelines on Data Protection Impact Assessment (DPIA) and Determining whether Processing Is "Likely to Result in a High Risk" for the Purposes of Regulation 2016/679. WP 248 rev.01

Article 29 Data Protection Working Party (2017b April 5) Guidelines on Data Protection Officers ('DPOs'). 16/EN WP 243 rev.01

Bjorge E, Zglinski J (2022) Chapter 11: The principle of proportionality in EU law and its domestic application: ni tout à fait le même, ni tout à fait un autre. In: Ziegler KS et al (eds) Research handbook on general principles in EU law. Edward Elgar Publishing, Cheltenham, UK

Christakis T, Bannelier K, Castelluccia C, Le Métayer D (2022 May) Mapping the use of facial recognition in public spaces in Europe – Part 2: Classification, Report of the AI- Regulation Chair. AI Regulation. https://ai-regulation.com/wp-content/uploads/2022/05/Facial-Recognition-in-Europe-Part2.-Classification.pdf. Accessed 12 Feb 2024

Cifaldi G (2022) Government surveillance and facial recognition system in the context of modern technologies and security challenges. Sociol Soc Work Rev 2:93–101

CNIL (2017 September) GDPR – Guide for Processors. https://www.cnil.fr/sites/cnil/files/atoms/files/gdpr_guide-for-processors_en.pdf. Accessed 17 Feb 2024

EDPB (2018 September 25) Opinion 6/2018 on the draft list of the competent supervisory authority of Estonia regarding the processing operations that are subject to the requirement of a data protection impact assessment (Art. 35.4 GDPR)

EDPB (2022 May 12) Guidelines 05/2022 on the use of facial recognition technology in the area of law enforcement. Version 1.0

EDPB (2023 April 26) Guidelines 05/2022 on the use of facial recognition technology in the area of law enforcement. Version 2.0

ENISA (2017) Handbook on Security of Personal Data Processing. https://doi.org/10.2824/569768

EU-LISA (2023 June 22) Consolidated Annual Activity Report 2022, Adopted by the eu-LISA Management Board. Document 2023-182 REV 3

European Commission (2017 September 13) Joint Communication to the European Parliament and the Council, Resilience, Deterrence and Defence: Building strong cybersecurity for the EU. JOIN/2017/0450 final

European Commission (2020 December 16) Proposal for a Directive of the European Parliament and of the Council on measures for a high common level of cybersecurity across the Union, repealing Directive (EU) 2016/114, COM(2020) 823 final, 2020/0359 (COD), Brussels, 16.12.2020

European Commission (2021a December 8) Proposal for a regulation of the European Parliament and of the Council on automated data exchange for police cooperation ("Prüm II"), amending Council Decisions 2008/615/JHA and 2008/616/JHA and Regulations (EU) 2018/1726, 2019/817 and 2019/818 of the European Parliament and of the Council. COM/2021/784 final

European Commission (2021b April 20) Quo Vadis Prum ? – Facial-image as a new biometric modality, DG Migration and Home affairs – Unit D1 – Police Cooperation and Information Exchange

European Commission (2022 September 15) Proposal for a Regulation on horizontal cyber security requirements for products with digital elements and amending Regulation (EU) 2019/1020. COM/2022/454 final

European Commission (2023 April 18) Proposal for a Regulation laying down measures to strengthen solidarity and capacities in the Union to detect, prepare for and respond to cyber security threats and incidents. COM/2023/209 final

FRA (2019 November 21) Facial recognition technology: fundamental rights considerations in the context of law enforcement. Publications Office of the European Union

Järvsoo M, Norta A, Tsap V, Pappel I, Draheim D (2018) Implementation of information security in the EU information systems. In: Al-Sharhan S et al (eds) Challenges and opportunities in the digital era, I3E 2018. Lecture Notes in Computer Science (LNTCS), vol 11195. Springer, Cham

Meng W, Yalin Q, Jiaojiao L, Weidong L (2023) Identifying personal physiological data risks to the Internet of Everything: the case of facial data breach risks. Humanit Soc Sci Commun 216:1–15

O'Connor N (2018 January 30) Reforming the U.S. Approach to Data Protection and Privacy. Council On Foreign Relations. https://www.cfr.org/report/reforming-us-approach-data-protection. Accessed 19 Feb 2024

Parker DB (1998) Fighting computer crim. John Wiley & Sons, New York

Raposo VL (2022) The use of facial recognition technology by law enforcement in Europe: a Non-Orwellian Draft Proposal. Eur J Crim Policy Res 29:515–533

Sauter W (2017) Proportionality in EU law: a balancing act? Camb Yearb Eur Leg Stud 15:439–466

FRT and Access to Public Services: What Acceptable Uses in Smart Cities?

Isadora Neroni Rezende

Abstract Digital technologies are the backbone of the smart city, where local governments rely on diversified solutions to make public services more accessible and efficient. Facial recognition technologies (FRT) are also a popular option to regulate access to public services. However, using FRT in this domain raises many privacy and data protection issues, for example, in terms of the legitimate legal basis and proportionality of the processing. Against this background, this chapter aims to assess what are the legitimate uses of FRT to access public services in smart cities. Preliminary, existing applications of the technology are mapped and categorized. In public service provision, FRT contribute to the efficiency of a service (i.e., by improving crowd flows) or detecting irregularities (i.e., violations of public facility rules). The legitimacy of such implementations is assessed against two of the legal bases for biometric processing under the EU General Data Protection Regulation (GDPR): consent (Article 9(2)(a) GDPR) and public interest (Article 9(2)(g) GDPR). In particular, firstly, I examine to which extent consent can legitimize FRT use for accessing public services and assess the role of the proportionality test in such processing vis-à-vis the determinations of data subjects. Secondly, I analyze if the employment of FRT to control the regular access to and use of services complies with proportionality, in light of data subjects' expectations of privacy in public venues. In conclusion, I summarise the findings of the legal analysis.

Keywords Smart cities · Public services · Privacy · Data protection · Surveillance

1 Introduction

Digital technologies are the backbone of the smart city, where local governments rely on diversified solutions to make public services more accessible and efficient. For example, Blockchain improves data privacy and security in e-government and

I. Neroni Rezende (✉)
University of Bologna, Department of Legal Studies, Bologna, Italy
e-mail: isadora.neroni2@unibo.it

N. Menéndez González, G. Mobilio (eds.), *Next Democratic Frontiers for Facial Recognition Technology (FRT)*, Law, Governance and Technology Series 74,
https://doi.org/10.1007/978-3-031-89794-8_7

provides greater accountability. Facial recognition technologies (FRT) are also a popular option to regulate access to public services. In Madrid, for example, Mastercard partnered with the *Empresa Municipal de Transporte* EMT to pilot a face recognition ticketing system in public transportation.[1] In France and the UK, FRT was used to monitor school attendance and make payments in canteens.[2] The Irish Department of Social Protection planned to employ the technology to identify welfare fraud.[3] In the US, instead, FRT systems were installed to monitor entrance in public housing buildings,[4] with worrisome implications for residents' privacy.

The use of facial recognition in the public arena raises a wide range of issues, for instance for democracy and accountability,[5] since biometric software is mostly developed by private companies, and its basic functioning is often opaque and prone to discrimination against women and dark-skinned people.[6] These problems are exacerbated by the threats that these technologies pose specifically to privacy and data protection rights, which are also instrumental in supplying power imbalances between individuals and government authorities.[7]

Against this background, this chapter aims to investigate what are the legitimate uses of FRT to access public services in smart cities under the European human rights framework on privacy and data protection. This comprises not only the Charter of Fundamental Rights of the European Union (CFREU) and relevant EU secondary law and case law, but also the European Convention on Human Rights (ECHR), as interpreted by the European Court of Human Rights (ECtHR). Before delving into the analysis, however, some caveats are necessary to clarify the scope and method of the research.

Using FRT in this domain raises many data protection problems, for example, in terms of the appropriate legal basis and proportionality of the processing. In the EU, data protection authorities (DPAs) have assessed FRT uses for authentication purposes in relation to consent (Article 9(2)(a) GDPR[8]) and public interest (Article 9(2)(g) GDPR).[9] In fact, these appear to be the most relevant legal bases for public authorities to collect personal data in public venues. Concerning the provision of

---

[1] del Castillo (2019).

[2] Baudino (2019); O'Murchu (2021).

[3] Horgan-Jones (2020).

[4] MacMillan (2023).

[5] On the impact of FRT on democracy, see Gentzel (2021); Smith and Miller (2022); Palmiotto and Menéndez González (2023). See also chapter 'Facial Recognition Technologies: Threats or Opportunities for Democracy?' in this volume by Mobilio.

[6] Lohr (2018).

[7] On the role of privacy and data protection in redressing power asymmetries, see in general Clifford and Ausloos (2018); Malgieri (2020); De Hert and Gutwirth (2006).

[8] Regulation (EU) 2016/679 of the European Parliament and of the Council of 27 April 2016 on the protection of natural persons with regard to the processing of personal data and on the free movement of such data, and repealing Directive 95/46/EC (General Data Protection Regulation) (Text with EEA relevance) OJ L 119, 4.5.2016, pp. 1–88.

[9] As outlined by Christakis et al. (2022).

services by public authorities, the grounds relating to the performance of a contract (Article 6(1)(b) GDPR), compliance with a legal obligation (Article 6(1)(c) GDPR), the protection of a vital interest of the data subject or another natural person (Article 6(1)(d) GDPR) do not sit well with a situation where a local government, while not complying with a strict legal obligation in terms of means, decides to rely specifically on FRT to manage relationships that have a public (and not private) nature.[10] Public authorities may, under some circumstances, rely on the legitimate interest basis, but not when they act "in the performance of their tasks" (Article 6(1)(second sentence) GDPR). Therefore, this ground will not be considered either in relation to the analysis of the provision of public services.

When the processing is based on consent, this is considered "free" only if alternative solutions are proposed,[11] meaning that data subjects should always have the possibility to opt out. Nonetheless, it is problematic to rely on consent as a legal basis in public spaces[12] and in the relations with the public sector.[13] In smart cities, specifically, individuals may not be aware that their data is being collected at all, especially when such data is gathered by sensors embedded in the infrastructure. Even where the processing is explicit to the data subject, such as in the case of facial authentication systems, their consent may not always be considered "freely given" because it might be impacted by external factors like time constraints and pressure from public authorities. Besides, when data subjects consent to the processing, they act as the "arbiters" of the underlying value balancing[14] and, in this case, this entails that they may choose freely whether to access public services more speedily with FRT. As we will see, this has important consequences for the assessment of the proportionality of the processing because it remains unclear to which extent DPAs may censure the decisions of the data subject.

Conversely, if the processing is based on public interest, as required by Recital 41 GDPR, an additional legal basis is needed that shall satisfy both "quality of the law" and proportionality requirements. Because the consent of the data subject is not

[10] For example, in a case involving the installation of a Wi-fi tracking system in the public streets of the municipality of Enschede, the Dutch data protection authority (*Autoriteit Persongegevens*, AP) observed that the only relevant GDPR bases for collecting personal data in such a context where consent, the performance of a public task, and legitimate interest. See Autoriteit Persoonsgegevens, *Gemeente Enschede*, Judgment of 11 March 2021.

[11] European Data Protection Board (2019), p. 20. This was highlighted too by the *Commission nationale du numérique et des libertés* (CNIL), in its decision about the ALICEM project, which aimed to establish a mobile FRT system to access online administrative services. See *Délibération n ° 2018-342 du 18 octobre 2018 portant avis sur un projet de décret autorisant la création d'un traitement automatisé permettant d'authentifier une identité numérique par voie électronique dénommé «Application de lecture de l'identité d'un citoyen en mobilité» (ALICEM) et modifiant le code de l'entrée et du séjour des étrangers et du droit d'asile (demande d'avis n° 18008244)*, Judgment of 18 October 2018. Non-biometric gates were also set up at the Molenbeek stadium to identify season ticket holders who did not consent to the 2019–2020 FRT trial.

[12] Van Zeeland et al. (2019), p. 8; Christofi and Wauters, pp. 24–28.

[13] Koops (2014), p. 253.

[14] Gellert (2016), p. 485.

necessary here, relying on this legal basis seems plausible when the system is meant to monitor every one of interest in a given area. Therefore, a system of this kind may be useful to control access to public premises such as public housing buildings, but such indiscriminate surveillance would hardly reconcile with proportionality requirements, if not in the security domain.

National DPAs have addressed these legal hurdles differently, creating legal ambiguity.[15] At the same time, tech companies are pushing these solutions to the market and could thus profit from this regulatory uncertainty. To address this problem, this chapter examines the effect of choosing a specific GDPR basis for the proportionality assessment of a given FRT processing. The aim is to provide more legal clarity for data controllers seeking to employ the technology in compliance with EU data protection.

As known, proportionality assessments in data protection are fact-based[16] and, methodologically speaking, this requires contextualizing the analysis and limiting its scope on multiple levels. At the outset, the investigation focuses only on FRT use to access to public services, while applications in the security domain (for example, in crime detection or border control) and in schools are excluded.[17] Both applications raise data protection issues of their own and therefore go beyond the scope of this chapter. In examining the relevant FRT uses, then, I first consider *why* the technology is employed to authorize users to access a public service. The purpose of the processing is a key element in assessing its proportionality and should thus be taken into account in the analysis. In this respect, FRT seek either (i) to improve people's experience or (ii) to detect irregularities in service provision. These applications should be examined separately: face verification systems used to buy tickets or to speed up crowd flows fall within the first category, while identification systems that control entries to public venues (e.g., public residences) refer instead to the second iteration. I shall see below how these objectives affect both the choice of the legal basis of the processing and the subsequent proportionality assessment.

Furthermore, a contextual approach also imposes to consider not only *how* FRT is used but also *where*, given that each setting where a given technology is deployed features specific normative elements that may impact the legal assessment. In this chapter, I address only applications used in (i) smart cities *and* (ii) in public places. This choice entails further preliminary considerations.

Concerning the first aspect, embracing a specific conception of the smart city plays a crucial role in setting the stage for the analysis. Certainly, there is no agreed definition of what "smart cities" are, least of all, in the legal domain.[18] The core idea behind this notion is using technologies to increase efficiency and sustainability in

---

[15] Christakis et al. (2022).

[16] European Data Protection Supervisor (2019), p. 11.

[17] For examples of FRT use in law enforcement and legal implications, see the contributions of Levantino and Jasserand in this volume, or if you wish, Neroni Rezende (2022); Neroni Rezende (2020).

[18] Albino et al. (2015); Cocchia (2014); Kummitha and Crutzen (2017).

cities, as well as citizens' quality of life.[19] However, on the normative level, there are diverging approaches as to how technologies shall be used to attain these objectives. In particular, there is a tension between *technology-driven* and *human-driven* conceptions of smart cities.[20] The former relies on the assumption that technologies alone can solve any challenge that cities face, with big corporations sponsoring technical solutions with a top-down approach and ignoring political, social, and cultural factors.[21] Instead, the latter focuses on the city as a political construct and looks at technologies as a means to reach broader societal goals,[22] meaning that smart projects are implemented with a bottom-up approach that considers both wider societal effects and citizens' human rights.[23]

For the purposes of this analysis, both outlooks express a specific equilibrium of values, which may affect the perspective taken in the proportionality assessments in data protection. For instance, the *technology-driven* approach prioritizes the need for innovation and economic attractiveness in the city but may also lead to a careless implementation of FRT technologies to the detriment of privacy and data protection rights. On the opposite, the *human-driven* conception values such instances while also resulting in a too-restrictive approach to FRT. Against this backdrop, in this analysis, I will combine elements of both conceptions to resolve some interpretative hurdles. From *technology-driven* approaches, I draw the emphasis on the need for innovation in the urban environment, which entails that no technology application—including FRT—should be rejected *a priori* in smart cities. At the same time, however, the *human-driven* approach requires keeping privacy and data protection rights, as well as the opinions of data subjects, at the forefront when implementing smart city projects.[24] This entails also avoiding top-down and paternalistic approaches, especially when data subjects can express their view on the legitimacy of the processing.

About the second aspect, deploying FRT in public places[25] raises specific challenges because such venues have always played a crucial role in cities[26] as they create room for political expression in liberal democracies, social integration, and

---

[19] Cardullo and Kitchin (2019), p. 815; Vanolo (2013), pp. 888–889.

[20] Ziosi et al. (2022).

[21] Cardullo and Kitchin (2019); Hollands (2008).

[22] De Waal (2017).

[23] Kitchin et al. (2019).

[24] Christofi et al. (2022).

[25] Although the terms "space" and "place" are often used interchangeably, it should be kept in mind that there is semantic difference the two, as clarified in human geography and other scholarly disciplines Koops and Galic (2017). On the one hand, in fact, "space" has a rather naturalistic and empirical connotation and shall be defined as the "backdrop against which human behaviour is played", as put it by Hubbard and Kitchin (2011), p. 4. On the other hand, a "place" is any "*meaningful* location" Altman and Zube (1989), p. 2; Cresswell (2004), p. 7, that is "a distinctive (and more-or-less bounded) type of space which is defined by (and constructed in terms of) the lived experiences of people" (Hubbard and Kitchin 2011, p. 6).

[26] Madanipour (2003).

identity-building.[27] Nonetheless, not all public places are alike: for example, airports and public squares do not raise the same privacy expectations or risks for public order.[28] Therefore, the specific nature and function of the place where FRT is deployed shall be another key element in the legal analysis, as we will see specifically in Sect. 3.

Given these caveats, the chapter is structured as follows. In Sect. 2, I examine to which extent consent can legitimize FRT use for accessing public services and assess the role of the proportionality assessment in such processing *vis-à-vis* the determinations of data subjects. In Sect. 3 instead, I analyze if the employment of FRT to control the regular access to and use of services complies with proportionality, in light of data subjects' expectations of privacy in public venues. In Sect. 4, I summarise the findings of the legal analysis.

2 FRT and Consent to Improve Service Flow

EU DPAs have consistently found that consent is often the right legal basis for FRT processing to access a public service. In EU data protection law, Article 4(11) GDPR defines consent as "any freely given, specific, informed and unambiguous indication of the data subject's wishes by which he or she, by a statement or by a clear affirmative action, signifies agreement to the processing of personal data relating to him or her.".[29] When FRT is used to manage access to a public service, then, the data subject must have a back-up solution allowing to access the service without the intermediation of the technology, as submitting biometric data to public administration must be a voluntary choice of the individual. Only if users have an alternative, their consent can be considered genuinely "free".

In the smart city context, this legal requirement does not pose particular issues, as controllers in the EU usually demonstrate that they have implemented alternative options.[30] However, as shown below, other issues remain unsolved. In particular, relying on this legal basis may be problematic to assess (i) the coherence of consent with the actual purpose of the processing, raising issues for the specificity of the wishes expressed by the data subject (ii) the authenticity of consent, and (iii) its relationship with the proportionality assessment. For each of these problems, some possible mitigation measures are suggested.

Concerning the first problem, using FRT for authentication purposes logically serves the objective of improving service experience. Face recognition makes

---

[27] Regan (2015).

[28] Ashworth and Zedner (2014), p. 130.

[29] For an analysis of the requirements of consent in EU data protection, see Article 29 Data Protection Working Party (2011); European Data Protection Board (2020); Kosta (2013); Kotschy (2020).

[30] Christakis et al. (2022), p. 13.

identity verification more seamless but only for those that accept such a processing. In smart cities, FRT could thus facilitate the purchase of tickets on public transport or speed up queues in public venues such as airports or postal services. Nonetheless, there are some grey areas, like border control, where it is not clear if the processing should still be based on consent or rather on public interest. In France, for example, EU citizens in airports and stations may voluntarily use the PARAFE biometric system to authenticate themselves while crossing borders.[31] The basis chosen for this processing is consent while its purpose is defined in Article R. 232-6 of the French Code of Internal Security, which provides that PARAFE "is intended, for *voluntary* air, sea and rail travellers, to *improve* and *facilitate* police controls at external borders".[32] In this context, the legal basis does not seem to grasp all the objectives of the operation, which exceed providing more comfort to travelers but have public interest (or even law enforcement purposes).[33] This ambiguity is further highlighted by the fact that, while the processing is grounded on data subjects' consent, it still needs an additional legal basis as it were based only on a public interest or law enforcement ground. In fact, foreseeability reasons impose that when authorities use FRT in public, the sensitive nature of processing and the context of application require that the operation is grounded in a clear and accessible law[34] which clarifies—inter alia—the voluntary participation in the processing. To satisfy the requirement of specific consent, however, the legal basis shall clearly inform individuals of the possible reuses of the data in other domains, in such a way that they fully understand all the consequences (and dangers) of submitting their biometric data.

Secondly, selecting consent as the legal basis for data processing in public is problematic for assessing the authenticity of data subjects' choices. In smart cities, FRT could simplify many activities for citizens leading a hectic lifestyle, allowing for example to buy tickets on public transportation or speed up queues in postal services and any other venue where identity verification is mandatory. Nonetheless, data subjects may not really understand the dynamics underlying the processing of their biometric data in such circumstances. It is unavoidable indeed that tension exists between improving services and making sure informed consent is granted: the more the information about the processing is accurate and lengthy, the more time-consuming authentication becomes. It is true that, differently from data collection by sensors,[35] citizens may choose to opt out of FRT processing. However, this may come at the cost of losing precious time, meaning that people may agree to go on with FRT authentication for convenience reasons but without a full understanding of its implications. One solution to this problem could be "anticipating" the provision of information in various ways. For instance, pre-enrolment in an FRT

[31] Ibid., p. 16.

[32] Emphasis added.

[33] *Contra* Christakis et al. (2022), p. 16.

[34] Christofi and Wauters, p. 50.

[35] Ibid., pp. 24–25; Kitchin (2016), p. 9.

authentication program should require assimilating background information (e.g., through small videos) a significant timeframe before the processing.[36] Likewise, public-facing initiatives could also assist public authorities in educating citizens on the implications of FRT and may be crucial for the future success of FRT initiatives. In fact, as shown by Alphabet's Sidewalk Labs experience in Toronto,[37] keeping citizens in the dark about the key features of smart city projects may cause public backlash and ultimately lead to their failure.

Even where consent is the right legal basis and is genuinely given by the data subject, a third problem arises with regard to the extent of the proportionality assessment. It is unclear whether and to which extent DPAs can censure the proportionality of the processing when data subjects have already assessed its means and purpose on their own. Any intrusion in this evaluation might conceal paternalistic attitudes and have problematic implications in smart cities, where patronizing attitudes toward the use of technologies are widespread.[38] Thus, in order to maximise user consent, it can be argued that DPAs should refrain from strictly assessing the legitimacy of FRT uses in relation to their *purposes*, thus leaving individuals the choice of whether or not to rely on the technology, even for trivial objectives (e.g. convenience). Conversely, DPAs should retain more discretion in assessing the *means* of FRT processing, ensuring that it remains within the limits of what is strictly necessary. Both aspects are examined below.

About the purpose of the processing, one could wonder whether using FRT at all merely to improve public services is acceptable in smart cities. In data protection, the Court of Justice of the European Union (CJEU) has considered that fostering performance in the public sector is a legitimate goal for the processing.[39] In the commercial domain as well, the French and Belgian DPAs have accepted that using FRT to achieve user comfort can meet the strict necessity test.[40] This could have ramifications for smart cities too, although in a context where public and private (i.e., economic) objectives overlap, as urban services are often delivered with public-private partnerships (PPPs).[41] In this context, indeed, DPAs seem to follow a similar approach even where the use of the technology in public places has strong

[36] A similar solution was proposed in relation to IoT sensors collecting data in public places. In particular, it was suggested that smart city services may equip lampposts and trams with QR codes redirecting data subjects to privacy policies or information campaigns. However, it is dubious whether individuals would dedicate time to read them while rushing to work or to buy groceries, as suggested by Christofi and Wauters, p. 27, that is why it would be important to anticipate somehow the provision of such information.

[37] Goodman and Powles (2019).

[38] Ranchordás (2020).

[39] Cf. Judgment in *Heinz Huber v Bundesrepublik Deutschland*, C-524/06 ECLI:EU:C:2008:724, §62.

[40] This was the case in the Molenbeek stadium trial and in the MONA project, see Christakis et al. (2022), pp. 25–26, mentioned above. For more on the strict necessity test, see chapter 'Facial Recognition in Public Spaces and the Principle of Necessity' in this volume by Jasserand.

[41] On PPPs, see Savas (2000); Vutsova (2014).

commercial connotations.[42] This could translate also for the use of FRT for authentication purposes, where citizens consent to the biometric processing in the framework of public services provided by private actors according to their corporate logic. In this way, however, citizens may be increasingly treated as *consumers* who experience different levels of services depending on how much data they decide to provide to the administration. Therefore, there might emerge legal and societal issues on the accessibility and quality of public services,[43] which compels public authorities to remain attentive to the collective implications of introducing such technologies to access public services. Specifically, they shall ensure that FRT simply enhances performance but does not affect the core service for those who do not consent to biometric processing. Again, to achieve more legitimacy at the collective level, these issues should be discussed within the citizenship, for instance, through participatory data protection impact assessments (DPIAs). In fact, Article 35(9) GDPR provides that "[w]here appropriate, the controller shall seek the views of data subjects or their representatives on the intended processing, without prejudice to the protection of commercial or public interests or the security of processing operations". Although this provision leaves wide discretion to the controllers in deciding whether to carry out participatory DPIAs,[44] the Belgian DPA has indicated that involving data subjects may not be entirely optional: the nature, context, scope, and purpose of the processing could make the consultation necessary,[45] although no further guidelines were given on the modalities of such an initiative. Participatory DPIAs may be a tool for controllers to be more transparent about the implications of the processing,[46] understand data subjects' potential concerns,[47] and examine all possible risks through the inputs of different segments of the population,[48] thus vesting the technology with greater democratic legitimacy.[49] Thus, in smart cities,

[42]This emerged, for instance, in a case where the company *JCDecaux France* lodged an authorisation request before the CNIL to implement a Wi-Fi tracking system in the esplanade of *La Défence* to measure pedestrian fluxes in the square. The project aimed at optimising the prices to promote adverts on the billboards in the esplanade, but it had public implications too, as the billboards also displayed messages for the public and were installed in a public place. In its decision, the CNIL recognized the legitimacy of the economic goals pursued by *JCDecaux France*. See *Délibération n° 2015-255 du 16 juillet 2015 refusant la mise en oeuvre par la société JCDecaux d'un traitement automatisé de données à caractère personnel ayant pour finalité de tester une méthodologie d'estimation quantitative des flux piétons sur la dalle de La Défense (demande d'autorisation n° 1833589).*

[43]On this issue, see Ranchordás (2018).

[44]Christofi et al. (2022), p. 504.

[45]Commission de la Protection de la Vie Privée (CPVP) (2018), §82.

[46]Irish Data Protection Commission (2019), p. 13; Agencia española de protección datos (2019), p. 149.

[47]Irish Data Protection Commission (2019), p. 13; Agencia española de protección datos (2019), p. 149.

[48]Commission de la Protection de la Vie Privée (2018), §82.

[49]On the relationship between FRT and democracy values, see chapter 'Facial Recognition Technologies: Threats or Opportunities for Democracy?' in this volume by Mobilio.

participatory DPIAs may serve not only to inform citizens of the technical features of the FRT but also of their impact on the accessibility of services. For instance, public authorities may address citizens' concerns by showing, preventively, that core service levels will not be affected for those who will not consent to the processing.

Conversely, proportionality should be strictly assessed when it comes to the *means* of the processing.[50] Specifically, this could be disproportionate if the processing involves people *other* than those who have consented. The EDPB stressed indeed that facial recognition checkpoints should be separated clearly, for example, by positioning them in gantries and avoiding that biometric templates of non-consenting people are collected.[51] Nonetheless, this requirement could make FRT authentication difficult in crowded venues, such as public transportation or squares, where other people's faces could easily be captured. In compliance with the *privacy-by-design* and *privacy-by-default* principles (Article 25 GDPR), such issues shall be addressed by private and public actors in the design phase of the project.

3 FRT and Public Interest to Detect Irregularities in Service Provision

Sometimes FRT is used for surveillance purposes beyond the law enforcement domain, such as to detect irregularities or little misbehavior in public facilities. In the US, for example, governments install facial recognition systems in public housing to spot violations of housing rules.[52] These aim to identify those who host guests overnight or misuse common facilities, like laundries, and identification could lead to negative consequences, such as fines or denied welfare benefits. In smart cities, we could imagine that biometric identification could be used to detect people who toss trash in parks and streets or do not respect recycling rules. In China, for example, FRTs are employed to identify and fine those who commit jaywalking, although such use would hardly be allowed in the EU under the new rules regulating artificial intelligence.[53]

Because in this case people do not consent to the biometric processing, the legal basis for such operation shall be public interest (Article 9(2)(g) GDPR). The proportionality assessment thus plays a crucial role when scrutinizing the legitimacy of the processing. As laid down in Article 52 CFREU, the proportionality assessment

---

[50] Christakis et al. (2022), p. 27.

[51] European Data Protection Board (2019), p. 20.

[52] MacMillan (2023).

[53] Cf. Article 5(1)(h) and (2–8) of the Regulation (EU) 2024/1689 of the European Parliament and of the Council of 13 June 2024 laying down harmonised rules on artificial intelligence and amending Regulations (EC) No 300/2008, (EU) No 167/2013, (EU) No 168/2013, (EU) 2018/858, (EU) 2018/1139 and (EU) 2019/2144 and Directives 2014/90/EU, (EU) 2016/797 and (EU) 2020/1828 (Artificial Intelligence Act).

first requires that a measure limiting fundamental rights is provided by the law and genuinely meets objectives of general interests recognized by the Union or the need to protect the rights and freedoms of others. The measure must also respect the essence of the rights, and be both necessary and proportionate to the objectives pursued.[54]

To establish whether the deployment of FRT to detect irregularities in public services may be proportionate under a public interest basis, I consider the case of such technologies applied to control the use of facilities in public housing where access is restricted to residents only. A preliminary issue to be examined is whether the right to privacy applies to this specific context[55] and, if so, what is the seriousness of the interference.

In relation to this problem, a relevant factor to take into account is whether the interference occurs in a public or private setting.[56] In the urban geography and privacy scholarship, the separation between public and private places does not revolve around the ownership regime of a given location but its accessibility by individuals.[57] Therefore, even if a space—for example, a shopping center—is privately owned, it should still be considered a public place if it is freely accessible by everyone. Conversely, individuals may claim to have an expectation of privacy in their offices, even if these are located in publicly owned premises like university buildings. In fact, there might be cases where there is an overlap between the public and private nature of the space, such as in publicly accessible places such as cafés and restaurants, where people may engage in private activities by retreating into their mental bubbles or having private conversations with friends.[58] Similar semi-private zones also include closed-off spaces where individuals may have some expectation

---

[54] EU data protection authorities have published studies to guide on the right interpretation of the essence of the right criterion, see González Fuster (2022); the necessity test, see European Data Protection Supervisor (2017); and the proportionality test, see European Data Protection Supervisor (2019). On technical solutions to make FRT compliant with the proportionality principle, see chapter 'Technical Solutions for a Proportional Use of Facial Recognition Technology' in this volume by Menéndez González.

[55] Conversely, as argued by Edwards (2016), p. 40, data protection law is not affected by "any crucial private/public distinction". Moreover, whether this application would be permissible under the AI Act, is different issue. Article 5 of the Regulation bans this practice only where carried out in a 'publicly accessible space and for law enforcement purposes, unless the specific conditions of paragraphs (2–7) apply. Recital 19 of the Regulation clarifies the notion of 'publicly accessible space' in similar terms as the scholarship outlined above. In particular, a space shall be considered publicly accessible if, regardless of its ownership regime, it can be accessed by an "undetermined number of natural persons". Because in the example proposed the buildings are not accessible by an indeterminate number of people, the deployment of an identification system shall not be considered to be *per se* against the Regulation.

[56] Since classical times, people have perceived the existence of a dividing line between the public and private (Westin 2018 original work of 1967) and, in the privacy domain, the separation between private and public places is still one of the most relevant for establishing the mechanisms of its legal protection Koops et al. (2017).

[57] Altman and Zube (1989); Ruppert (2006).

[58] Koops (2018), pp. 647–648.

of secrecy or discretion, such as in toilets, changing cubicles, hotel or hospital rooms, and library desks.[59]

In the case under consideration, the common facilities (e.g., the laundry and the garden) of a public housing building are an example of a space where both private and public elements converge. Such facilities are located in a closed-off space where users may expect to carry out their chores or spend their free time privately, away from the eyes of non-residents. However, the level of secrecy experienced in these venues is not as high as that of the home, because the facilities are likely located in an open space within the infrastructure to be shared with the rest of the residents, who might thus intrude on each other's private activities. Moreover, there is also a public interest in the right management of such facilities as far as energy consumption and facility deterioration are concerned, as the infrastructure is publicly funded. Therefore, while residents may expect to have some expectation of privacy in such venues, these cannot be considered very high.

We shall see how such expectations are assessed in the European human rights framework, and what is their impact on the proportionality assessment, by relying on the theory of reasonable expectations of privacy endorsed by the ECtHR.

When the applicant claims that a privacy violation occurred in public, Strasbourg relies on the reasonable expectations of privacy test to establish if, in that specific case, Article 8 of the Convention applies beyond the strict boundaries of the 'home'.[60] The concept of reasonable expectations of privacy, although elaborated in the jurisprudence of the United States Supreme Court, has also been integrated into the case law of the ECtHR.[61] The Court acknowledges that there is "a zone of interaction of a person with others, even in a public context, which may fall within the scope of 'private life'".[62] The right to live a 'private social life' extends to a variety of public settings, including the workplace: for example, in *Antović and Mirković v. Montenegro*, the Court contended that two professors could claim an expectation of privacy against the video surveillance carried out at their university, as this represented a place "where they not only [taught] students, but also interact [ed] with them, thus developing mutual relations and constructing their social identity".[63]

[59] Ibid., pp. 643–644.

[60] See, e.g., ECtHR, *Peck v. the United Kingdom,* judgment of 28 January 2003, App. no. 44647/98, §58; ECtHR, 5 September 2017, *Bărbulescu v. Romania*, App. no. 61496/08, §73; ECtHR, *Benedik v. Slovenia,* judgment of 24 April 2018, App. no. 62357/14, §101; ECtHR, *López Ribalda and Others v. Spain,* judgment of 17 October 2019, App. nos. 1874/13 and 8567/13, §89.

[61] ECtHR, *P.G. and J. H. v. United Kingdom,* judgment of 25 September 2001, App. no. 44787/98, §56; ECtHR, *Peck v. the United Kingdom,* §57. In the US context, *compare* USSC, *Katz v. United* States, 389 U.S. 347, 351 (1967) and *Carpenter v. United States*, 585 U.S._(2018).

[62] ECtHR, *P.G. and J. H. v. United Kingdom,* judgment of 25 September 2001, App. no. 44787/98, §56; ECtHR, *Peck v. the United Kingdom,* §57.

[63] ECtHR, *Antović and Mirković v. Montenegro,* judgment of 28 February 2018, App. no. 70838/13, §44.

Although the reasonable expectation of privacy test is not carried out consistently, a review of the relevant case law highlights that the ECtHR usually relies on a set of criteria to assess the seriousness of the interference in public, such as: the relevant regulatory framework (e.g., legal rules, principles, workplace instructions, acceptable uses of the data); the characteristics of the individual targeted by the surveillance; the activity intercepted by the operation; the means of employed in the surveillance, as far as they are relevant for how the data will further be used; the place and time of surveillance.

For instance, concerning the relevant legal framework, the instructions given by the employer about the surveillance carried out in the workplace are relevant to determine the level of privacy expectations,[64] although they cannot exclude the applicability of the right to privacy altogether.[65] Public figures do not enjoy the same expectations of privacy in public, while people in a situation of vulnerability, such as in *Peck,* might claim a higher level of protection.[66] The Court also considers the public or private nature of the activity subject to surveillance, downsizing—or sometimes even excluding[67]—privacy expectations when the actions do not bear any intimate nature. For example, in the Grand Chamber judgment *López-Ribalda and Others v. Spain,* the Court assessed the legitimacy of a covert video surveillance system implemented in a supermarket. When assessing the level of privacy expectations of the employees, the Court observed that a "supermarket [...] was open to the public and [...] the activities filmed there, namely the taking of payments for purchases by the customers, were not of an intimate or private nature. Their expectation as to the protection of their private life was thus necessarily limited".[68] This assessment suggests that also the physical features of the space where the surveillance occurs are relevant in the test, as further argued by the Court: "[The expectation of privacy] is very high in places which are private by nature, such as toilets or cloakrooms, where heightened protection, or even a complete ban on video-surveillance, is justified [...]. It remains high in closed working areas such as offices. It is manifestly lower in places that are visible or accessible to colleagues or, as in the present case, to the general public".[69] As for the means of surveillance, Strasbourg arguably tends to take a neutral approach, making no distinction between surveillance through analogical and digital means. What seems to be relevant is whether the technologies used rely on the (automated) processing of personal data

[64] Cf. ECtHR, 25 June 1997, *Halford v. United Kingdom,* App. no. 20605/92, §45; ECtHR, 3 April 2007, *Copland v. United Kingdom*, App. no. 62617/00, §42; ECtHR, *Bărbulescu v. Romania*, §78; ECtHR, *López Ribalda and Others v. Spain*, §93; ECtHR, *Akhlyustin v. Russia*, §39.

[65] Cf. ECtHR, *Bărbulescu v. Romania*, §80; ECtHR, *Antović and Mirković v. Montenegro*, §44.

[66] ECtHR, *Peck v. the United Kingdom,* §62.

[67] Cf. ECommHR, 19 May 1994, *Friedl v. Austria*, App. no. 15225/89 (referred to the participation to anti-government demonstration) and ECtHR, 24 November 2009, *Friend and Others v. United Kingdom*, App. nos. 16072/06 and 27809/08, §43 (referred to the case of a fox hunt carried out in open fields).

[68] ECtHR, *López Ribalda and Others v. Spain*, §89.

[69] ECtHR, *López Ribalda and Others v. Spain*, §125.

and if they can generate a permanent record of the operations.[70] In *Glukhin*, specifically, the ECtHR found that privacy considerations arise especially when a person's picture is captured by the camera, as the image represents one of the chief attributes of the personality.[71] For an interference with privacy to arise, however, it might also be necessary that the data is further used to identify the target of surveillance.[72] This emerged, for instance, in *Friedl*, where the Commission excluded that the applicant's right to private life had been at stake because police forces had never taken the initiative to identify him from his photographs.[73]

Continuing with the example proposed, it is important to highlight that, although public housing regulations may forbid the presence of non-residents or the unreasonable use of common facilities, such rules cannot reduce to zero the privacy expectations of the residents in relation to their social interactions and daily chores. Activities such as doing the laundry or spending free time with friends still bear a private nature with regard to the other residents and public administrators, even if they are carried out in open spaces within the infrastructure. Moreover, it should be underlined that, although there is a public interest in the right management of the facilities, these do not raise the same concerns as high-risk areas like airports, stations, and other overcrowded venues. Surveillance in public housing may also systematically target people belonging to the poorest segments of the population, who could be further penalized due to the violation of housing rules.

Against this background, the interference with privacy rights shall be considered serious and calls for a strict approach in the proportionality assessment.

Under the proportionality principle, biometric processing of several non-consenting individuals would not be justified only to detect minor irregularities and improve resource management in public housing facilities. At the outset, it might be difficult to assess whether such interference violates the essence of the residents' privacy rights, as this requirement is assessed only on a case-by-case basis by the CJEU,[74] and was never analyzed in this context. It may be argued that, as long as the interference occurs in a semi-public setting and not within a fully private space, this might not violate the essence of the right to privacy of those involved. Regardless of the outcome of this first evaluation, however, the lack of proportionality of FRT surveillance in this context emerges with the other requirements of the test. In fact, even admitting that FRT is an appropriate means to attain the public

---

[70] ECtHR, *Perry v. United Kingdom*, §38; ECtHR, *P.G. and J. H. v. United Kingdom,* §57; ECtHR, *Peck v. the United Kingdom,* §59 (and cited jurisprudence).

[71] ECtHR, *Glukhin v. Russia*, App no 11519/20, 4 July 2023, §66, commented by Neroni Rezende (2023); Palmiotto and Menéndez González (2023).

[72] ECtHR, *Perry v. United Kingdom*, §38; ECtHR, *Leander v. Sweden*, judgment of 26 March 1987, App. no. 9248/81, §48; ECtHR, 16 February 2000, *Amann v. Switzerland*, App. no. 27798/95, §§65–67; ECtHR, 4 May 2000, *Rotaru v. Romania*, App. no. 28341/95, §§43–44.

[73] See ECtHR, *Peck v. the United Kingdom,* §61.

[74] Brkan (2018); González Fuster (2022), p. 8; Ojanen (2016), p. 326. Conversely, this requirement is not mentioned in Article 8(2) ECHR and is rarely used by the ECtHR.

interest pursued, the processing would fall short of the strict necessity and proportionality *stricto sensu* requirements, as argued below.

Concerning the first aspect, to argue that FRT is strictly necessary, public authorities should demonstrate that CCTV surveillance, as well as other tracking instruments like RFID cards, are not enough to address entry control and efficiency needs in resource management. Likely, it would be difficult to provide such evidence in restricted environments like public housing facilities, where residents are registered and known to the administrators. Such venues do pose the same risks as unrestricted environments, where security needs may require identifying people in large crowds. Moreover, in terms of strict proportionality, a *human-rights* approach to the smart city would require prioritizing fundamental rights in the balancing between privacy expectations and the need for efficiency. For instance, for an identification system to work, a centralized database of residents' pictures would have to be created and fed to the machine. Arguably, such invasive surveillance would be disproportionate if used only to detecting minor misbehavior. In addition, an identification system may disproportionally target vulnerable people, like the poor, the undereducated, the homeless, and those belonging to ethnic minorities, who might be overrepresented in similar venues. As known indeed, FRT performs badly with women and people of color,[75] posing a significant risk of discrimination that may not be counterbalanced by the public interest pursued.

In conclusion, differently from the examples shown in Sect. 2, the use of FRT to regulate access to public services would hardly reconcile with proportionality when the surveillance pursues a public interest beyond the law enforcement domain. Overall, then, this analysis suggests that FRT may be implemented very differently in smart city scenarios and that the assessment of its legitimacy should be molded accordingly.

4 Conclusions

This chapter aimed to shed light on the legitimate uses of FRT to access public services. The context chosen for the analysis was the *human-rights* smart city, which aims to reproduce an adequate balance of values between innovation needs and fundamental rights like privacy and data protection. The assessment further considered how FRT contribute to the efficiency of a service, i.e., by improving crowd flows or detecting irregularities. From a data protection perspective, this choice affects the legal basis and subsequent proportionality assessment. The analysis conducted highlights that FRT can be leveraged only to improve the "customer experience" of those who agree with the processing. This, however, does not exempt smart city bodies from all responsibilities. These should continue to make efforts to gather *meaningful* consent and exclude the fortuitous collection of other biometric

[75] Castelvecchi (2020), p. 348.

templates. Conversely, using FRT to detect irregularities in welfare services imposes a stricter proportionality assessment that excludes its legitimacy in democratic societies. Ultimately, it seems that such initiatives implement surveillance mechanisms that are incompatible with the *human-rights* approach to the smart city.

References

Agencia española de protección datos (2019) Gestión del riesgo y evaluación de impacto en tratamientos de datos personales.

Albino V, Berardi U, Dangelico RM (2015) Smart cities: definitions, dimensions, performance, and initiatives. J Urban Technol 22:3–21. https://doi.org/10.1080/10630732.2014.942092

Altman I, Zube EH (eds) (1989) Public places and spaces. Plenum Press, New York

Article 29 Data Protection Working Party, Opinion 15/2011 on the definition of consent, 2011

Ashworth A, Zedner L (2014) Preventive justice, 1st edn. Oxford University Press, Oxford

Baudino H (2019) Reconnaissance faciale dans les lycées: la fin justifie-telle les moyens ? numériqueétique.fr

Brkan M (2018) The concept of essence of fundamental rights in the EU legal order: peeling the onion to its core. Eur Const Law Rev 14:332–368. https://doi.org/10.1017/S1574019618000159

Cardullo P, Kitchin R (2019) Smart urbanism and smart citizenship: the neoliberal logic of 'citizen-focused' smart cities in Europe. Environ Plan C Polit Space 37:813–830. https://doi.org/10.1177/0263774X18806508

Castelvecchi D (2020) Beating biometric bias. Nature 587:347–349

Christakis T et al (2022) Mapping the use of facial recognition in public spaces in Europe - Part. 3: Facial recognition for authorisation purposes

Christofi A, Wauters E. Smart cities and the data protection framework in context

Christofi A, Breuer J, Wauters E et al (2022) Data protection, control and participation beyond consent - seeking the views of data subjects in data protection impact assessments. In: Kosta E, Leenes R, Kamara I (eds) Research handbook on EU data protection law. Edward Elgar Publishing, pp 503–529

Clifford D, Ausloos J (2018) Data protection and the role of fairness. Yearb Eur Law 37:130–187

Cocchia A (2014) Smart and digital city: a systematic literature review. In: Dameri RP, Rosenthal-Sabroux C (eds) Smart city. Springer International Publishing, Cham, pp 13–43

Commission de la Protection de la Vie Privée (CPVP) (2018) Recommandation d'initiative concernant l'analyse d'impact relative à la protection des données et la consultation préalable, (CO-AR-2018-001).

Cresswell T (2004) Place: a short introduction. Blackwell Pub, Malden

De Hert P, Gutwirth S (2006) Privacy, data protection and law enforcement: opacity of the individual and transparency of power. In: Claes E, Duff A, Gutwirth S (eds) Privacy and the criminal law. Intersentia, Antwerp-Oxford, pp 61–104

De Waal M (2017) A city is not a galaxy. In: Kitchin R, Lauriault TP, McArdle G (eds) Data and the city, vol 2018, 1st edn. Routledge, Abingdon, Oxon; New York, pp 17–30

del Castillo C (2019) Madrid probará el pago con reconocimiento facial en autobuses públicos. elDiario.es.

Edwards L (2016) Privacy, security and data protection in smart cities: a critical EU law perspective. Eur Data Prot Law Rev 2:28–58

European Data Protection Board, Guidelines 3/2019 on processing of personal data through video devices, 2019

European Data Protection Board, Guidelines 05/2020 on consent under Regulation 2016/679, 2020

European Data Protection Supervisor, Assessing the necessity of measures that limit the fundamental right to the protection of personal data: A Toolkit, 11 April 2017
European Data Protection Supervisor, EDPS Guidelines on assessing the proportionality of measures that limit the fundamental rights to privacy and to the protection of personal data, 19 December 2019
Gellert R (2016) We have always managed risks in data protection law. Eur Data Prot Law Rev 2: 481–492. https://doi.org/10.21552/EDPL/2016/4/7
Gentzel M (2021) Biased face recognition technology used by government: a problem for liberal democracy. Philos Technol 34:1639–1663. https://doi.org/10.1007/s13347-021-00478-z
Goodman EP, Powles J (2019) Urbanism under Google: lessons from Sidewalk Toronto. SSRN Electron J. https://doi.org/10.2139/ssrn.3390610
González Fuster G (2022) Study on the essence of the fundamental rights to privacy and to protection of personal data, EDPS 2021/0932.
Hollands RG (2008) Will the real smart city please stand up?: Intelligent, progressive or entrepreneurial? City 12:303–320. https://doi.org/10.1080/13604810802479126
Horgan-Jones J (2020) Facial recognition used in public services card programme, department says. Ir Times
Hubbard P, Kitchin R (eds) (2011) Key thinkers on space and place, 2nd edn. Sage, Los Angeles
Irish Data Protection Commission (2019) Guide to Data Protection Impact Assessments (DPIAs).
Kitchin R (2016) The ethics of smart cities and urban science. Philos Trans R Soc Math Phys Eng Sci 374:20160115. https://doi.org/10.1098/rsta.2016.0115
Kitchin R, Coletta C, Leighton E, Liam H (2019) Creating smart cities. In: Creating smart cities, 1st edn. Routlege
Koops B-J (2014) The trouble with European data protection law. Int Data Priv Law 4:250–261. https://doi.org/10.1093/idpl/ipu023
Koops B-J (2018) Privacy spaces. W Va Law Rev 121:611–666
Koops B-J, Galic M (2017) Conceptualizing space and place: lessons from geography for the debate on privacy in public. In: Timan T, Newell BC, Koops B-J (eds) Privacy in public space: conceptual and regulatory challenges. Edward Elgar Publishing, pp 19–46
Koops B-J, Newell BC, Timan T et al (2017) A typology of privacy. Univ Pa J Int Law 38:483–575
Kosta E (2013) Consent in European data protection law. Brill | Nijhoff
Kotschy W (2020) Article 6. Lawfulness of processing. In: Kuner C, Bygrave LA, Docksey C (eds) The EU General Data Protection Regulation (GDPR): a commentary. Oxford University Press, pp 321–344
Kummitha RKR, Crutzen N (2017) How do we understand smart cities? An evolutionary perspective. Cities 67:43–52. https://doi.org/10.1016/j.cities.2017.04.010
Lohr S (2018) Facial Recognition Is Accurate, if You're a White Guy. New York Times.
Madanipour A (2003) Public and private spaces of the city. Routlege, London and New York
Malgieri G (2020) The concept of fairness in the GDPR: a linguistic and contextual interpretation. In: Proceedings of the 2020 Conference on Fairness, Accountability, and Transparency. ACM, Barcelona Spain, pp 154–166
Neroni Rezende IN (2020) Facial recognition in police hands: assessing the 'Clearview case' from a European perspective. New J Eur Crim Law 11:375–389. https://doi.org/10.1177/2032284420948161
Neroni Rezende I (2022) Facial recognition for preventive purposes: the human rights implications of detecting emotions in public spaces. In: Bachmaier Winter L, Ruggeri S (eds) Investigating and preventing crime in the digital era. Springer International Publishing, Cham, pp 67–98
Neroni Rezende I (2023) Glukhin and the EU regulation of facial recognition: lessons to be learned? Eur Law Blog
Ojanen T (2016) Making the Essence of Fundamental Rights Real: The Court of Justice of the European Union Clarifies the Structure of Fundamental Rights under the Charter: ECJ 6 October 2015, Case C-362/14, Maximillian Schrems v Data Protection Commissioner. Eur Const Law Rev 12:318–329. https://doi.org/10.1017/S1574019616000225

O'Murchu C (2021) Facial recognition cameras arrive in UK school canteens. Financial Times.
Palmiotto F, Menéndez González NM (2023) Facial recognition technology, democracy and human rights. Comput Law Secur Rev 50:105857. https://doi.org/10.1016/j.clsr.2023.105857
Ranchordás S (2018) Citizens as consumers in the data economy. EuCML 4
Ranchordás S (2020) Nudging citizens through technology in smart cities. Int Rev Law Comput Technol 34:254–276. https://doi.org/10.1080/13600869.2019.1590928
Regan PM (2015) Privacy and the common good: revisited. In: Roessler B, Mokrosinska D (eds) Social dimensions of privacy, 1st edn. Cambridge University Press, pp 50–70
Ruppert ES (2006) Rights to public space: regulatory reconfigurations of liberty. Urban Geogr 27: 271–292. https://doi.org/10.2747/0272-3638.27.3.271
Savas (2000) Privatization and public-private partnerships. Sage Publications
Smith M, Miller S (2022) The ethical application of biometric facial recognition technology. AI Soc 37:167–175. https://doi.org/10.1007/s00146-021-01199-9
Vanolo A (2013) Smartmentality: the smart city as disciplinary strategy. Urban Stud 51:883–898. https://doi.org/10.1177/0042098013494427
van Zeeland DJ, Breuer J, Christophi A, Pierson J (2019) Personal data protection in smart cities: Roundtable report: for Chair 'Data Protection on the Ground'.
Vutsova A (2014) The role of public-private partnership for effective technology transfer. Appl Technol Innov 10:83–90. https://doi.org/10.15208/ati.2014.14
Westin A (2018) Privacy and freedom. Ig Publishing
Ziosi M, Hewitt B, Juneja P et al (2022) Smart cities: reviewing the debate about their ethical implications. AI Soc. https://doi.org/10.1007/s00146-022-01558-0

From Identity to Emotional Dominance? "Early Warnings" on Emotion Recognition Uses by Police Forces

Francesco Paolo Levantino

Abstract While AI-based technologies designed to analyse inner states—including human emotions—are spreading across different domains, this chapter points at some "early warnings" regarding the use of emotion recognition technology by police forces. The chapter opens by emphasising key factors contributing to this emerging trend, including the growing use of facial recognition and other biometric-based tools in the post-09/11 security era. In fact, these technologies have significantly shifted police forces' approach from reactive responses to crimes that have already been committed to proactive monitoring and surveillance practices. In this context, the integration of emotion recognition and similar technologies into existing surveillance infrastructures could serve well public authorities by flagging suspicious individuals and behaviours. However, such technologies and their uses in this sensitive domain create significant interferences with international and European human rights law standards. This chapter proceeds by identifying a broad range of interferences through the concept of "emotional dominance" and presents the risks it poses to democratic societies. It then uses the right to privacy and the right to the protection of personal data as a framework to highlight the severity of these interferences, suggesting that they may challenge the inviolable core of these rights, as well as the respect for human dignity. In framing these issues, the chapter draws on relevant definitions and provisions in EU secondary legislation that is functional to the protection of these rights, including the recently adopted AI Act. This contribution concludes by emphasising that, while there is a strong case for asserting the inconsistency of emotion recognition used for monitoring purposes by police forces with the frameworks discussed, reactive approaches may be inadequate in light of the rapid adoption of these tools and the severity of the risks they pose. In this regard, there is a growing interest towards complementary *ex ante* protection mechanisms, such as fundamental rights impact assessments and AI literacy obligations. Although these mechanisms are highly regarded, at this stage, they do not

F. P. Levantino (✉)
Sant'Anna School of Advanced Studies, DIRPOLIS Institute (Institute of Law, Politics and Development), Pisa, Italy
e-mail: f.levantino@santannapisa.it

N. Menéndez González, G. Mobilio (eds.), *Next Democratic Frontiers for Facial Recognition Technology (FRT)*, Law, Governance and Technology Series 74,
https://doi.org/10.1007/978-3-031-89794-8_8

seem to be adequate solutions to prevent individuals and democratic societies from sleepwalking into a reality where even our emotions could become a source of discrimination, criminalisation, and social control.

Keywords Emotion recognition · Surveillance · Security · Law enforcement · Fundamental rights

1 Biometrics in Action: Setting the Stage

The question "how do you feel today?" embodies several assumptions about human nature. It presupposes that humans are generally aware of their feelings and emotions, recognises that these states can change over time, and acknowledges that others can perceive our emotional states and their variations by observing physical and behavioural clues. Yet, as technology advances, humankind seems to no longer have any monopoly on the perception and interpretation of feelings and emotions. Today, different sub-fields of Artificial Intelligence (AI)—affective computing, in particular—enable the "recognition" of emotional states such as anger, disgust, fear, happiness, sadness, and surprise through the analysis of physical, physiological or behavioural attributes.[1] Among others, these attributes encompass our characteristic facial features or expressions, voice prints, gait, and eye movements[2]—or a combination of these or other factors.

As these technologies increasingly permeate various domains, the degree of intrusiveness associated to their deployment by Law Enforcement Agencies (LEAs) can be considered as contributing to blurring the lines that separate their powers and activities from those traditionally reserved for the military or intelligence agencies.[3] In this connection, it is essential to recognise that these public bodies perform inherently different functions. And some of their operations are guided by distinct paradigms and logics, sometimes even falling under different bodies of law, such as international human rights law and international humanitarian law.[4]

The converge among these and other elements—analysed in more detail later—finds symbolic expression in urban environments increasingly equipped with sensors, also for security purposes.[5] In that context, this analysis sees the AI-driven

[1]McStay (2018), pp. 20–21; Clifford (2024), p. 3.

[2]Ienca and Malgieri (2022), p. 3.

[3]Haggerty and Ericson (1999); Malgieri and De Hert (2017).

[4]Melzer and Gaggioli Gasteyger (2015); see also Levantino *(forthcoming)*.

[5]Sadowski and Pasquale (2015); see also Melgaço and van Brakel (2021) on the symbolic use of surveillance practices in smart cities, turning them into "surveillance theatres". See chapter 'FRT and Access to Public Services: What Acceptable Uses in Smart Cities?' in this volume by Neroni Rezende.

"disembodiment"[6] and parallel "objectification"[7] of inner states—like emotions, mental states, personality traits or intentions—as intensifying the traditional tension between security needs and fundamental freedoms, civil rights, and democratic values. Thus, calling into question the very foundations of the international and European human rights frameworks, especially in relation to human dignity as a legal concept, a meta-principle,[8] and a standalone right[9] which 'is [also] to be considered while interpreting other human rights', including the right to privacy.[10]

From these premises, this chapter aims at providing some "early warnings" on risks associated with deployments of emotion recognition and similar tools by LEAs. In Sect. 2, it examines some paradigm shifts following events like 09/11 and other factors shaping the evolution of LEAs' surveillance and security practices. With these changes being considered as conducive to the growing interest in, and adoption of, biometric-based tools by LEAs. Section 3 opens by briefly highlighting the critical role of Facial Recognition Technology (FRT) in military operations under the Global War on Terrorism (GWOT). In fact, it will draw connections between the military concept of "identity dominance" consisting in armed forces' capacity to deny enemies anonymity and its application in domestic settings through LEAs uses of FRT. This Sect. will specifically link "identity dominance" with the chilling effects of widespread deployments of FRT, while examining broader implications for democratic societies. Considering potential variations of the "identity dominance" concept in view of the diffusion of Emotion Recognition Technology (ERT), Sect. 3 also outlines key components of a shift that could be defined as "emotional dominance". In Sect. 4, the implications of this development will be framed through the lenses of international and European human rights law, focusing specifically on the rights to privacy and the protection of personal data in relation to human dignity. These rights and relevant provisions of the recently adopted AI Act[11] will be used to point out critical issues surrounding ERT uses by police forces. Section 5 concludes the chapter by critically drawing together the most relevant threads and findings from the discussion, offering some final thoughts.

---

[6] Teo (2023), pp. 26 ff.

[7] On the concept of "objectification" in feminist theory, see Nussbaum (1995).

[8] Bublitz (2024).

[9] Teo (2024), p. 9.

[10] Le Moli (2021), p. 241.

[11] Regulation (EU) 2024/1689 of the European Parliament and of the Council of 13 June 2024 laying down harmonised rules on artificial intelligence and amending Regulations (EC) No 300/2008, (EU) No 167/2013, (EU) No 168/2013, (EU) 2018/858, (EU) 2018/1139 and (EU) 2019/2144 and Directives 2014/90/EU, (EU) 2016/797 and (EU) 2020/1828 (Artificial Intelligence Act).

2 Mixed Factors in the Materialisation of Surveillance and the Datafication of the Body After 09/11

Western conceptions of security were significantly impacted by dramatic events such as 09/11 and the terrorist attacks that struck Europe in the early 2000s.[12] These events demonstrated that threats to public and national security can materialise through actions involving "ordinary individuals", amidst the weaves of ordinary days. Initially conceived as emergency responses, surveillance and security measures have since stabilised in daily practices—'[t]he war on terror came home, and it walked in like it owned the place'.[13] Heightened vigilance became the *status quo*, and reactive investigative paradigms shifted towards vast-scale pre-emptive monitoring activities.[14] Nowadays 'peace is a coded [state of] war',[15] be it the general "war" against crime or the ever-emerging sector-specific "wars" on drugs, irregular migration, terrorism, and so forth.[16]

Surveillance practices now involve also 'groups which were previously exempt from routine surveillance',[17] making individuals more familiar with security rituals shaping daily life.[18] Among these, "visual surveillance" has gained *momentum*,[19] also encompassing the possibility of 'techno-visualis[ing] the intangible and invisible: mental thoughts directed at prospective or potential acts'.[20] In this direction, recent studies suggest that within 5–10 years, biometric-based systems will be more and more used to infer future behaviours and emotional states.[21] This trend already includes ERT applications for security purposes[22] or the assessment of the emotional states of customers and users in various settings—such as art exhibitions[23] and workout sessions.[24] Additionally, emotion recognition capabilities can be applied more extensively among users of headsets for Extended Reality (EX),[25] Brain-Computer Interfaces (BCI),[26] or AI-powered smart glasses.[27]

12 Lyon and Haggerty (2012); De Hert (2005).
13 Lozada (2021).
14 Wilson and McCulloch (2017).
15 Foucault (1997), pp. 50–51.
16 Cf. Andreas and Price (2001).
17 Haggerty and Ericson (2000), p. 606.
18 Balzacq et al. (2010).
19 De Hert and Bouchagiar (2022).
20 Pugliese (2012), p. 108.
21 Stockwell et al. (2024), p. 3.
22 Wright (2023).
23 Hermes Center (2021).
24 AlgorithmWatch (2021).
25 Hammond-Errey and Barrett (2024).
26 Ibid.
27 Ashworth (2024).

Despite growing awareness of these developments, individuals actively contribute to their own monitoring and surveillance[28] through "wearable" smart devices allowing the direct "extraction" of biometrics, vital metrics, and health-related data.[29] As an example of this continually evolving landscape, the company Emteq Labs recently developed the "Sense (smart)glasses" to monitor users' emotional states and link specific feelings to particular moments or events. Thus, allegedly making it easier for mental healthcare professionals to "understand" their patients' emotions and associate them with potential triggers for specific conditions.[30] Functions of this device, such as capturing images of what people are eating and monitoring the speed at which they chew, could also support nutrition specialists in treating patients with eating disorders.[31]

For now putting aside privacy and data protection concerns related to these developments, it is important to emphasise how the widespread integration of these technologies into consumer-grade devices is "acclimating" people to intrusive technologies, surveillance practices, and their normalisation.[32] At the same time, the benefits of advanced AI-based technologies in combating crime push for their adoption,[33] while some sectors of civil society have raised serious concerns, including calls to ban biometric mass surveillance.[34] In fact, given the significant impact of Biometric Identification Systems (BISs) on protected rights and freedoms, expert opinions on their use by LEAs remain divided.[35] Similarly, the views of both law enforcement professionals and the general public appear fragmented, with surveys revealing sharply opposing perspectives, even within the same respondent groups. Overall, these findings suggest increasing acceptance of biometric-based tools in the security sector.[36]

Yet, the mainstreaming of biometric-based tools—such as FRT—in this domain is not solely related to its widespread adoption among the general public, as also states' obligations under international law have driven the increased use of biometrics in law enforcement. This is the case of a binding resolution adopted under Chapter VII of the UN Charter by the Security Council of the United Nations (UNSC). In its 2017 Resolution 2396, the UNSC '[d]ecide[d]'—*inter alia*—that:

> Member States shall develop and implement systems to collect biometric data, [including] fingerprints, photographs, facial recognition, and other relevant identifying biometric data,

---

[28] Lyon (2018).

[29] Deerwater and Scarff (2021).

[30] Ashworth (2024).

[31] Ibid.

[32] Hartzog et al. (2024); Selinger and Rhee (2021).

[33] Gikay (2023).

[34] Reclaim your face (n.d.).

[35] Policing Insight (2024).

[36] Cf. Ada Lovelace Institute (2019); McStay (2020); Urquhart and Miranda (2021); AP4AI (2022); Policing Insight (2024); IE University (2024).

> in order to responsibly and properly identify terrorists, including foreign terrorist fighters, in compliance with domestic law and international human rights law […].[37]

In this connection, the former UN Special Rapporteur on the promotion and protection of human rights while countering terrorism, Fionnuala Ní Aoláin, reported to the UN General Assembly (UNGA) that before Resolution 2396 'States had no previous obligation under international law to set up watch lists [and] develop biometric databases'.[38] In this sense, specific criticisms emerged regarding the UNSC's inadequacy in addressing the human rights implications of similar measures—except for scattered references to international human rights law and "responsible practices".[39] In fact, as it will be briefly specified in the following Section, counter-terrorism efforts following 09/11 contributed to the expansion of biometric technologies uses from military contexts to national security uses, acting as a bridge for their further diffusion in general LEAs' practices. Today, many initiatives align with Resolution 2396 and go even further. Examples include INTERPOL and EUROPOL's creation of biometric databases for 'criminals, fugitives, [and] persons of interest',[40] while EU Member States such as Germany, the Netherlands, Poland, Belgium, France, Hungary and Italy are reported to have both legal and technical infrastructures for deploying FRT.[41]

After having mapped just some key factors contributing to the growing diffusion of biometric technologies in the post-9/11 security landscape and given the role such technologies played in the GWOT, the next Section connects the notion of chilling effects generated by FRT use in LEAs' practices with the heightened intrusiveness and deterrent impact that the mainstreaming of ERT by police forces could give rise to.

3 Beyond "Identity Dominance" in Military Deployments: Towards the Rise of "Emotional Dominance"?

In the military context, the concept of "identity dominance" originated as the 'operational capability to achieve an advantage over […] adversar[ies] by denying [them] the ability to mask [their] identity […]'.[42] The latter was widely operationalised in Afghanistan through the use of several BISs by US armed forces. Concerns over the large amount of sensitive data of local informants, activists, and journalists left in the hands of the Taliban following the US withdrawal of 2021 are,

[37] UNSC (2017), para. 15.

[38] Report of the Special Rapporteur on the promotion and protection of human rights and fundamental freedoms while countering terrorism (2018), paras. 29 ff.

[39] Ibid.

[40] INTERPOL (2020); Avramopoulos (2018).

[41] EDRi (2021); Ragazzi et al. (2021); Coluccini et al. (2024).

[42] CALL (2011), p. 71.

to some extent, side-effects of this phenomenon.[43] In that setting, FRT was originally deployed to enhance the safety of the US-led coalition by *verifying* identities before access to sensitive facilities, or to obtain "actionable intelligence" by *identifying* enemies, detecting threats, and disrupting their networks and actions.[44]

As BISs are increasingly used also by LEAs, the prism of "identity dominance" in domestic settings could entail both positive and negative implications for fundamental human rights. These could include the denial of anonymity to current or potential criminals, thus fulfilling states' obligations 'to protect the lives and security of individuals under their jurisdiction',[45] while generating unintended consequences also affecting common citizens . Let us consider the vulnerabilities the disclosure of certain habits or the mere association with specific locations—such as places of worship, clinics for alcohol or substance abuse, abortion facilities, or places from which political/social views can be inferred—that uncontrolled uses of FRT could expose us to. Indeed, empowering public authorities with the ability to remotely and silently[46] identify passersby, track their activities, companions, interests—and more—can lead to broader systemic consequences,[47] particularly considering the lack of transparency surrounding who, when, how, and for what purposes deploys such instruments. The balance among these elements is crucial in assessing power dynamics within democratic societies,[48] whereas instances of "digital authoritarianism" advance through the (ab)use of technology to control, manipulate, and repress political opponents, activists, minorities or other "troublemakers".[49]

In fact, besides providing potential for targeted repression, one of the major risks associated with widespread deployments of BISs is the exacerbation of traditional "chilling effects"—i.e., behavioural restrains or changes due to the consciousness of "being watched" by others,[50] even when the exercise of protected civil rights and fundamental freedoms is at stake.[51] Empirical research indicates that individuals may modify their behaviour to avoid even indirect associations with groups, ideas, or individuals potentially monitored by public authorities.[52] While chilling effects may have positive implications when they deter unlawful or undesirable behaviours, the psychological impact of pervasive surveillance should not be underestimated. Recent studies reveal that awareness of being monitored not only influences

---

[43] Human Rights Watch (2022).

[44] CALL (2011).

[45] Nowak and Charbord (2018), p. 60 and references therein.

[46] On the notion of 'silent technologies', see Introna and Nissenbaum (2010), p. 183.

[47] Murray (2023).

[48] Rudschies (2022).

[49] Dragu and Lupu (2021).

[50] Cf. diffusely Rautenberg and Murray (2024) and references therein.

[51] Roy (2022).

[52] Stevens et al. (2023).

'controlled behaviours' but also affects 'basic [brain functions of] human cognition', potentially implicating public mental health.[53]

At this point, considering how surveillance-related chilling effects may evoke negative feelings such as fear and anxiety,[54] or phenomena like self-censorship, one could argue that instances of "emotional dominance" are already among us. In this connection, recent news reveal that states are aware that the general population feels intimidated when deployments of FRT are publicised to actively discourage the participation in demonstrations viewed unfavourably by the government.[55] And these concerns could be further aggravated if one considers that FRT and similar instruments are increasingly designed to delve "beyond the surface" of the body. With highly debated academic papers asserting the possibility of making 'Automated Inference[s] on Criminality using Face Images',[56] and AI systems on the market to identify terrorists or paedophiles from video streams.[57]

Building on the definition of "identity dominance" provided above, for the limited purposes of this contribution, the concept of "emotional dominance" refers to public authorities' practices involving the use of biometric-based data and behavioural analytics to infer emotional states, intentions, or personality traits for detecting, investigating, prosecuting and preventing criminal offences—even through enhanced forms of deterrent effects.[58] This phenomenon could affect liberal democracies in two ways: [1] by hindering the free development and exchange of ideas[59] and "emotions", thus constraining individual autonomy and self-representation, core concepts tied to privacy rights and human dignity;[60] and [2] by enabling the exploitation of "emotional states" to gain 'political or social control', hence 'providing greater [...] potential for a fascist or totalitarian regime'.[61]

In this respect, while assessing the intrusiveness of ERT uses for security purposes, it is important to consider that in high-risk areas, such as train stations and airports, the use of sensors to detect passengers 'concealing weapons, explosives or drugs and other contraband'[62] could even be considered as a form of "ethical surveillance". In this sense, such practices allow the pursuit of security goals while preserving bodily integrity, avoiding the more intrusive impact of traditional

[53] McNicoll et al. (2024), p. 2.

[54] Svenonius (2018).

[55] AlgorithmWatch (2024).

[56] Wu and Zhang (2016).

[57] Faception (n.d.).

[58] Cf. Levantino *(forthcoming)*.

[59] Cf. Richards (2008, 2015).

[60] Cf. Teo (2023), pp. 36 ff.; Rautenberg and Murray (2024).

[61] Andalibi and Buss (2020), pp. 9–10. See also Teo (2023), p. 37, with reference to the limitations to personal autonomy, as a component of human dignity, occurring when 'choice architectures' are tailored on individuals to influence them.

[62] Adey (2012), p. 195.

searches.[63] However, given the manifold problematic nature of ERT, this reasoning does not seem to extend to biometric-based instruments that scan and analyse human bodies to infer emotions, intentions, or personality traits.

Such states are subjective and hard to interpret, even for those directly experiencing them. Numerous factors—including past experiences and cultural background—influence how we perceive and express our emotions.[64] For instance, describing our emotions to others, including people close to us, often involves ‘insurmountable difficulties [in] adequately [expressing] thoughts or feelings’.[65] Moreover, the main psychological theories underlying ERT have been recently refuted. Empirical studies challenge the reliability of using micro-expressions to assess emotions.[66] Consequently, the detection of “suspicious behaviours or emotions” that deviate from rigid and/or arbitrary AI-readable patterns risks leading to highly discriminatory outcomes.[67] Following this line of reasoning, there seem to be low chances of having training data and processes able to take into account the diverse factors—including clinical conditions—that could influence individual “emotional attitudes”.[68] Even attempts to behave in a non-suspicious manner could inadvertently trigger false positives and “self-fulfilling prophecies”. This is the case of the psychological phenomenon known as “Othello error”, where a “watcher” may mistakenly interpret truthful individuals as lying due to visible stress under observation.[69]

Additionally, it is important to consider the implications that similar AI-based determinations may have on someone’s life. For instance, LEAs interventions prompted by ERT outputs might shift the burden of proof onto those flagged by the system through an “emotional lead”. This potentially undermines the respect of basic defence rights, such as the presumption of innocence.[70] Individuals may feel under constant scrutiny, akin to being in a “perpetual line-up”.[71]

All of this considered, the first component of “emotional dominance” could, in the long run, foster instances of behavioural and emotional standardisation towards “accepted/imposed” forms of “emotional expression”. This raises serious concerns on possible interferences with fundamental human rights as enshrined—*inter alia*—in the Charter of Fundamental Rights of the European Union (CFREU) and the European Convention on Human Rights (ECHR). This broad set of rights includes various dimensions of human dignity, for instance, as it relates to the prohibition of discrimination, freedom of expression and information, the respect for private life,[72]

---

[63] Cf. Stoddart (2012), pp. 369–376.

[64] Barrett et al. (2019).

[65] Ligthart et al. (2023b), p. 466.

[66] Barrett et al. (2019).

[67] Cf. Le Moli (2022).

[68] Vemou and Horvath (2021), pp. 1–5.

[69] Cf. Article 19 (2021), p. 39.

[70] Neroni Rezende (2022); see also Sachoulidou (2023).

[71] Garvie et al. (2015); AlgorithmWatch (2024).

[72] Cf. Teo (2023).

the protection of personal data—as well as each of these rights taken individually. In particular, all these rights would be affected from an unprecedented "emotional perspective". This includes the possibility of being discriminated against when stopped by the police based on inner states and emotions, having to limit the free expression and socialisation of our emotions with others for fear of being "noticed" by public authorities, or, once again, feeling compelled to self-reflect on our emotional states and responses due to the awareness of having them constantly monitored—thereby *de facto* violating our autonomy and self-determination, i.e. the innermost spheres of our privacy.

These significant constraining effects can be linked to the second component of the concept of "emotional dominance", consisting in the possible exploitation of "emotions"—also in their inferred and "datafied" form—for manipulative purposes aiming at gaining or maintaining political or social control. In many jurisdictions, instances of 'participatory authoritarian persuasion 2.0'[73] already involve "emotional engineering" through data collection, analysis, and targeted propaganda.[74] Some ERT deployments are also part of broader 'ideological campaign[s] to encourage certain kinds of expression and limit others'.[75] And analogous deployments have been reported in some workplaces, where companies like Canon have equipped their facilities with ERT to foster an environment where 'everyone would be, or appear to be, happy at work all the time'.[76] Even clinical AI applications, although conceived to predict diseases or mental health conditions,[77] such as psychosis, suicidal ideation, or self-harm[78] could actually broaden the *spectrum*, granularity and intrusiveness of possible AI-based inferences, corresponding vulnerabilities, and possibilities for their exploitation by malicious actors, including authoritarian governments.

At this point, it seems that by putting into relation the original deployment of biometric-based tools aiming at achieving "identity dominance" in military operations with the chilling effects of surveillance practices, there are reasons to argue that applications of ERT in law enforcement would likely intensify the impact of such effects on the enjoyment of several fundamental human rights in a previously unexamined emotional dimension. In this sense, two limbs of a new concept referred to as "emotional dominance" have been proposed: one concerning the influence of "emotional surveillance" on the unconditioned development and exchange of human emotions in democratic societies, the other referring to the possible use and manipulation of emotional states for social control.

Given the potential for ERT and its use by LEAs to conflict with democratic principles and European human rights standards, the next Section will offer just some "early warnings" regarding its use in law enforcement. This analysis will draw

---

[73] Repnikova and Fang (2018), p. 760 ff.

[74] Burnay (2021), p. 204.

[75] Standaert (2021).

[76] Alegre (2023), p. 221.

[77] Gregory (2022).

[78] Corsico (2019).

upon relevant *dicta* by the European Court of Human Rights (ECtHR) and the Court of Justice of the European Union (CJEU) in the context of interferences and violations of the rights to privacy and data protection from surveillance practices conducted by public authorities through analogue and technological means. Moreover, given the recent adoption of the EU AI Act, which explicitly addresses some uses of ERT and other biometric-based tools by LEAs, Sect. 4 will also explore how some of its key provisions intersect with international and European human rights law.

4 Beyond Privacy and Data Protection: Intricacies in LEAs' Uses of ERT

Uses of ERT could support LEAs in conducting anticipatory interventions, apprehending criminals in the act or even preventing certain serious offences—as in the case of acts of terror.[79] In fact, unlike traditional Closed-Circuit Television systems (CCTV), the use of ERT and similar tools in public spaces would allow the detection and monitoring of individuals flagged by emotion recognition systems as presenting "a suspicious behavior".[80] However, considering that LEAs are state-authorised and/or controlled bodies empowered to use force and/or special powers to maintain public tranquility, law and order, prevent, detect and combat crime,[81] the fact that 'respect for human rights is part of public order' should not be underestimated.[82] In turn, as the ECtHR has noted, public order also inherently 'consists of the respect for human dignity'.[83] This raises the question of how to reconcile these complementary yet seemingly opposing imperatives in the context of LEAs' activities.

On this matter, human rights law provides mechanisms that allow for flexibility through deviations from the full enjoyment of certain rights considering factors such as the imminence, likelihood, and severity of a threat, the potential harm and societal impact posed by a particular offence, the public interests a certain police action protects, and whether these actions target minor offences, serious crimes, national security challenges, or intervene in the context of counter-terrorism efforts. In fact, all these variables contribute to balancing security needs with respect for, and the

[79] Levantino (2023a).

[80] Neroni Rezende (2022); Shehabi (2022); Vigliarolo Brandon (2024).

[81] Cf. United Nations General Assembly (UNGA) Code of Conduct for Law Enforcement Officials, Resolution 34/169 (1979); Council of Europe (CoE) The European Code of Police Ethics, Committee of Ministers Recommendation 10 (2001).

[82] American Association for the International Commission of Jurists, Siracusa Principles on the Limitation and Derogation of Provisions in the International Covenant on Civil and Political Rights (1984).

[83] Cf. Teo (2023), p. 10.

protection of, fundamental human rights. Importantly, irrespective of the purpose of a police operation, the degree of intrusiveness of any interference must never compromise the essence or core of any given right, which remains inviolable under international and European human rights law.[84] Since ERT in law enforcement presents unprecedented challenges to the rights to privacy and data protection, it is crucial to consider whether interferences linked to forms of "emotional dominance" threaten the core of these rights. However, identifying the exact essence of these interconnected civil rights *in abstracto* is not a simple task and considerations regarding their relationship to values such as 'human development, [...] autonomy, creativity, [and] social identity experimentation'[85] will help in understanding how ERT challenges core elements underlying the rights mentioned above,[86] as well as human dignity as the mother-right of every human right.[87]

Building on these premises, the rights to privacy and data protection are considered as "qualified rights"—i.e., they may be limited under certain conditions.[88] Any limitations must comply with the law, serve legitimate purposes—including public and national security—and meet standards of necessity and proportionality.[89] Reviewing relevant cases by the ECtHR suggests that blanket uses of ERT would likely integrate violations of the right to privacy. For instance, in *Kopp v Switzerland*, surveillance practices as such were considered as constituting interferences with Article 8 ECHR.[90] The ECtHR has also recognised the existence of private spheres even in public spaces, mentioning 'the right to live a "social private life", *that is the possibility for an individual to develop his or her social identity*'.[91] Then, in counter-terrorism investigations, the Court acknowledged 'reasonable expectations' of privacy in public spaces and expressed particular concerns over the 'systematic or permanent record of video material'.[92] At this stage, the ECtHR has already labelled some basic uses of FRT as creating risks of arbitrariness, rendering the exercise of state powers 'obscure'.[93] Moreover, considering that general monitoring entails the processing of data of various subjects, such as individuals without criminal records, witnesses, known offenders, or those that are deemed as potential threats, it is likely that similar deployments would not adhere to the "data subject

[84] Thielbörger (2019).

[85] Büchi et al. (2020).

[86] Van der Sloot (2015).

[87] Le Moli (2021), pp. 216–260.

[88] Mobilio (2023).

[89] Lavrysen (2018); Peers and Precha (2021). See chapters 'Technical Solutions for a Proportional Use of Facial Recognition Technology' by Menéndez González and 'Facial Recognition in Public Spaces and the Principle of Necessity' by Jasserand in this volume.

[90] ECtHR, *Kopp v Switzerland*, No 23224/94, (25 March 1998), para. 53.

[91] ECtHR, *Niemietz v Germany*, No 13710/88, (16 December 1992), para. 29, *emphasis* added by the author.

[92] ECtHR, *Unuz v Germany*, No 35623/05, (2 September 2010), paras. 43 ff.

[93] ECtHR, *Gaughran v United Kingdom*, No 45245/15, (13 June 2020), para. 86.

categorisation" principle established in *S. and Marper v the United Kingdom*. In that case, the indiscriminate processing of sensitive data of different categories of people created risks of stigmatisation, conflicts with the presumption of innocence, and resulted in a disproportionate interference—i.e., a violation of Article 8 ECHR.[94]

Other forms of indiscriminate data processing, which lack proportionality or necessity, have been deemed by the CJEU to exceed the limits of "legitimate interferences", as established in cases such as *Digital Rights Ireland* and *Tele2*—among others.[95] Here, it is essential to distinguish between schemes of mass surveillance, as exposed by Snowden's 2013 revelations, which involved the pre-emptive and indiscriminate monitoring of private communications and data flows,[96] and forms of targeted surveillance, which are based on pre-identified suspicion or ongoing criminal investigations, thus involving one or more specific individuals.[97] In this light, deploying ERT for monitoring purposes would not only fall into the category of pre-emptive dragnet surveillance but—considering how such uses would screen emotions, feelings, and intentions of each passersby—also the nature of what is actually surveilled should be taken into account.

Leaving aside for now reflections on the nature of the data ERT processes—covered in more detail later—and focusing instead on how "emotional dominance" through the use of ERT might reshape traditional conceptions of surveillance, it seems interesting to underline that some surveillance practices vary in intrusiveness depending on whether they involve the interception of "external" or "internal" dimensions of communications and data flows. Typically, content data—pertaining to the substantive content of a communication—is regarded as more sensitive, whereas metadata—the "external" facet of that communication that includes details like sender, receiver, timing, location, devices used, etc.—is generally considered as less sensitive.[98] From this perspective, it is both intriguing and somewhat disturbing to reflect on how biometric technologies, such as FRT, enable the identification of individuals and the association of their "recognition" with the spatial and temporal coordinates at which their identification occurs, offering metadata-like insights into people's lives in the physical word and turning them into living sources of metadata.[99] By the same token, emotion recognition and related technologies go even

[94] ECtHR, *S and Marper v United Kingdom*, Nos 30562/04 and 30566/04, (4 December 2008), paras. 122; 125.

[95] CJEU, *Digital Rights Ireland and Others*, Joined Cases C-293/12 and C-594/12, (8 April 2014), ECLI:EU:C:2014:238; *Tele2 Sverige and Watson and Others*, Joined Cases C-203/15 and C-698/15, (21 December 2016), ECLI:EU:C:2016:970. See also Hijmans (2021).

[96] Mitsilegas (2021), pp. 101 ff.

[97] Hijmans (2021), pp. 240 ff.

[98] Except for the significant intrusiveness characterising in the opinion of the CJEU the aggregation of metadata which 'may allow very precise conclusions to be drawn concerning the private lives of the persons whose data has been [processed]', see CJEU, *Digital Rights Ireland and Others*, paras. 26–27, 37.

[99] Levantino (2023b).

further by analysing beneath the body's surface, thus allowing the interception and analysis of elements akin to the content data of our emotional lives and interactions.[100] These points serve as a basis for understanding the heightened intrusiveness of mass scale deployments of ERT, particularly when compared to the use of FRT in analogous contexts. Based on the jurisprudence reviewed thus far, there are indeed reasons to consider *pre-emptive* uses of ERT by LEAs as even more intrusive than current uses of FRT, particularly in light of the broader "enabling function" that privacy rights play within the system of human rights protection by allowing individuals possibilities to freely enjoy other civil rights that are fundamental for the correct functioning of pluralistic and democratic societies.

While also the deployment of ERT would be required to occur in force of an adequate legal basis, when necessary in a democratic society, respecting the principle of proportionality—also through the provision of adequate safeguards, in connection to the specific circumstances and the gravity of the offences involved, the view of this author is that a crucial consideration in assessing the seriousness of the interferences that LEAs' uses of ERT could imply lies in the very intimate nature of human emotions.

Particularly when it comes to the operationalisation of the right to the protection of personal data through data protection law, the sensitive nature of emotions deserves further attention. On this point, if one considers that ERT detects and analyses emotions on the basis of biometric features, and that biometric data is granted a particularly protective discipline also when processed by LEAs, one might intuitively consider the analysis of emotional or other intimate states as even more sensitive than that of biometric data. However, from a purely technical standpoint, these conclusions should not be taken for granted, and further investigation is needed to understand the limits of this reasoning, especially in light of some specific aspects related to current EU law provisions governing biometric data processing and emotion recognition systems.

It is true, in *Glukhin v Russia*, the ECtHR recently emphasised the sensitive nature of biometric data, also referencing EU data protection law, and found the deployment of both retrospective and real-time FRT by LEAs to identify and arrest a "solo demonstrator" to be in violation of Articles 8 and 10 ECHR. With these violations being linked to broader implications for democratic societies,[101] particularly through considerations on the chilling effects generated by such technologies.[102] Yet, the application of the EU data protection provisions on biometric data processing to ERT is more complex than it appears, and an analysis of this issue calls into question the innovations introduced by both the definitions of biometric data and that of emotion recognition systems provided in the AI Act. On this issue, initial scepticism surrounded the direct applicability of provisions on biometric data processing to uses of ERT, since the processing of biometric data technically occurs only when it

[100] Cf. Ibid.

[101] Palmiotto and Menendez González (2023).

[102] Cf. ECtHR, *Glukhin v. Russia*, App no 11519/20, 4 July 2023.

allows or confirms the unique identification of natural persons.[103] With that being something that largely depends on what "identification" actually means under the same regime. In fact, the interpretation of this definition has a variable scope, ranging from the association of persons to their "civil identity" to merely 'individualising' a given person among a crowd.[104] By applying these variables to the use of ERT in public spaces to detect "suspicious behaviours", intentions, or emotions, uncertainty could surround the suitability of EU data protection law to limit the widespread use of such technologies, as the analysis of sensitive inner states does not automatically involve the unique identification of those individuals an emotion recognition systems has flagged as worth of further attention. An identification in the broad sense of individualising a person among many is certainly what would occur in most cases, while e.g., coupling ERT with facial recognition capabilities is the case that would imply the association of natural persons to their civil identity and corresponding identifiers.

In this connection, a few steps of the legislative process behind the adoption of the final text of the AI Act, which includes specific provisions on ERT, also merit further attention. In fact, different approaches followed one another, including the European Parliament's proposal (EP) for a ban on LEAs' uses of ERT—as these practices were deemed to pose an unacceptable level of risk to EU values and fundamental rights. Provided that, according to the final text of the AI Act, only uses of such technologies in 'the areas of workplace and education institutions' are prohibited,[105] while uses in the security sector are not, an analysis of some relevant provisions in the AI Act will help in shedding light on some critical issues both of definitional and substantive nature affecting LEAs uses of this technology. A case in point is the definition of "emotion recognition systems" in Article 3(39) AI Act, the latter has changed several times as this regulation moved towards its final version. Initially referring to AI systems used to identify or infer 'emotions or intentions of natural persons on the basis of biometric data', this definition saw variations including references to 'psychological states', or 'thoughts, states of mind 'of 'individuals or groups on the basis of their biometric and *biometric-based data*'.[106] Ultimately, the final text published in the Official Journal of the European Union (OJEU) on 12 July 2024, largely reflects the Commission's proposal.[107]

Nevertheless, the fact that the draft text put forward by the EP explicitly distinguished between biometric and biometric-based data demonstrated a certain degree of sensitivity on the loopholes presented above concerning the applicability of the

---

[103] Cf. Wendehors and Duller (2021), pp. 20–22.

[104] Cf. Purtova (2022).

[105] Article 5(1)(f) AI Act.

[106] Papakonstantinou and Zarkadoulas (2023). See also the Proposal for a Regulation of the European Parliament and of the Council laying down harmonised rules on Artificial Intelligence and amending certain Union legislative acts, COM/2021/206 final, Article 3(34), and the corresponding amendments proposed by the EP and the Council, *emphasis* added by the author.

[107] See Article 3(39) AI Act.

biometric data processing regime to AI systems that analyse biometric characteristics without directly "allowing or confirming the unique identification" of natural persons. And this distinction could have paved the way to introducing a new category of data potentially encompassing the AI-based analysis of emotional states. However, even this approach would have left considerable uncertainty regarding the substantive regulatory framework applicable to the processing of biometric-based data.

Although the final AI Act text does not seem to unequivocally resolve these issues, it reduces the uncertainty surrounding how emotion recognition systems relate to the application of data protection provisions concerning the processing of biometric data. This is largely due to the broader definition of 'biometric data' provided in Article 3(34) AI Act compared to corresponding GDPR and LED provisions. While it maintains the requirement for a 'specific technical processing' of certain 'physical, physiological or behavioural characteristics [...]', it omits the reference to the 'purpose of uniquely identifying a natural person'.[108] This omission, combined with other definitions and provisions in the AI Act[109] suggest that, at this stage, processing biometric data merely serves as a 'proxy'[110] to infer what are considered as manifestations of a given emotion—e.g., through specific facial expressions, thereby triggering the application of a regime analogous to that data protection law traditionally affords to biometric data.

Still, if the intersection of relevant provisions in the AI Act and the EU data protection framework would seem to allow the application of the biometric data processing regime to the performance of ERT, a few additional observations are necessary. As a matter of fact, considering the AI Act's definitions of emotion recognition systems (which reference both "identification or inference" of human emotions) and that of biometric data (which now refers also to the "recognition" of emotions of natural persons), in this author's opinion greater precision towards what seems to be the interchangeable use of concepts such as identification, recognition, and inference applied to the functions of ERT would have been beneficial. Indeed, the reasoning connecting biometric data to the *inference* of "emotions"—or their representation—may not apply equally to cases where the actions performed are defined as "identification" or "recognition" of emotions. Considering that AI systems designed to assess human emotions are generally referred to as emotion *recognition* technology or emotion *recognition* systems, terms like *identification* and *recognition* seem to imply that emotions are something objectively identifiable/recognisable. In contrast, the concept of *inference* acknowledges that the AI system merely assigns an assumed emotional state to a specific expression, such as a facial

[108] Cf. Article 3(39) AI Act, Articles 3(13) and 10 LED; Articles 4(14) and 9 GDPR as well as corresponding Recitals.

[109] This is the case of the definition of "emotion recognition system" contained in Article 3(39) AI Act, which refers to 'AI system[s] for the purpose of identifying or inferring emotions or intentions of natural persons on the basis of their biometric data', or Recital (14) AI Act, where '[b]iometric data can allow for [...] the recognition of emotions of natural persons'.

[110] McStay (2024), p. 94.

cue. On this point, the formulation of these provisions and their overly vague language create some discrepancies.

The decision to adopt a broad definition of the activities emotion recognition systems can perform likely reflects both the challenges encountered by EU policymakers in fully understanding an emerging technology like emotion recognition and an effort to account for several technologies that could analyse human emotions. This approach can be interpreted as functional to ensure the effectiveness of AI Act's provisions by preventing tech companies from bypassing them due to narrowly tailored definitions. However, if the rationale for applying data protection provisions concerning biometric data to ERT hinges on the idea that such systems *infer* emotions and other states from the processing of biometric characteristics, then references to activities such as the *recognition* and *identification* of emotions or intention are inconsistent with this reasoning and suggests that the protections from the AI-based assessment of inner states through these mechanisms may be inadequate. In this connection, also the fact that Recital (18) AI Act defines "emotions" as encompassing 'happiness, sadness, anger, surprise, disgust, embarrassment, excitement, shame, contempt, satisfaction and amusement',[111] but excludes the 'mere detection of readily apparent expressions, gestures or movements', such as 'basic facial expressions, [...] a frown or a smile, or gestures such as the movement of hands, arms or head [...] *unless* they are used for identifying or inferring emotions'[112] is problematic. Taking into account the main argument that—as also the AI Act explicitly acknowledges—'[t]here are serious concerns about the scientific basis of AI systems aiming to identify or infer emotions, particularly as expression of emotions vary considerably across cultures and situations, and even within a single individual',[113] and with the scientific validity of such tools being disputed to the point of being considered "pseudoscience",[114] the exclusion from the scope of relevant provisions in the AI Act of "basic facial expressions" or other simple actions, like movements of the head, is at odds with the premise that a broad definition of what tasks ERT can perform would enhance the protection afforded by the AI Act.

To begin with, it seems challenging to distinguish and verify in practice the difference between AI systems that detect facial movements, like a frown or a smile, to identify or infer emotions, and those that perform these activities for other purposes. To elaborate further, precisely these movements serve as proxies for inferring or allegedly identifying inner states, such as emotions. Additionally, AI-based tool that analyse micro-movements, including head and facial vibrations, have already been developed and deployed—even for security purposes—to assess inner states like emotions, mental states, or personality traits.[115] Finally, also the lack

[111] Recital (18) AI Act.

[112] Ibid, *emphasis* added by the author.

[113] Recital (44) AI Act.

[114] Stark and Hutson (2021).

[115] Wright (2023).

of a specific definition of what intentions are according to the AI Act opens a significant regulatory gap, which can be analysed in conjunction with the exclusion of other gestures and bodily movements from the definition provided above. Bearing this in mind, it seems worth reflecting on whether the deployment of increasingly diffused automated surveillance systems e.g., for 'the [...] purpose of detecting, in real time, predetermined events that may present or reveal [risks]'[116] foreseen by France in view of the 2024 Olympics would fall under this definition and corresponding discipline or not. In fact, official sources specify that while this surveillance system is designed to identify 'unusual behaviours' or 'anomalies',[117] it is neither a BIS nor it uses FRT—and it does not process biometrics.[118] Once again, the interpretation of the concept of 'identification' adopted could play a crucial role at least when it comes to the application of the discipline on biometric data processing in the lack of a specific regime on certain "behavioural analytic systems" designed to detect "risks", "unusual behaviours" or "anomalies", whose functionalities may overlap significantly with ERT uses for security purposes.

Rather recently, considering how the definition of biometric data seems already outdated in the face of ever-evolving technological advancements[119]—like ERT and similar tools, substantive proposals have been introduced to shift the focus of possible regulation from the centrality of elements like the specifical technical means used to process certain data, the purposes of such processing or the kind of activities specific AI systems can perform, to the "nature" of the inferences that such AI systems can make. In this sense, the category of "cognitive biometrics" has emerged within parallel yet increasingly convergent areas of study, where tools such as ERT, EX headsets, BCIs, neurotechnologies, or AI-powered smart glasses are all grouped together due to the possibilities these offer to interpret cognitive states. In that context, the term "cognitive" has to be interpreted *latu sensu*, as it includes 'cognitive, affective, and conative states'.[120] In turn, each of such sub-categories specifically encompasses 'processes related to knowledge, understanding, and thinking, [...] emotions and feelings, and [...] desires, volition, and related behavioural intentions', respectively.[121]

If these proposals partially address some of the definitional challenges presented so far, it is important to specify that this debate is currently focused primarily on issues related to the processing of sensitive data by private companies. As a result, it has not yet been adapted to the unique challenges posed by the deployment of ERT by police forces. Nevertheless, these reflections offer valuable insights that may also benefit the objectives of this contribution. In fact, current EU secondary law sources,

[116] Cf. Article 10, loi n° 2023-380, du 19 mai 2023 relative aux jeux Olympiques et Paralympiques de 2024 et portant diverses autres dispositions, Légifrance.

[117] Carroll (2024).

[118] Cf. Article 10 loi n° 2023-380.

[119] Stockwell et al. (2024), pp. 3, 13.

[120] Magee et al. (2024), p. 3022.

[121] Ibid.

including the frameworks governing the processing of personal data and some provisions in the AI Act, can be understood as operationalising the right to the protection of personal data which, in turn, originated from the evolutive interpretation of the right to private life, home, and correspondence. From this perspective, also discussions on how to protect cognitive, affective, and conative states may similarly be interpreted as operationalising debates premised on the assertion that current fundamental human rights standards are inadequate in the face of the unprecedented interferences and challenges posed by emerging technologies. In this sense, these debates advocate for either evolutive interpretations of existing rights, such as the right to privacy, the right to the protection of personal data, and freedom of thought, or the introduction of new rights, specifically the right to the protection of mental privacy.[122]

Now, what stands out is that even those more moderate viewpoints maintaining that stretching the interpretation of current rights would be preferable—as some of them have not seen their protective potential fully realised yet—link concerns on ever evolving technologies designed to "read" human emotions and other inner states with the concept of mental privacy.[123] According to those opinions, the latter could be viewed as constituting the inviolable core or essence of privacy rights, or again, could be associated with the *forum internum* of the right to freedom of thought which, under international and European human rights law, is also regarded as inviolable.[124]

Retracing the key findings of this Section, it seems that an analysis aiming at verifying the compatibility of some "early warnings" on the use of ERT connected to its deployment by police forces—especially given the unprecedented interferences it may pose to the rights to privacy and data protection—reveals significant concerns. These interferences, including chilling effects on the free expression and exchange of emotional states—here described as "emotional dominance", reflect considerations emerging from relevant caselaw from supranational courts on surveillance matters, including cases involving the use of AI-based tools like FRT. Moreover, also definitional issues concerning ERT, as identified through relevant provisions of EU secondary law, and ongoing debates calling for substantive changes in international and European human rights frameworks highlight the severe challenges emerging technologies and their use pose to the effective protection of such rights in their current understanding—to the point of suggesting that these practices may infringe upon the core, inviolable aspects of these rights. Given that reforms—whether through amendments to existing human rights frameworks, changes to EU law, or judicial interpretation—would require a considerable amount of time, a pressing question remains: how can we prevent individuals and democratic systems

[122] Ligthart et al. (2023a); Brown (2024).

[123] Alegre (2023).

[124] Cf. Ibid.

from sleepwalking into a reality where even our emotions could become a source of discrimination, criminalisation, and social control?

Drawing on considerations that see AI-powered tools and their use progressively eroding possibilities for the protection of fundamental human rights and how,[125] particularly the automated analysis of emotional and other inner states raises doubts about its coherence with key elements of the whole system of protection, including the core of enabling rights, such as the rights to privacy and to the protection of personal data, and human dignity, which stands at the core of the entire human rights protection system, the next Section will present some final reflections.

5 Taking "Emotion Recognition" and Its Regulation Seriously: Is a Shift from Reaction to Pre-emption Enough?

After having explored just some intersections between the AI Act and the use of ERT by LEAs, it is now time for some concluding remarks. As a recent contribution on the role of emotions in international law advocated, we must 'acknowledge that emotions are not biases or untruths that need to be weeded out, [...] rather [they] ought to be understood and embraced as a central component of reasoned decision-making'.[126] This reflection certainly denotes that emotions and other intangible human traits might well become increasingly relevant in supporting decision-making processes, including through the use of AI systems by LEAs. In this regard, this chapter has attempted to highlight different dimensions of risk posed by the rise of "emotional dominance"—where secondary effects of advanced surveillance practices hinder the spontaneous development and exchange of social interactions and emotions—exposing vulnerabilities that our multilayered system of fundamental rights protection present when facing modern and emerging technologies. Independently of the technical relevance of certain open issues concerning ERT, that create favourable conditions for its deployment, international and European human rights law frameworks should, in the first place, constitute a compass guiding the flourishing of our societies rather than merely setting limits to possible interferences with individual rights. Although current regulations might technically allow pseudoscientific claims on the possibility of detecting, analysing, or otherwise inferring emotions and other sensitive attributes of human beings, deploying these tools for surveillance and security purposes seems to raise questions about the compatibility of such uses with the core or essence of some fundamental human rights. This chapter has highlighted the rights to privacy and the protection of personal data as just two paradigmatic examples of how emerging technologies challenge the very foundations of these rights in ways that were previously unimaginable. Considering

[125] Teo (2024).

[126] Saab (2021), p. 10.

factors including sector-specific frameworks permitting the use of ERT by LEAs, the proliferation of related tools like FRT, and the expansion of ERT in civilian applications, it seems that risks associated with the rise of "emotional dominance" should not be relegated to the realm of science fiction fantasy.

This is because the automated scrutiny of cognitive, affective, and conative states, personality traits, predispositions, or assessments of individuals as "threats" or "anomalies" to be monitored confronts the core of the right to privacy, whose respect has to be granted even in public spaces and in relational terms. Precisely from similar reflections, what emerges is the potential ERT has to undermine values essential to individual and societal flourishing,[127] such as autonomy, self-determination, the free development of one's personality, or again, of opinions, ideas, emotions, and their exchange with others. Beyond privacy, these frictions also impact the right to the protection of personal data, which helps in understanding how the issue is not only one that has to do with the freedom to be oneself, but it is also "representational".[128] In fact, while interferences with the core of the right to privacy allow to reflect on the detrimental effects that being "emotionally surveilled" could have on the authentic development of our identities, doubts on the effectiveness of basic data protection rights—such as the right to rectification, or the principle of data accuracy[129]—undermine and erode the foundations that have made EU data protection law a global standard, especially when individuals are misrepresented through the processing of personal data. In other words, whenever an emotion recognition system flags someone as warranting public authorities' attention, with the serious implications this might entail—particularly if individuals do not recognise themselves in an AI-based assessment—is our freedom to be humans that is questioned. In this respect, such practices challenge the very notion of "human dignity", which, in turn, constitutes the core of international and European human rights law, the mother right of every human right and, at the EU level, the first right enshrined in the CFREU. In this light, it seems crucial to further stimulate open debates on the opportunity, necessity, and desirability of deploying these tools. At this point in time, considering their current level of technical (im)maturity and scientific validity, uses of ERT—as discussed in this chapter—seem not to respond to any pressing social need. As there seem to be reasonable grounds to argue that the risks they could pose might outweigh the potential benefits deriving from their deployment in very sensitive domains, like the law enforcement area.

If reactive approaches to these issues might be inadequate for addressing the rapid proliferation of controversial technologies, such as the use of ERT in sensitive domains, a growing trend consists in the adoption of *ex ante* mechanism to identify, mitigate, and prevent the implications arising from the deployment of certain AI systems. While also this chapter has aimed at contributing to a deeper understanding of the risks of ERT use by police forces through an interdisciplinary analysis

[127] Cf. Rautenberg and Murray (2024).

[128] Cf. Teo (2024).

[129] Cf. Custers and Vrabec (2024); Duchoňová (2023).

revolving around the concept of "emotional dominance", the AI Act establishes some mechanisms intended to guide pre-deployment practices, including those for the use of ERT by LEAs. For example, Article 27 AI Act introduces a new tool complementary to the Data Protection Impact Assessment (DPIA) that competent authorities should carry out according to Article 27 LED.[130] Prior to the first use of a "high-risk" AI system, deployers are required to perform a Fundamental Rights Impact Assessment (FRIA) by taking into account several factors including expected duration, frequency, and context of use of a given AI system, as well as the corresponding risk of harm for the specific subjects that could be affected by such uses. This process also entails the identification of oversight measures, as well as response mechanisms in case such risks materialise.[131] Despite recent efforts to develop methodologies and approaches for assessing the impact socio-technical advancement can have on fundamental rights and our societies,[132] at this stage, diffused scepticism remains on the capacity of deployers, their organisations and procedures to effectively identify the full scope of affected rights and individuals, thus establishing effective monitoring mechanisms and reactive measures.[133] In this connection, a potentially impactful yet overlooked provision that has so far received limited attention and that could fill this gap is Article 4 AI Act, which mandates that AI providers and deployers ensure AI literacy for system operators—as well as affected persons—considering their individual characteristics and those of the AI system being deployed, in any given context of use, and with in mind 'opportunities and risks of AI and possible harm it can cause'.[134]

However, while the introduction of FRIAs and AI literacy obligations—also involving LEAs as deployers of "high-risk" AI systems—is intended to prevent interferences with protected rights and freedoms, it does not seem that similar mechanisms would account for the risks associated to the rise of "emotional dominance" as described here. In this direction, it suffices to recall the lack of clarity revolving around what protections does data protection law afford in the face of ever evolving technologies designed to "read" human emotions, or the vague and imprecise definitions of key terms in relevant AI Act provisions, such as what constitutes "intentions". All these considerations urge a renewed focus on the impact of ERT uses in law enforcement on the protection of fundamental human rights as such, and their role in democratic societies. In this context, mitigating mechanisms such *ex*

[130] Cf. Arts. 27 AI Act and 27 LED, Directive (EU) 2016/680 of the European Parliament and of the Council of 27 April 2016 on the protection of natural persons with regard to the processing of personal data by competent authorities for the purposes of the prevention, investigation, detection or prosecution of criminal offences or the execution of criminal penalties, and on the free movement of such data, and repealing Council Framework Decision 2008/977/JHA (Law Enforcement Directive or LED).

[131] Ibid.

[132] Mantelero (2024).

[133] Cf. Waem et al. (2024); De Capitani (2024).

[134] Cf. Arts 3(56) and 4 and Recitals (20), (91), (165) AI Act.

ante FRIAs or basic AI literacy requirements are not new and should already inform LEAs' practices. In the law enforcement area, the introduction of new technologies inherently heightens risks to fundamental rights and demands specific safeguards,[135] especially for intrusive and debated instruments like ERT. Past cases, including the deployment of controversial tools like Clearview AI by both Member States' LEAs and EUROPOL,[136] Snowden's 2013 revelations,[137] or even recent cases adjudicated by the CJEU,[138] tell us a lot on how, in many instances, we are still far from being fully protected through the *ex ante* respect of substantive and procedural safeguards.

Ultimately, while the substantive issues associated with those identified here as shortcomings in the protection against intrusive technologies fuelling unprecedented forms of surveillance can be framed as fundamental human rights issues, envisioning complimentary forms of protection consisting in *ex ante* FRIAs and AI literacy obligations seem like a tiger paper in the face of the broader rule of law issues Europe and its democratic foundations are currently facing—as the examples just presented illustrate. More broadly, if a regulation aiming at protecting fundamental rights while fostering innovation has been adopted with EU legislators implicitly accepting the materialisation of technologies that screen, abstracts, and analyse inner states for security purposes, what is at stake is something much greater: namely, the ambitions, aims, effectiveness, and current state of fundamental rights protection in the EU.

References

Ada Lovelace Institute (2019, September 10) Beyond face value: public attitudes to facial recognition technology. https://www.adalovelaceinstitute.org/case-study/beyond-face-value/

Adey P (2012) Borders, identification and surveillance – new regimes of border control. In: Ball K, Haggerty K, Lyon D (eds) Routledge handbook of surveillance studies. Routledge International Handbooks, London, pp 193–200

Alegre S (2023) Freedom to think: protecting a fundamental right in the digital age. Atlantic Books, London

AlgorithmWatch (2021) At Danish gyms, face recognition technology checks your COVID-19 certificate (and your mood?). https://algorithmwatch.org/en/tracers/in-danish-gyms-face-recognition-technology-checks-your-covid-19-certificate-and-your-mood/

AlgorithmWatch (2024, October 24) Show Your Face and AI Tells Who You Are. https://algorithmwatch.org/en/biometric-surveillance-explained/

American Association for the International Commission of Jurists, Siracusa Principles on the Limitation and Derogation of Provisions in the International Covenant on Civil and Political Rights (1984). https://www.icj.org/wp-content/uploads/1984/07/Siracusa-principles-ICCPR-legal-submission-1985-eng.pdf

[135] Consultative Committee of Convention 108 (2018), pp. 9 ff.

[136] EDPS (2021).

[137] Milanovic (2015).

[138] CJEU, *Direktor na Glavna direktsia "Natsionalna politsia" pri MVR - Sofia* C-118/22, 30.1.2024, ECLI:EU:C:2024:97.

Andalibi N, Buss J (2020) The human in emotion recognition on social media: attitudes, outcomes, risks. Proceedings of the 2020 CHI Conference on Human Factors in Computing Systems, pp 1–16. https://doi.org/10.1145/3313831.3376680

Andreas P, Price R (2001) From war fighting to crime fighting: transforming the American national security state. Int Stud Rev 3(3):31–52. https://doi.org/10.1111/1521-9488.00243

AP4AI (2022) Accountability Principles for Artificial Intelligence in the Internal Security Domain. Summary Report on Expert Consultations. https://www.ap4ai.eu/sites/default/files/2023-09/AP4AI_Report1_27Jan2022.pdf

Article 19 (2021) Emotional Entanglement: China's emotion recognition market and its implications for human rights. https://www.article19.org/wp-content/uploads/2021/01/ER-Tech-China-Report.pdf

Ashworth B (2024, October 15) These smart glasses will read your emotions and watch what you eat. Wired. https://www.wired.com/story/emteq-smart-glasses-read-emotions-watch-what-you-eat/

Avramopoulos D (2018) Answer given by Mr Avramopoulos on behalf of the European Commission. EP, Parliamentary question - E-002894/2018(ASW). https://www.europarl.europa.eu/doceo/document/E-8-2018-002894-ASW_EN.html

Balzacq T, Basaran T, Bigo D, Guittet EP, Olsson C (2010) Security practices. In: Oxford research encyclopedia of international studies. https://doi.org/10.1093/acrefore/9780190846626.013.475

Barrett LF, Adolphs R, Marsella S, Martinez AM, Pollak SD (2019) Emotional expressions reconsidered: challenges to inferring emotion from human facial movements. Psychol Sci Pub Int 20(1):1–68. https://doi.org/10.1177/1529100619832930

Brown CML (2024) Neurorights, mental privacy, and mind reading. Neuroethics 17(2):34 ff. https://doi.org/10.1007/s12152-024-09568-z

Bublitz C (2024) Neurotechnologies and human rights: restating and reaffirming the multi-layered protection of the person. Int J Human Rights: 1–26. https://doi.org/10.1080/13642987.2024.2310830

Büchi M, Fosch-Villaronga E, Lutz C, Tamò-Larrieux A, Velidi S, Viljoen S (2020) The chilling effects of algorithmic profiling: mapping the issues. Comput Law Secur Rev 36:105367 ff. https://doi.org/10.1016/j.clsr.2019.105367

Burnay M (2021) Privacy and surveillance in a digital era: transnational implications of China's Surveillance State. In: Miltsilegas V, Vavoula N (eds) Surveillance and privacy in the digital age: European, transatlantic and global perspectives. Hart, Oxford, pp 197–213

Carroll J (2024, March 8) Paris to use AI surveillance at Olympics. The Washington Post. https://www.washingtonpost.com/video/sports/paris-to-use-ai-surveillance-at-olympics/2024/03/08/cd77cfb5-710f-41ea-9c7b-637adf7a8b67_video.html

Center for Army Lessons Learned (CALL) (2011) Handbook – Commander's Guide to Biometrics in Afghanistan. No. 11-25, pp 1–99. https://info.publicintelligence.net/CALL-AfghanBiometrics.pdf

Clifford D (2024) Data protection law and emotion. Oxford University Press, Oxford

Coluccini R, Giannini A, Sottile L (2024, July 24) Il Viminale ci tiene all'oscuro su come e quanto usa il sistema di riconoscimento facciale. IRPIMedia. https://irpimedia.irpi.eu/sorveglianze-viminale-riconoscimento-facciale-trasparenza/

Consultative Committee of Convention 108 (2018) Practical guide on the use of personal data in the police sector. Co E, T-PD(2018)01. https://rm.coe.int/t-pd-201-01-practical-guide-on-the-use-of-personal-data-in-the-police-/16807927d5

Corsico P (2019) The risks of risk. Regulating the use of machine learning for psychosis prediction. Int J Law Psychiatry 66:101479. https://doi.org/10.1016/j.ijlp.2019.101479

Council of Europe (CoE) – Committee of Ministers (2001) The European Code of Police Ethics (ECPE). Rec(2001)10. https://rm.coe.int/16805e297e

Custers B, Vrabec H (2024) Tell me something new: data subject rights applied to inferred data and profiles. Comput Law Secur Rev 52:105956. https://doi.org/10.1016/j.clsr.2024.105956

De Capitani E (2024) The COE Convention on Artificial Intelligence, Human Rights and the Rule of Law. Is the Council of Europe losing its compass? European Area of Freedom Security & Justice. https://free-group.eu/2024/03/04/the-coe-convention-on-artificial-intelligence-human-rights-democracy-and-the-rule-of-law-is-the-council-of-europe-losing-its-compass/
De Hert P (2005) Balancing security and liberty within the European human rights framework. A critical reading of the Court's case law in the light of surveillance and criminal law enforcement strategies after 9/11. Utrecht Law Rev 1(1):68–96. https://doi.org/10.18352/ulr.4
De Hert P, Bouchagiar G (2022) Visual and biometric surveillance in the EU. Saying 'no' to mass surveillance practices? Inf Polity 27:193–217. https://doi.org/10.3233/IP-211525
Deerwater M, Scarff R (2021) How are you feeling today? Surveill Soc 19(4):448–457. https://doi.org/10.24908/ss.v19i4.15114
Dragu T, Lupu Y (2021) Digital authoritatianism and the future of human rights. Int Organ 75:991–1017. https://doi.org/10.1017/S0020818320000624
Duchoňová T (2023) Voice as the Window to the Soul: Analysis of the level of protection granted by the GDPR to emotions inferred from one's voice. Oslo. https://www.jus.uio.no/ifp/om/organisasjon/seri/aktuelle-saker/2024/complex_03_2023.pdf
European Data Protection Supervisor (EDPS) (2021, February 12) Swedish DPA: Police unlawfully used facial recognition app. https://www.edpb.europa.eu/news/national-news/2021/swedish-dpa-police-unlawfully-used-facial-recognition-app_en
European Digital Rights (EDRi) (2021) The rise of biometric mass surveillance in the EU. https://edri.org/wp-content/uploads/2021/11/EDRI_RISE_REPORT.pdf
Faception (n.d.) Facial Personality Analytics. https://www.faception.com/our-technology. Accessed 31 Mar 2024
Foucault M (1997) "Society Must Be Defended": Lectures at the Collège de France (1975-1976). Picador, New York
Garvie C, Bedoya AM, Frankle J (2015) The perpetual line-up – unregulated police face recognition in America. Georgetown Law University, Center on Privacy & Technology, Georgetown. https://www.perpetuallineup.org/
Gikay AA (2023) Regulating use by law enforcement authorities of live facial recognition technology in public spaces: an incremental approach. Camb Law J 82(3):414–449. https://doi.org/10.1017/S0008197323000454
Gregory A (2022, October 4) AI eye checks can predict heart disease risk in less than minute, finds study. The Guardian. https://www.theguardian.com/society/2022/oct/04/ai-eye-checks-can-predict-heart-disease-risk-in-less-than-minute-finds-study
Haggerty KD, Ericson RV (1999) The militarization of policing in the information age. J Polit Mil Sociol 27(2):233–255
Haggerty KD, Ericson RV (2000) The surveillance assemblage. Br J Sociol 51:605–633. https://doi.org/10.1080/00071310020015280
Hammond-Errey M, Barrett T (2024, February 1) The only privacy we have left is what's in our heads, and that will soon be public. The Sydney Morning Herald. https://www.smh.com.au/technology/the-only-privacy-we-have-left-is-what-s-in-our-heads-and-that-will-soon-be-public-20240123-p5eziu.html
Hartzog W, Selinger E, Gunawan J (2024) Privacy nicks: how the law normalizes surveillance. Wash Univ Law Rev 101:717–789
Hermes Center (2021, July 14) No Place for Emotion Recognition Technologies in Italian Museums. European Digital Rights (EDRi) (blog). https://edri.org/our-work/no-place-for-emotion-recognition-technologies-in-italian-museums/
Hijmans H (2021) Data protection and surveillance: the perspective of EU law. In: Mitsilegas V, Vavoula N (eds) Surveillance and privacy in the digital age. European, transatlantic and global perspectives, Hart, Oxford, pp 235–254
Human Rights Watch (2022) New Evidence that Biometric Data Systems Imperil Afghans. https://www.hrw.org/news/2022/03/30/new-evidence-biometric-data-systems-imperil-afghans

IE University (2024, October 10) 67% of Europeans fear AI manipulation in elections, according to IE University research. IE European Tech Insights. https://www.ie.edu/university/news-events/news/67-europeans-fear-ai-manipulation-elections-according-ie-university-research/

Ienca M, Malgieri G (2022) Mental data protection and the GDPR. J Law Biosci 9(1):1–19. https://doi.org/10.1093/jlb/lsac006

INTERPOL (2020) Facial recognition. https://www.interpol.int/content/download/15013/file/FS-04_Facial%20R_Factsheets_EN_2020-03.pdf

Introna L, Nissenbaum H (2010) Facial recognition technology a survey of policy and implementation issues, Working Paper 2010/030. Lancaster University Management School. https://core.ac.uk/download/pdf/1555646.pdf

Lavrysen L (2018) System of restrictions. In: Van Dijk P et al (eds) Theory and practice of the European Convention on Human Rights, 5th edn. Intersentia, Antwerp, pp 307–330

Le Moli G (2021) Human dignity in international law. Cambridge University Press, Cambridge

Le Moli G (2022) AI vs Human Dignity: when human underperformance is legally required. Groupe d'études géopolitiques. https://geopolitique.eu/en/articles/ai-vs-human-dignity-when-human-underperformance-is-legally-required/

Levantino FP (2023a) "How do you feel today?" Exploring IHRL and IHL perspectives on law enforcement and military uses of emotion recognition technology. Opinio Juris. https://opiniojuris.org/2023/11/15/how-do-you-feel-today-exploring-ihrl-and-ihl-perspectives-on-law-enforcement-and-military-uses-of-emotion-recognition-technology/

Levantino FP (2023b) Meta- and content data in the "real world": some rule of law reflections. The Digital Constitutionalist. https://digi-con.org/meta-and-content-data-in-the-real-world-some-rule-of-law-reflections/

Levantino FP (forthcoming) Assessing the risks of emotion recognition technology in domestic security settings: What safeguards against the rise of "emotional dominance"? In: Kosta E, Hallinan D, De Hert P, Nusselder S (eds) Data protection, privacy and artificial intelligence: to govern or to be governed, that is the question, vol 17. Hart Publishing, Oxford

Ligthart S, Bublitz C, Alegre S (2023a) Neurotechnology: we need new laws, not new rights. Nature 620:950 ff. https://doi.org/10.1038/d41586-023-02698-z

Ligthart S, Ienca M et al (2023b) Minding rights: mapping ethical and legal foundations of 'Neurorights'. Camb Q Healthc Ethics 32(4):461–481. https://doi.org/10.1017/S0963180123000245

Lozada C (2021, September 3) 9/11 was a test. The books of the last two decades show how America failed. The Washington Post. https://www.washingtonpost.com/outlook/interactive/2021/911-books-american-values/

Lupo N, Piccirilli G (2012) European Court of Human Rights and the quality of legislation: shifting to a substantial concept of 'law'? Legisprudence 6(2):229–242. https://doi.org/10.5235/175214612803596668

Lyon D (2018) The culture of surveillance: watching as a way of life. Polity Press, Cambridge

Lyon D, Haggerty KD (2012) The surveillance legacies of 9/11: recalling, reflecting on, and rethinking surveillance in the security era. Can J Law Soc/La Revue Canadienne Droit et Société 27(3):291–300. https://doi.org/10.1017/S0829320100010516

Magee P, Ienca M, Farahany N (2024) Beyond neural data: cognitive biometrics and mental privacy. Neuron 112(18):3017–3028. https://doi.org/10.1016/j.neuron.2024.09.004

Malgieri G, De Hert P (2017) European human rights, criminal surveillance, and intelligence surveillance: towards "good enough" oversight, preferably but not necessarily by judges. In: Gray D, Henderson SE (eds) The Cambridge handbook of surveillance law. Cambridge University Press, Cambridge, pp 509–532

Mantelero A (2024) The Fundamental Rights Impact Assessment (FRIA) in the AI Act: roots, legal obligations and key elements for a model template. Comput Law Secur Rev 54:106020

McNicoll J, Koening R, Seymour K (2024) Big brother: the effects of surveillance on fundamental aspects of social vision. PsyArXiv. https://doi.org/10.31234/osf.io/3buaq

McStay A (2018) Emotional AI: the rise of empathic media. Sage Publications, Singapore

McStay A (2020) Emotional AI, soft biometrics and the surveillance of emotional life: an unusual consensus on privacy. Big Data Soc 7:1. https://doi.org/10.1177/2053951720904386

McStay A (2024) Automating empathy: decoding technologies that gauge intimate life. Oxford University Press, Oxford

Melgaço L, van Brakel R (2021) Smart cities as surveillance theatre. Surveill Soc 19(1):244–249. https://doi.org/10.24908/ss.v19i2.14321

Melzer N, Gaggioli Gasteyger G (2015) Conceptual distinction and overlaps between law enforcement and the conduct of hostilities. In: Gill TD, Fleck D (eds) The handbook of the international law of military operations. Oxford University Press, Oxford, pp 63–92

Milanovic M (2015) Human Rights Treaties and Foreign Surveillance. EJIL: Talk!. https://www.ejiltalk.org/human-rights-treaties-and-foreign-surveillance/

Mitsilegas V (2021) The privatisation of surveillance in the digital age. In: Mitsilegas V, Vavoula N (eds) Surveillance and privacy in the digital age. European, transatlantic and global perspectives. Hart, Oxford, pp 101–158

Mobilio G (2023) Your face is not new to me–regulating the surveillance power of facial recognition technologies. Internet Policy Rev 12:1–31. https://doi.org/10.14763/2023.1.1699

Murray D (2023) Police use of retrospective facial recognition technology: a step change in surveillance capability necessitating an evolution of the human rights law framework. Mod Law Rev 1–31. https://doi.org/10.1111/1468-2230.12862

Neroni Rezende I (2022) Facial recognition for preventive purposes: the human rights implications of detecting emotions in public spaces. In: Bachmaier Winter L, Ruggeri S (eds) Investigating and preventing crime in the digital era – new safeguards, new rights. Springer, Cham, pp 67–98

Neroni Rezende I (2023) Glukhin and the EU regulation of facial recognition: lessons to be learned? European Law Blog, Blogpost 39/2023. https://europeanlawblog.eu/2023/09/19/glukhin-and-the-eu-regulation-of-facial-recognition-lessons-to-be-learned/

Nowak M, Charbord A (2018) Key trends in the fight against terrorism and key aspects of international human rights law. In: Nowak M, Charbord A (eds) Using human rights to counter terrorism. Edward Elgar Publishing, Cheltenham, pp 12–91

Nussbaum M (1995) Objetification. Philos Public Aff 24(4):249–291

Palmiotto F, Menendez González N (2023) Facial recognition technology, democracy and human rights. Comput Law Secur Rev 50:105857. https://doi.org/10.1016/j.clsr.2023.105857

Papakonstantinou V, Zarkadoulas E (2023) Remote biometric identification and emotion recognition in the context of law enforcement. Eucrim 2:237–240. https://doi.org/10.30709/eucrim-2023-021

Peers S, Precha S (2021) Article 52 – scope and interpretation of rights and principles. In: Peers S et al (eds) The EU Charter of Fundamental Rights: a commentary, 2nd edn. Hart Publishing, Oxford, pp 1611–1674

Policing Insight (2024, June 25) Game changer, or dangerous tech? Policing Insight report gives you all you need to know about facial recognition. https://policinginsight.com/news/game-changer-or-dangerous-tech-policing-insight-report-gives-you-all-you-need-to-know-about-facial-recognition/

Pugliese J (2012) Biometrics: bodies, technologies, biopolitics. Routledge, London

Purtova N (2022) From knowing by name to targeting: the meaning of identification under the GDPR. Int Data Priv Law 12(3):163–183. https://doi.org/10.1093/idpl/ipac013

Ragazzi F, Mendos Kuskonmaz E, Plájás I, van de Ven R, Wagner B (2021) Biometric and behavioural mass surveillance in EU Member States. Report for the Greens/EFA in the European Parliament. https://www.greens-efa.eu/biometricsurveillance/

Rautenberg N, Murray D (2024) Making tangible the long-term harm linked to the chilling effects of AI-enabled surveillance: can human flourishing inform human rights? Hum Rights Rev 1–23. https://doi.org/10.1007/s12142-024-00727-6

Reclaim Your Face (n.d.). https://reclaimyourface.eu/news/

Repnikova M, Fang K (2018) Authoritarian Participatory Persuasion 2.0: netizens as thought work collaborators in China. J Contemp China 27(113):763–779. https://doi.org/10.1080/10670564.2018.1458063

Report of the Special Rapporteur on the promotion and protection of human rights and fundamental freedoms while countering terrorism (2018). UN Doc A/73/361, paras. 29 ff. https://documents.un.org/doc/undoc/gen/n18/274/67/pdf/n1827467.pdf?token=l2EHR9JLuWV0s8bUwB&fe=true

Richards NM (2008) Intellectual privacy. Tex Law Rev 87(2):387–446

Richards NM (2015) Intellectual privacy: rethinking civil liberties in the digital age. Oxford University Press, Oxford

Roy KE (2022) Defrosting the chill: how facial recognition technology threatens free speech. Roger Williams Univ School Law Rev 27(1):185–210

Rudschies C (2022) Power in the modern 'surveillance society': from theory to methodology. Inf Polity 27:275–289. https://doi.org/10.3233/IP-211536

Saab S (2021) Emotions and international law. ESIL Reflections 10(3):1–10. https://esil-sedi.eu/wp-content/uploads/2021/09/ESIL-Reflection-Saab.pdf

Sachoulidou A (2023) Going beyond the "common suspects": to be presumed innocent in the era of algorithms, big data and artificial intelligence. Artif Intell Law 1–54. https://doi.org/10.1007/s10506-023-09347-w

Sadowski J, Pasquale FA (2015) The spectrum of control: a social theory of the smart city. First Monday, 20.7. https://firstmonday.org/ojs/index.php/fm/article/view/5903/4660

Selinger E, Rhee HJ (2021) Normalizing surveillance. Sats 22(1):49–74. https://doi.org/10.1515/sats-2021-0002

Shehabi OY (2022) Surveillance, data collection and data mining in occupied territory. In: Lubin A, Buchan R (eds) The right to privacy and data protection in times of armed conflict. NATO CCDCOE Publications, Tallin. https://ccdcoe.org/uploads/2022/06/The-Rights-to-Privacy-and-Data-Protection-in-Armed-Conflict.pdf

Standaert M (2021, March 3) Smile for the camera: the dark side of China's emotion-recognition tech. The Guardian. https://www.theguardian.com/global-development/2021/mar/03/china-positive-energy-emotion-surveillance-recognition-tech

Stark L, Hutson J (2021) Physiognomic artificial intelligence. Fordham Intell Prop Media Ent Law J 32:922–978

Stevens A, Fussey P, Murray D, Hove K, Saki O (2023) 'I started seeing shadows everywhere': the diverse chilling effects of surveillance in Zimbabwe. Big Data Soc 10(1):1–14. https://doi.org/10.1177/20539517231158631

Stockwell S et al (2024) The future of biometric technology for policing and law enforcement. Centre for Emerging Technology and Security. https://cetas.turing.ac.uk/sites/default/files/2024-03/cetas_research_report_-_the_future_of_biometric_technology_for_policing_and_law_enforcement_0.pdf

Stoddart E (2012) A surveillance of care: evaluating surveillance ethically. In: Ball K, Haggerty K, Lyon D (eds) Routledge handbook of surveillance studies. Routledge International Handbooks, London, pp 369–376

Svenonius O (2018) The body politics of the urban age: reflections on surveillance and affect. Palgrave Commun 4(1):1–10. https://doi.org/10.1057/s41599-017-0057-5

Teo SA (2023) Human dignity and AI: mapping the contours and utility of human dignity in addressing challenges presented by AI. Law Innov Technol 15(1):241–279

Teo SA (2024) Artificial intelligence and its 'slow violence' to human rights. AI Ethics 1–16. https://doi.org/10.1007/s43681-024-00547-x

Thielbörger P (2019) The "essence" of international human rights. German Law J 20(6):924–939. https://doi.org/10.1017/glj.2019.69

United Nations General Assembly (UNGA) (1979) Code of Conduct for Law Enforcement Officials. Resolution 34/169. https://www.ohchr.org/en/instruments-mechanisms/instruments/code-conduct-law-enforcement-officials

United Nations Security Council (UNSC) (2017) Resolution S/RES/2396, para 15. https://www.un.org/securitycouncil/content/sres23962017. Accessed 31 Mar 2024

Urquhart L, Miranda D (2021) Policing faces: the present and future of intelligent facial surveillance. Inf Commun Technol Law 31(2):194–219. https://doi.org/10.1080/13600834.2021.1994220

Van der Sloot B (2015) Privacy as personality right: why the ECtHR's focus on ulterior interests might prove indispensable in the age of big data. Utrecht J Int Eur Law 31(80):25 ff. https://doi.org/10.5334/ujiel.cp

Vemou A, Horvath A (2021) Facial Emotion Recognition. EDPS, TechDispatch #1/2021. https://doi.org/10.2804/014217

Vigliarolo Brandon (2024, October 29) US Army turns to 'Scylla' AI to protect depot. The Register. https://www.theregister.com/2024/10/29/us_army_scylla_ai/

Waem H, Dauzier J, Demircan M (2024) Fundamental Rights Impact Assessments under the EU AI Act: who, what and how? Technology's Legal Edge (DLA Piper). https://www.technologyslegaledge.com/2024/03/fundamental-rights-impact-assessments-under-the-eu-ai-act-who-what-and-how/

Wendehors C, Duller Y (2021) Biometric recognition and behavioural detection. Policy Department for Citizens' Rights and Constitutional Affairs (European Parliament). https://www.europarl.europa.eu/RegData/etudes/STUD/2021/696968/IPOL_STU(2021)696968_EN.pdf

Wilson D, McCulloch J (eds) (2017) Pre-crime: pre-emption, precaution and the future. Routledge, London

Wright J (2023) Suspect AI: Vibraimage, emotion recognition technology and algorithmic opacity. Sci Technol Soc 28(3):468–487. https://doi.org/10.1177/09717218211003411

Wu X, Zhang X (2016) Automated inference on criminality using face images. arXiv preprint arXiv:1611.04135: 4038–4052

MIX
Papier aus verantwortungsvollen Quellen
Paper from responsible sources
FSC® C105338

If you have any concerns about our products,
you can contact us on
ProductSafety@springernature.com

In case Publisher is established outside the EU,
the EU authorized representative is:
Springer Nature Customer Service Center GmbH
Europaplatz 3, 69115 Heidelberg, Germany

Printed by Libri Plureos GmbH
in Hamburg, Germany